The Collected OZ

Volume Three

Richard Neville et. al.

Edited by Jonathan Downes
Typeset by Jonathan Downes
Cover and Internal Layout by Jon Downes for Gonzo Multimedia
Using Microsoft Word 2000, Microsoft , Publisher 2000, Adobe Photoshop.

First edition published 2016 by Gonzo Multimedia

c/o Brooks City,
6th Floor New Baltic House
65 Fenchurch Street,
London EC3M 4BE
Fax: +44 (0)191 5121104
Tel: +44 (0) 191 5849144
International Numbers:
Germany: Freephone 08000 825 699
USA: Freephone 18666 747 289

ISBN: 978-1-908728-64-7

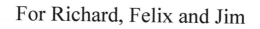
For Richard, Felix and Jim

Trial begins 22 June
Any information contact Friends of Oz,
39a Pottery Lane, London W11. 01-229 5887.

Introduction

Back in the day, and this particular day was about twenty years ago, I was friendly with a notorious Irish Republican musical ensemble known as *Athenrye*, and particularly with their guitarist, a guy called Terry Manton. I was very angry about a lot of things at the time, and quite how drinking with various groups of slightly dodgy Hibernians actually made me feel any better I am not sure, but it seemed to have the desired effect.

09

On one of their albums there is a song about Éamon de Valera. For those of you not in the know, over to those jolly nice people at Wikipedia.

"Éamon de Valera first registered as George de Valero; changed some time before 1901 to Edward de Valera; 14 October 1882 – 29 August 1975) was a prominent politician and statesman in twentieth-century Ireland. His political career spanned over half a century, from 1917 to 1973; he served several terms as head of government and head of state. He also led the introduction of the Constitution of Ireland.

De Valera was a leader in the War of Independence and of the anti-Treaty opposition in the ensuing Irish Civil War (1922–1923). After leaving Sinn Féin in 1926 due to its policy of abstentionism, he founded Fianna Fáil, and was head of government (President of the Executive Council, later Taoiseach) from 1932 to 1948, 1951 to 1954, and 1957 to 1959, when he resigned after being elected as President of Ireland. His political creed evolved from militant republicanism to social and cultural conservatism.

Assessments of de Valera's career have varied; he has often been characterised as

Lucky man of our times

Chorus
He was loved he was hated he was cherished despised
There were rivers of tears when the chieftain he died
But love him or hate him I cannot decide
What to make of old Dev this man of our times."

And it ended up:

"Now Spain had it's Franco and France it's De Gaulle
We had our Dev and god rest his soul"

It has been many years since I bounced up and down in a weird Gaelic moshpit shouting "Tiocfaidh ár lá" and I strongly doubt whether I shall ever do so again. My foray into such things had more to do with my reaction to the way that I perceived that I had been treated by my family over my particularly scabrous divorce, than any genuine political fervour, although I thought then (and think now) that the British history in Ireland has not been our greatest or most honourable hour. However, today I have had that song going round and around my head, ever since I read an email from Tony Palmer telling me that Richard Neville had died at the age of 74, in Byron Bay, New South Wales, the Australian hippy enclave where Gilli Smyth breathed her last only a few days before.

Now I never met Neville. Our acquaintanceship was confined to two emails about five years ago when I was working on the new edition of Tony Palmer's *The Trials of Oz*. I exchanged a few more emails with Jim Anderson, and had no contact whatsoever with Felix Dennis, so I cannot really be called an insider of the *Oz* scene. But Neville came out with one of my favourite quotes from the counterculture: "There is some corner of a foreign field that is forever Woodstock", and was an undeniably major figure in that much maligned social movement.

He seemed to be someone who brought out strong reactions in people. Whilst I was working on *The Trials of Oz* I discovered that people were either terribly fond of the man or disliked him intensely. I never found anyone who was ambivalent towards him. Even after his death, as I sent emails around the usual suspects asking for their memories of him, most people refused to be drawn one way or the other, with those who had been friends with him at various periods of their lives being totally devastated that they had woken up this morning to a planet on which Richard Neville was no longer alive.

Me? I am no better than any of the others. I have no knowledge of him personally, and whereas I found large chunks of *Oz* unreadable, I was impressed by his book *Playpower* and in the passages about him in Tony Palmer's book he struck an undeniably heroic figure against the same sort of establishment malice which had (as alluded to above) turned me against my parents twenty years back.

His book *Hippy Hippy Shake* was entertaining, even though its hedonism left a slightly bitter taste in one's mouth, but I remember being told that the movie that was made from it was so bad that several of the major figures portrayed refused to let it come out. In July 2007, in a piece for *The Guardian*, feminist author Germaine Greer vehemently expressed her displeasure at being depicted, writing, "You used to have to die before assorted hacks started munching your remains and modelling a new version of you out of their own excreta." Greer refused to be involved with the film, just as she declined to read Neville's memoir before it was published (he had offered to change anything she found offensive). She did not want to meet with Emma Booth, who portrays her in the film, and concluded her article with her only advice for the actress: "Get an honest job."

So where is this taking me? I truly don't know, but if there had not been a Richard Neville, there might well not have been a *Gonzo Weekly* magazine. I first read *The Trials of Oz* whilst on holiday with my patients back when I was a Registered Nurse for the Mentally Subnormal [RNMS] nearly thirty years ago, and it was one of the sacred texts, together with *A Series of Shock Slogans and Mindless Token Tantrums* by Penny Rimbaud et al, that set me on the path that I am on now. But when I finally read the *Schoolkid's Oz*, I thought it was puerile bollocks, and was massively underwhelmed.

And I too find it hard to adjust to the fact that I have woken up this morning to a planet on which Richard Neville was no longer alive.

So, if I may:

"He was loved he was hated he was cherished despised
There were rivers of tears when the Oz editor died
But love him or hate him I cannot decide
What to make of old Nev this man of our times."

Hare Bol Mr Neville

GOD SAVE US

ELASTIC OZ BAND

OUTCRY AS OZ EDITORS ARE JAILED

Labour MPs attack 'act of revenge'

Daily Telegraph

FURY OVER OZ JAILINGS

Angry MPs join the wave of protest

The Sun

OZ: OBSCENE! BUT WHY THE FEROCIOUS SENTENCES?

Fury as three editors are jailed

Daily Mirror

Oz sentences — Labour MPs sign protest

MPs condemn OZ gaolings as 'Establishment revenge'

The Guardian

Demonstrations and protests against 'Oz' jail sentences

Shocked MPs protest: It looks like revenge

Apple are donating royalties on this record to the Oz Obscenity Fund

STORM OVER OZ SENTENCES

Daily Mail

THE print system on these sides of the magazine sounded a crop of sentences for style

In Mitigation

So what was *Oz?* And why was it so important?

OZ was an underground alternative magazine. First published in Sydney, Australia, in 1963, a second version appeared in London, England from 1967 and is better known.

The original Australian *OZ* took the form of a satirical magazine published between 1963 and 1969, while the British incarnation was a "psychedelic hippy" magazine which appeared from 1967 to 1973. Strongly identified as part of the underground press, it was the subject of two celebrated obscenity trials, one in Australia in 1964 and the other in the United Kingdom in 1971. On both occasions the magazine's editors were acquitted on appeal after initially being found guilty and sentenced to harsh jail terms. An earlier, 1963 obscenity charge was dealt with expeditiously when, upon the advice of a solicitor, the three editors pleaded guilty.

The central editor throughout the magazine's life in both Australia and Britain was Richard Neville. Co-editors of the Sydney version were Richard Walsh and Martin Sharp. Co-editors of the London version were Jim Anderson and, later, Felix Dennis.

In early 1966 Neville and Sharp travelled to the UK and in early 1967, with fellow Australian Jim Anderson, they founded the London *OZ*. Contributors included Germaine Greer, artist and filmmaker Philippe Mora, illustrator Stewart Mackinnon, photographer Robert Whitaker, journalist Lillian Roxon, cartoonist Michael Leunig, Angelo Quattrocchi, Barney Bubbles and David Widgery.

With access to new print stocks, including metallic foils, new fluorescent inks and the freedom of layout offered by the offset printing system, Sharp's artistic skills came to the fore and *OZ* quickly won renown as one of the most visually exciting publications of its day. Several editions of *Oz* included dazzling psychedelic wrap-around or pull-out posters by Sharp, London design duo Hapshash and the Coloured Coat and others; these instantly became sought-after collectors' items and now command high prices. Another innovation was the cover of *Oz* No.11, which included a collection of detachable adhesive labels, printed in either red, yellow or green. The all-graphic "Magic Theatre" edition (*OZ* No.16, November 1968), overseen by Sharp and Mora, has been described by British author Jonathon Green as "arguably the greatest achievement of the entire British underground press". During this period Sharp also created the two famous psychedelic album covers for the group Cream, Disraeli Gears and Wheels Of Fire.

Sharp's involvement gradually decreased during 1968-69 and the "Magic Theatre" edition was one of his last major contributions to the magazine. In his place, young Londoner Felix Dennis, who had been selling issues on the street, was eventually brought in as Neville and Anderson's new partner. The magazine regularly enraged the British Establishment with a range of left-field stories including heavy critical coverage of the Vietnam War and the anti-war movement, discussions of drugs, sex and alternative lifestyles, and contentious political stories, such as the magazine's revelations about the torture of citizens under the rule of the military junta in Greece.

In 1970, reacting to criticism that *OZ* had lost touch with youth, the editors put a notice in the magazine inviting "school kids" to edit an issue. The opportunity was taken up by around 20 secondary school students (including Charles Shaar Murray and Deyan Sudjic), who were responsible for *OZ* No.28 (May 1970), generally known as "Schoolkids OZ". This term was widely misunderstood to mean that it was intended for schoolchildren, whereas it was an issue that had been created by them. As Richard Neville said in his opening statement, other issues had been assembled by gay people and members of the Female Liberation Movement. One of the resulting articles was a highly sexualised Rupert Bear parody. It was created by 15-year-old schoolboy Vivian Berger by pasting the head of Rupert onto the lead character of an X-rated satirical cartoon by Robert Crumb.

OZ was one of several 'underground' publications targeted by the Obscene Publications Squad, and their offices had already been raided on several occasions, but the conjunction of schoolchildren, and what some viewed as obscene material, set the scene for the *Oz* obscenity trial of 1971.

The trial was, at the time, the longest obscenity trial in British legal history, and it was the first time that an obscenity charge was combined with the charge of conspiring to corrupt public morals. Defence witnesses included artist Feliks Topolski, comedian Marty Feldman, artist and drugs activist Caroline Coon, DJ John Peel, musician and writer George Melly, legal philosopher Ronald Dworkin and academic Edward de Bono.

At the conclusion of the trial the "OZ Three" were found not guilty on the conspiracy charge, but they were convicted of two lesser offences and sentenced to imprisonment; although Dennis was given a lesser sentence because the judge, Justice Michael Argyle, considered that Dennis was "very much less intelligent" than the others. Shortly after the verdicts were handed down, they were taken to prison and their long hair forcibly cut, an act which caused an even greater stir on top of the already considerable outcry surrounding the trial and verdict.

The best known images of the trial come from the committal hearing, at which Neville, Dennis and Anderson all appeared, wearing rented schoolgirl costumes.

At the appeal trial (where the defendants appeared wearing long wigs) it was found that Justice Argyle had grossly misdirected the jury on numerous occasions and the defence also alleged that Berger, who was called as a prosecution witness, had been harassed and assaulted by police. The convictions were overturned. Years later, Felix Dennis told author Jonathon Green that on the night before the appeal was heard, the *OZ* editors were taken to a secret meeting with the Chief Justice, Lord Widgery, who reportedly said that Argyle had made a "fat mess" of the trial, and informed them that they would be acquitted, but insisted that they had to agree to give up work on *OZ*. Dennis also stated that, in his opinion, MPs Tony Benn and Michael Foot had interceded with Widgery on their behalf.

Despite their supposed undertaking to Lord Widgery, *OZ* continued after the trial, and thanks to the intense public interest the trial generated, its circulation briefly rose to 80,000. However its popularity faded over the next two years and by the time the last issue (*OZ* No.48) was published in November 1973 Oz Publications was £20,000 in debt and the magazine had "no readership worth the name".

We are publishing these magazines in these collected editions, partly as a tribute to the late Richard Neville (1943-2016) and partly because we believe that they constitute a valuable socio-political document reflecting the counterculture of 1967-74. This collection has been made available due to its historical and research importance. It contains explicit language and images that reflect attitudes of the era in which the material was originally published, and that some viewers may find confronting. However, we have taken the decision to blank out a very few images which would be seen as unacceptable in today's society.

Times have changed a lot in the past half century. The magazine's obsession with pornography, for example, has not stood the test of time very well, and some of the typography is so muddy as to be unreadable. Every effort has been made by the present publishers to clean up the typography, but in most cases it proved to be impossible, so we have left it as it was. The *Oz* readers of the late 1960s were unable to read it. Why should the present generation be any different?

Some of the pictures in the original magazine, especially artwork by Martin Sharp, was printed so it could fold out into a poster. We have therefore included these twice - as per the original pages so they can be read easily, and as extrapolations of the original artwork. Richard Neville stipulated in the extract from the notorious *Schoolkid's Oz* reproduced below that the material in these magazines could be used for any purpose, and we are taking him at his word.

Peace and Love

Ronnie Rooster
September 2016

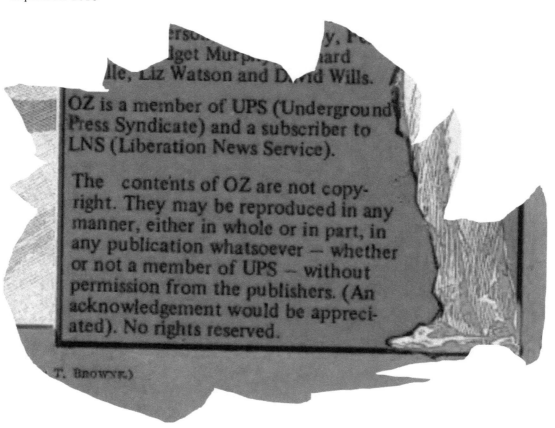

...rso... ...y, ...
...lget Murp..., ...ard
...lle, Liz Watson and D...id Wills.

OZ is a member of UPS (Underground Press Syndicate) and a subscriber to LNS (Liberation News Service).

The contents of OZ are not copyright. They may be reproduced in any manner, either in whole or in part, in any publication whatsoever — whether or not a member of UPS — without permission from the publishers. (An acknowledgement would be appreciated). No rights reserved.

.T. Brown.)

BIG O POSTER SHOW

price 3s. № 13

WORLD REVOLUTION!
BRIAN JONES TALKS!
BOB DYLAN FILM SCRIPT!
LEGALISE POT POSTER!
THE GREAT SPACE ODYSSEY!

CATHERINE AND THE WHEEL OF FIRE /a space poem revealed.

OZ13

London OZ is published approximately monthly by OZ Publications Ink Ltd, 38a Palace Gardens Terrace, London W8. Phone: 01-229 4623 . . . 01-603 4205.

Editor: Richard Neville

Deputy Editor: Paul Lawson

Design: Jon Goodchild assisted by Felix Dennis

Art: Martin Sharp and Virginia Clive-Smith

Advertising: John Leaver 2 Walsingham Mansions, Fulham Road, SW6. Phone: 01-385 4639

Writers: Andrew Fisher, David Widgery, Angelo Quattrocchi, John Wilcock, Dave Phillips & Nigel Fountain

Photography: Keith Morris

Pushers: Felix Dennis and Louise Ferrier

Distribution: (Britain) Moore Harness Ltd, 11 Lever Street, London EC1. Phone: CLE 4882. (New York) D G B Distribution Inc, 41 Union Square, New York 10003. (Holland) Thomas Rap, Regulierdwarstraat 91, Amsterdam. Telefoon: 020-227065. (Denmark) George Streeton, The Underground, Larsbjørnstraede 13, Copenhagen K.

Printing: Steel Bros. (Carlisle) Ltd, Phone: 0228-25181. Printed Web Offset.

Typesetting: Jacky Ephgrave Big O Press Ltd, 49 Kensington High Street, London W8. Phone: 01-937 2614. ECAL, 22 Betterton Street, London WC2. Phone: 01-836 8606.

Dear OZ,

After living in one roomed communes of the love/hate type in the Notting Hill Gate area, since I dropped out in September last year I have come to the conclusion that the city drop-out scene is a pathetic one.

I would like to list some of my observations.

1. People thrown together by necessity (usually financial), although sharing in the true community spirit, food (usually stolen), experiences (usually hallucinatory) and pot (usually not enough), still tend to split into little camps, ie Joe hangs up Bill and Bill hangs up Fred which upsets Jim because Jim likes everyone. Which is a big hang up for Him, for if he refuses to bend in one direction or another, he's on his own man!

2. Speed kills—not only people, but scenes as well. Someone suffering (and they do!) from speed hang ups and come downs really drag the whole scene down. Watching a friend becoming an addict, drifting into the misty world of Boot's disposables, is a soul searing experience not to be forgotten easily.

Perhaps if many dealers sold decent acid and not disappointments, a lot of the speed thing might disappear.

3. Most conversation in turned-on scenes, is mainly turned in to 'My best trip' or various 'Freak you out cocktail recipes', and little else is discussed.

4. Even the people wanting to be in on the love commune thing, seem to be sitting around on their arses, drawing the NAB and waiting. Waiting for what?

For things to be arranged for them by the diggers? (That mythical race of people) or perhaps for guidance from our friends? in space? Whilst this situation exists it just isn't going to happen.

Dharma—Karma—Smarma! Each of us should be a digger for fucks sake, otherwise there's not going to be any communes 'cos we'll all die of old age, waiting!

My grumbles may seem slanted from one angle, but walk around NHG and ask any drop out on the scene where they've been lately (apart from MOSS or Middle Earth) its a strange land surrounding a strange land.

As for myself, I'm giving up my cherished freedom (and the NAB), my long locks are to be shorn and I'm dropping IN decked out in my blue suit, white shirt and tie, to become a purveyor of holiday shell ashtrays and other plastic goodies for the grey people (poor bastards) in Sunny Jersey (from whence I came) for as long as I can stand it.

Then along with my brother and anyone else who wants to create something, by raising bread, we're going to buy a cottage and land in the country, grow our own food etc, and build a commune out of our own efforts.

A 20th century city of Electric Gardens is no place for anyone to find their relationship with the things which will always be here.

Love and peace
(if you can find it)

Michael Escott
7 Foxhill Close
Greatfield, Hull
Yorks

Dear Sir,

We are shocked by the Prime Minister associating himself with Monsieur Roche, Rector of the Sorbonne, whose one chapter in history can be written with a sentence. He closed the Sorbonne.

That our Prime Minister as Chancellor of Bradford University should confer the honour of a degree on a man who abused the trust of more than seven centuries of students by violating the right to maintain the University as a centre of free thought, and who, apparently in the name of the State, called the armed representatives of that State, and violated one of the worthiest of French traditions, the sanctuary of the Sorbonne, suggests that our Prime Minister would follow Monsieur Roche and the french government if the liberties of our own Universities were ever put to the test.

Yours sincerely,

MW Watson Todd
David Schreiber
R Deane Edwards
Michael N Momache

The English Revolutionaries

When they broke into the town hall guns at the ready the town clerk said "I'm sorry you'll have to write for an appointment." So they went away and came back three weeks on tuesday in their best suits.

Steve Sneyd
Aldmondbury
Huddersfield, Yorks

We need you
Cohn-Bendit, because

1. We are fed and watered by the State's Almighty Hand, and do exactly as we are told.

2. We are told that the Government knows what's best for us; the big Corporations know what's best for us; BBC, TV and the Press know what is good for us to hear; Advertising Agencies know what is good for us to buy; teachers know what is good for us to know; Law and Order is good for us, because it excludes anybody who tells us that we ourselves might know best what is good for us.

3. In return for being well looked after, we PAY taxes to the Government, to buy noisy aeroplanes for Corporation men to deafen us with; we PAY for the BBC, TV, and Press, and give them our trust; we PAY the Advertisers, and they don't need our trust because there is nothing but their products to buy; we PAY for our teachers and pretend they are all profound and knowledgeable; we PAY for Law and Order with cash and obedience, and agree to call you 'irresponsible'.

4. We do not know how to want to be responsible for our own lives and our own environment.

5. We are superior to all foreigners, who are (1) oppressed (2) untrustworthy (3) violent (4) backward (5) far away.

2.

6.   We admire America, and are the only country in Europe who like the Americans to be in Vietnam.

7.   We have a good trade going in poison gases . . . and you can tell us how they work.

8.   Our policemen are wonderful.

9.   Our Leaders are a bunch of fixers, our politicians their pimps, our businessmen arrogant bloodsuckers, our universities teach us only how to be teachers, our parents fear and hate (1) negros (2) jews (3) jews (4) foreigners (5) the Lower Orders (6) us; our Press tells us lies about you, and loves our politicians, businessmen, pundits and parents; and our Law orders us to obey them all.

10.   Our debt to all of them has made us morally bankrupt.

11.   We think we owe our lives to Society, and forget that we ARE society.

12.   We are made oblivious with Welfare; blind with parochial pride; childish with obedience; petulant wtih disobedience; anxious for a pension; taught to be ignorant. We do not like FACTS.

13.   We are very young for our age; very insulated; devoted to cash and status.

14.   Sex and pot are our substitutes for Freedom.

15.   WE HAVE NO PASSION.

16.   Although we don't believe in god, we let him make our laws and frighten our children.

17.   We don't believe in politicians, but we act as if we do.

18.   We don't believe our Press, but we buy it.

19.   We want what you want, but we support the other side.

20.   We call police violence and the violence of the State . . . "student violence", and make it our excuse.

21.   WE ARE VERY, VERY FRIGHTENED.

Issued by the Surrealist Group: Ian Breakwell, Alan Burns, Rupert Cracknell, Sophie Kemp, John Lyle, Conroy Maddox, George Melly, Peter Rider, John Rudlin, Ken Smith.

Dear Sir,

Sorry to say that there were not 50 but 25 of us, ('Police arrest Poets') sorry to say that Christopher Logue was not a participant in the event but a watcher.

Yours sincerely,
Sonia Sharkey (known as Wendy)
52 Queensway
London W2

Dear Sir,

This year will be the last year that mankind will have in the consciousness they have manifested hitherto.

On our part, we have planned everything, and everything has been prepared carefully. The message is a message of joy, and I wish that it be treated as a message of joy. Serious events will strike Earth, they will end in the Second Coming. And this is what should be stressed; speak of the spiritual side of the matter more than the violent part of it. Violence does not belong to us,—it belongs to Man; but violence will come to an end for Man now.

Certainty and knowledge are to be preferred to faith; but in order to attain certainty in this matter, one must believe. When the events begin to speed up you should group together and talk about these subjects. Never discuss, but talk—and be calm and harmonious within. The more calm and harmonious one is, the more one will understand about the nature of this message. Many individuals will receive messages themselves during the forthcoming days.

Confusion begets confusion. Only he who will not receive confusion within himself will escape confusion. Do not allow outer things to disturb your innermost being, and it will apply now more than ever before in the situation in which you will come to stand. Find peace and harmony within yourselves; they will be necessary during these latter days of Earth.

Au Revoir !

Universal Link
PO Box 13
4140, Borup, Denmark

Dear Sir,

These ideas might interest you . . . Over the past ten years I have been the author of numerous un-American letters to the local newspapers. It has always been my basic purpose in writing letters to the newspapers to present ideas, to make people think. In this small way, I have been contributing to the increase of consciousness. A deliberately subversive enterprise I admit.

With the widespread increase of consciousness society will mature, and authoritarian institutions such as governments and religions will lose their power over the human spirit. The maturing of society means precisely the increase of consciousness, on a general or collective scale.

Psychedelic drugs are the best way to achieve a radical increase of consciousness, although there are clumsier drugless methods such as fasting, breathing exercises, and concentration, as in yoga or

meditation. This is why psychedelics are felt to be a threat to the present order. In spite of persecution, the advent of psychedelics will have the effect of accelerating the growth of the human race.

To experience an altered state of consciousness, such as intoxication is educational and broadening, like speaking a foreign language or playing a musical instrument. But psychedelic drugs do not merely alter the consciousness, they literally increase or expand consciousness. The mind opens up, everything is more real. This is the minimum effect; it may be followed by psychological hallucinations or by spiritual insight, depending on the temperament or personality of the drug user.

The basic conflict in society is between the forces of growth and the forces of inertia (sometimes called 'stability'). Psychedelic drugs are a powerful force for growth, too important to be confined by legalism or medicalism.

Dave Reissig
402 Arthur St
Syracuse NY 13204

Along with some 'Smalls' advertisements, offers of crashpads have been lost. If you want to add your name to the world wide list of crashpads being prepared, please write to OZ, c/o Crashpads. Please write again if we lost you.

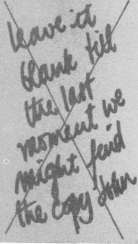

leave it blank till the last moment we might find the copy John

EVA

I have had many letters in response to the appeal in OZ 12 to get Eva into the country. It is impossible to answer them all, and so I'd like to thank you all here. Eva has 'chosen' her man, and will be in touch with him by June 10. Thank you again—love Judy.

Dear Judy,

If she **really** needs someone in order to gain entry into England, being a man of leisure, I guess I'll give it a try. (No strings, of course.)

About myself, am 22, live in Spain, teacher by profession, 6'1½" and believe in trying everything once. Anyhow, all this apart, will help Eva out if I can.

A. Q.

Dear Judy,

With respect to Eva, OK.

Yours,
MHD

Dear Judy,

I would be more than happy to marry your friend Eva. As divorce is now quite simple in England it would be of advantage to both of us: Eva would get into this country and as I'm in the air force I would get a pay rise of £3 a week, and the added advantage of her company for 1 week.

Yours faithfully,
JF

Dear Judy,

I think I should start by telling

you a few things about myself. I am twenty-eight years old, and a University lecturer in physical chemistry. My main interests are surfing, swimming and rally-driving. I am also interested in photography and am a keen hi-fi enthusiast.

I have every sympathy with Eva's problem of getting British citizenship, and would be willing to help her in any way possible, the more so because I believe this could be a stimulating and enjoyable experience for us both.

Yours,
Dr DB

Dear Judy,

I have just read the **thing** about your friend, Eva, in the OZ. I have just been sentenced to Borstal for being in possession of hashish. I would be glad to help her as the prison authorities should allow me a days freedom to get married.

Marriage means nothing whereas freedom be it only for a day is everything.

As from next Tuesday my postal address will be Wormwood Scrubs Prison, London. If your friend is still willing to enter England you can reach me there.

Yours hopefully,
JB
HM Prison, Leicester.

To Judy,

23 yr old, free thinker requests the hand of EVA.

Sincerely,
JD

Due to the urgency of the content of this issue, the final part of Ray Duignat's article, the continuation of Meat Pack and Hipocrates are held over till issue 14

FUGS

Begun in 1965, The Fugs are probably the world's first underground rock group. They are the fathers of 'The Mothers of Invention', and known for such pop poems as Kill for Peace, Coca Cola Douche, Group Grope and the Virgin Forest. They've released four LP's in the US and all but one of their songs have managed to avoid the charts. You haven't heard their dulcet acrobatics on Radio Yawn because, according to John Peel, the dj's are not allowed to announce even the word Fugs.

One of the unannouncables, Tuli Kupferberg, was in London recently. Tuli's a poet, publisher, pacifist, vegetarian and author of such Grove Press classics as A Thousand and One ways to Live without Working and A Thousand and One ways to Beat The Draft. His next book is A Thousand and One ways to Make Love.

Kupferberg spent much of his time in London conferring with the Anti Vaccination League to equip himself for the fight against his country's compulsory smallpox vaccination laws. He points out that smallpox is virtually extinct and that in the last 30 years more people have died from the vaccination than have caught smallpox.

In between arming himself with Doctor's letters confirming that "that there has been no recent outbreak of smallpox in Earls Court," Tuli Kupferberg spoke to OZ:

TK I have come to a rather simplified outlook: As long as you're getting more from them than they are taking from you then its worth working with the establishment. But you have to be very careful. Sometimes you wake up and say I really shouldn't be doing this—how did I get here and then you should leave.

How often do you compromise?

TK At Santa Monica we were playing in this place and the sound system was awful and the whole atmosphere was bad—we came onto the band stand and looked down and there were 11 and 12 year old kids which would be alright except their

parents were with them—so we really couldn't do our kind of show. And that's happened a few times. This happens in my publishing also. There are certain things I wanted to publish and don't dare to and in a sense that's a compromise. But then if I had always told the truth by now I would be dead. And I don't really believe in paying rent. I think it's unjust. But if I didn't pay rent then my landlord would throw me out and I'd end up having to pay it to another. And that's a sort of daily compromise. One should compromise as little as possible though. And always push yourself. I have published many things where I was afraid that the next day the police would be there. I was the first one to print the word shit on a cover. I'm sort of proud of that. But this seems like nothing today which just shows how fast the revolution is going.

And where is it going to?

TK Well I think the best examples are on the west coast of California. Thousands and thousands of young people have moved out of the society and for them the revolution has occured. They have enough money and enough leisure to do whatever they want.

Where does the money come from?

TK Firstly they bypass a lot of people's ideals. I mean they don't care where they live or what they eat or how they dress. And in California the climate is warm. Some of them still have money coming from their families. A lot of them live communally which makes things a lot easier. And most of them don't even care if they get into trouble with the authorities. They are considered just like a natural force, nothing to worry about. And they have drugs too. But what they're going to do with it we don't know yet. They spend their freedom playing with a frisby—a plastic disc you throw back and forth. At first this annoyed me but what else is there to do?

Have the Fugs been as successful as you would have liked?

TK Well at the beginning I didn't care, but now I think it should have been more successful. I felt it should have evolved into theatre, we should have read poetry. And done more extensive skits. So it hasn't been a success artistically. The others in the Group don't realise what our popularity is based on. Its not based on the fine music in quote marks, but on our vitality. Our energy. And our kind of amateurishness. A kind of anything goes bit. Most important with the material. But also technically. It would be beautiful if we were all inspired musicians but we're not. What we really needed was someone like Jimmi Hendrix or the Stones as musicians. So we could have had a fusion of music, theatre, poetry and politics.

Why didn't you play in London?

TK Various technical reasons. We will be here in September. But I think its a pity we didn't play here at our peak. I think each group has one special contribution to make to music and then they fade. I am afraid that we may have already made ours.

LEBEL ?

Jean-Jacques Lebel led the storming of the Paris Odeon. Now he is in geol and the building has been cleared by police. Many complicated, contradictory elements are united against French fascism; not the least of which is Lebel, who sometimes inspires derision from his more stubbornly political colleagues (who also regard the Odeon as a tourist's revolution). But the eloquence of Lebel is considered dangerous enough to have him gaoled. Here he speaks to Bryan Willis a few days before his arrest:

We are for the total end of the human rapport which is established between the governor and the governed, the ruler and the ruled. We are for self management in each profession and each category of the people by themselves, but we are also for the destruction of the categories. In other words one of the reasons that we occupied the universities is not only for the students or for the workers: it is for everyone to come and use this university for whatever they want to use it. Not only for education, but if they want to eat there, sleep there, fuck there, get high there or live there. We are for the total destruction of categories.

One of the main ways the Capitalist system maintains its total control over bodies and minds is by categorising everybody into social groups. They say "You're the workers you're the students, you're the intellectuals, you're the doctors or whatever". We are for the destruction of this division into small groups. The fact that a tremendous number of workers now come to the Sorbonne or to other faculties that are occupied means that they feel that these are their places. These places belong to them. They do not just belong to the students or to the teachers.

As far as the Cultural industry is concerned, one of the main industries of the capitalist state is culture, in the sense that the propaganda of the ideology of the ruling class goes through everything that is called artistic. The movies for instance, were first an art and are now an industry— the same thing has happened to writing, to theatre to painting. Whatever is done in the way of culture is completely counter-revolutionary because it is the culture of money. The main thing about all cultural activity in the capitalist state is that it makes money. Whether you make money by playing Brecht or by playing Moliere it is exactly the same thing. You are giving a spectacle to people who do not participate in any way in what's happening. They consume the spectacle in exactly the same way as they consume when they buy a car or a refrigerator or chewing gum.

The society has made everybody into consumers and everything including art and political ideology has become consumer goods. We want to demolish completely the structure of the consumer society. It is possible for the people to make their own art. Some artists who pretend to be revolutionaries exhibit at the museum of modern art, which is a temple of capitalism just as much as the stock exchange we burned the other day. Some painters want to bring their paintings to the factories but that is a completely counter-revolutionary attitude. The workers don't need pseudo avant-garde paintings in the factories they need the total destruction of the social rapport between the bosses and the workers. They have to make their own paintings or invent their own art which will probably not be with brushes and canvases, but an art which will be completely integrated into the life process itself. Art can can become, when the revolutionary process has really demolished a number of mental and social taboos, something completely integrated in daily life.

Our action is to demolish even the left. For years the unions have been trying to stop the students and the workers coming together. Our main work is now in the factories, talking to the workers and telling them how the unions are helping the government to alienate them. The unions manipulate the workers into obeying the government. The workers get a shilling a day more to continue doing the same work, when it is the concept of work that needs to be questioned. Self-management would enable people to cease working for others and break down their work into what was necessary for economic exchange with others. We are trying to, beginning to, reinvent the concept of life, language, and political expression itself.

De Gaulle is trying to sell an image of France abroad which does not correspond at all to the corruption and pseudo liberal fascism that is going on inside the country So one of the aims was to destroy this image and I think that we succeeded in that. We took over one of the centres of propaganda, the Odeon. This used to represent the French culture from Warsaw to Tokyo and everywhere. So we took it over and decided that was the end of the cultural industry there. It would never be a theatre any longer, just a place, an ordinary place where anybody could come and learn, inform other people, talk with other people and exchange information and ideas.

What happened later, alas, and this we must criticize, was that a bureaucracy installed itself in there. It started making the usual little bureaucratic decisions which were cut off completely from the general movement.

What we are doing today is denouncing completely what is going on inside the Odeon. It re-institutionalized itself within a few weeks. It became again a sort of Ministry of Culture, a micro Ministry of Culture. What we are doing today is throwing all those people out and giving it again to who ever wants to express themselves there.

We didn't take it to re-establish a leftish bureaucracy there.

John Esam is rumoured to have begun a new publishing project. It is said to be a magazine scheduled to appear each fortnight in a format similar to 'The History of the 20th Century' entitled 'The History of the Future'. It will begin with the end of the world and work its way back. A number of famous but at present unknown writers will be writing for it, many of whom have yet to be born but all of whom have died.

John Wilcock's Other Scenes is now being distributed in London by ECAL 22 Betterton Street, WC2. Phone: TEM 8606.

HAROLD MUGGINS IS A MARTYR, (play/festival/freakout/gala/funfair/trial) uses movement, sound, light, projections, and more audience involvement from moment they enter front gate with carnival funfair, amusement arcade, guest orators, and Harold Muggins appealing for support in environment slapped onto Unity Theatre by students from Bradford School of Art; late night shows after performances on Fridays and Saturdays of poets, singers, short plays, films, whatever comes; discussion on the alternative society; children's carnival processions through Camden.

Unity Theatre is old, seedy left-wing theatre club near Kings Cross or Mornington Crescent tube stations. Good stage and auditorium, licensed bar, people don't know about it so hardly used, one of the assets of the Underground that should be developed. Run by committee, ineffective, needs people who want to get things done and just do them. Full membership gives right to take part in shows, vote and stand for election to management (£1 a year plus 1/- on joining).

6

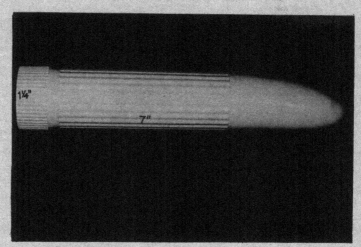
We shall attack, consistently, every
kind of bureaucratic humbug that
believes that "They" should control
"Us". HELP wants participation democracy, at all levels. And a genuine
belief in people. Not shadow-boxing
and public relations.

We're backing the underdog. The
squeezed-out, unaffluent, not-politically-
important minorities. The mentally
sick. The gypsies. The handicapped.

We're looking at protest groups because
they are the Davids in a Goliath society.
They have the sniff of truth for what's
wrong. Perhaps because they have no
power and money.

In 10 years more cause groups have been
formed in Britain than in any other
decade in our history. From Consumers
Associations to Shelter, from Child
Poverty Action to Stansted. Draw your
own conclusions.

We see HELP as a movement. A gathering of people who care. We will use
volunteers. Pool information. Try and
act as some kind of publishing ombuds-
man.

We see HELP developing a computer
service to readers, publishing subsidiary
material to the order and interests of the
individuals and groups working with us.

HELP staff are young. And they are
sick and tired of the cynicism they have
inherited. Not just in politics. In just
about everything.

Send No Money now.
Please let me have a copy. I'd like to see it. **HELP**
Name:

Address:

We will send you a copy, plus subscription form for £3.3.0d. If you
don't like it, you don't pay.
Send to: 2 Arundel Street, London WC2.
Do you want extra copies to rope in your friends? If so, say how
many in the box. We'll pay £1 to any group you nominate for
every subscription that comes via you.

ANDY

From John Wilcock's 'Other Scenes'

Andy Warhol is alive and well. He's sitting up in his room at New York's Columbus Hospital, reading magazines, unable to talk to anybody. Despite bullets in his head and chest he'll be fine. Meanwhile, Grove Press goes ahead with plans to publish his novel, "Twenty Four Hours" in the fall.

Having produced the ultimate in deadpan paintings, the totally static movie, a pop group that wanders offstage while feedback entertains the audience and pop-up] book that can't be read so much as looked at, Warhol has now turned his attention to tape recording. "Twenty Four Hours" is an untouched taped record of 24 hours in the life of Andy (carrying the NOrelco tape recorder), Ondine, articulate star of Chelsea Girls and other movies (who does most of the talking) and whoever they run into on their serendipitous journeys around Manhattan. It sounds revealing—but isn't.

To the average reader, in fact, the book might as well be in code. To start with, Andy is referred to throughout as Drella or "D", short for the nickname 'Cinderella', known only to intimates. Ondine is clearly identified and some of the Warhol gang or friends (Gerard Malanga, Billy Name, Paul Morrissey, Steve Schorr, Jonas Mekas, Allen Ginsberg, Ed Sanders) are featured by name, but how many people are going to identify references to or by Taxine, the Duchess, the Mayor, Billy Bedroom, Norman or 'the number one artist' ?

As for subject matter, it shifts almost every sentence in a surrealistic manner that resembles James Joyce more than anything else. It's important to remember that the book is *documentary*—god knows, it's surely too freaky to have been made up.

Despite their clamorous indignation about our liberties, Tory MPs are taking great care that the case of Sir Frederick Crawford, the Rhodesian who lost his British passport, doesn't get pushed to the point of an actual investigation. For they know as well as everybody in Rhodesia that Sir F and his wife are pillars of Rhodesian reaction, as long as it makes money.

His wife, an obsessive busybody, is even more famous than the Queen Mother for monumentally unfortunate remarks, and dining at the Crawfords is gracious living indeed: 1 black servant per guest on informal occasions, 3 blacks per guest on formal occasions. It's no secret in Salisbury that Sir F was over here to arrange a big, devious, sanctions-busting deal in asbestos and tobacco. But the whole Tory line on Rhodesia confirms that, where Tory loyalty is concerned, class ('kith and kin' being the smooth phrase) comes first, the Queen a very poor second, and the rest of us, nowhere.

Goodluck to the Manchester Arts Laboratory, which opened on June 22nd.

Congratulations to John Hopkins and Suzy Creamcheese on their marriage trip.

Hilary Barrow and Adrian Rifkin are helping form a White Peoples Association to promote the aims of Black Power and help black people. They plan day nurseries in Notting Hill, cottages in the country for orphaned children, films, plays, dances and summer events. Anyone interested write to Hilary c/o OZ.

OZ

Thank you everyone who helped so generously with the OZ benefit. We're sorry about the girl who rang us weeping over the exploding parrot ("Everyone else was laughing . . . it was horrible") and for the man who freaked out when the mercanaries freaked in for the crucifixion scene.

The World's Most Boring Man had over 40 customers; some of whom competed with him; and the World's Longest Joke Teller is droning on to this day. The girl wrestlers were sexy, cruel dedicated, deliciously young and are coming back for more on June 30. Yes; we're having another one at Middle Earth next Sunday. It will be wilder, more unexpected totally integrated, and dangerous. Come. It will make our first one seem like a nursery party.

Meanwhile; warm thankyous to The Pink Floyd, Pretty Things, Social Deviants, Blonde on Blonde, Alexis Korner, Miss Kelly, The Flamingoes, Louise, Buzby Loyd, John Peel, Jeff Dexter, Carolyn Coon, Transcendental Aurora (The Light Show), Ian Knight, Jeff Shaw, Sean Kelly, Peter the popcorn man, Sebastian Jorgensen, Michael Newman, Bruce Beresford, Felix Dennis, the Mercenaries, Dave Hausman, Paul Waldman, Middle Earth, Michael Ramsden, Tony Crerar and the Human Family, David Spode and everyone else who helped OZ at Middle Earth.

Some who couldn't make it to Middle Earth sent a donation instead. We've added a section to the subscription coupon for the convenience of any other philanthropists. The Black Dwarf has a sweet old Scottish lady (she sent them £1000), Private Eye has celebrities, IT has a lovely

---

banker's son, but OZ, dear readers, has only you.

TOM

A few weeks ago Mr Tom Morton was arrested and roughed-up outside the Royal Courts of Justice for distributing a pamphlet entitled The Crown of England and the Throne Stinks of the Corruption of Her Majesty's Judges.

Under the sub heading; The Palaces of Perjured Judicial Ponces, Mr Morton alleges, among other things: "That I was brought to secret trial by the Director of Public Prosecutions, on false charges and false evidence, designed to deprive me of my freedom of speech, in order to protect Judge . . . , whom he knew to be criminally corrupt . . ."

Under another heading; Your

Majesty's Judges are Posturing, Petrified Pestilential, Perjured Pimps; Mr Morton calls for a public inquiry into his case on the grounds that the Judiciary cannot try a charge against itself.

Mr Morton's contempt for the legal profession derives from the mis-handling of his divorce proceedings in 1953 and he has been fighting the law ever since.

In 1964 he produced a 350,000 word book single handedly, on an electric duplicator, entitled "Treason by Dilhorne and His Corrupt Judges Hilbery Salmon and Rawlins" which is the complete story of a marriage, narrative accounts and the official records of the "corrupt and extraordinary" legal proceedings which followed. He has since persisted with a series of pamphlets written in traditional inflammatory style which he has distributed himself in strategic areas. The penultimate paragraph in one pamphlet reads:

As an artist, I greatly admire Your Majesty. Like many of my fellow citizens, I was filled with pride, when you appeared in France some years ago, looking beautiful and splendid, before an official banquet. We all know you to be the very personification of chivalry and honour, but your judges have placed the filth of perjury and suppression into your mouth. A person who commits perjury spits in the face of God. In condoning these terrible crimes, that is what your judges have done in your name and until you spit this filth out in their faces, you defile heaven and must be known as, The Perjured Queen.

When Mr Morton appeared at Bow Street Magistrates Court on a charge of disturbing the peace he was convicted and put on a good behaviour bond. The court treated him with a bored paternalism, telling him to go home to Polperro and forget all about his bizarre allegations. "We've heard it all before", said the magistrate.

Tom Morton is a friendly, elegant artist from Polperro in Cornwall, intelligent and courageous. When young, he was a policeman, joined the army, became a landscape artist and now runs his own gallery.

OZ has no opinion about what he says; but defends to the last column inch, the flair with which he says it. Ho! HO!

The tradition of all the dead
generations weighs like a nightmare on the brain of the living.
Karl Marx The Eighteenth Brum-
aire of Louis Napoleon.

"The quotations and historiography are aimed at demonstrate the partisan and unseemly belief that socialism means popular power and human liberation and requires the overturning of advanced capitalism by the industrial workers themselves. Dewey, Laing and even Marcuse are important and serious Marxist thinkers but largely irrelevant to our here and now. (Excellent left critiques of Marcuse's pessimism and hey nonny no Freudianism are the Alisdair Macintyre in Survey Jan 67 and Peter Sedgewick in Socialist Register 66). Above all else read Victor Serge's "Memoirs of a Revolutionary", an Oxford paperback at 12/6d."

"The best Marxist paperback selections are the Bottomore and Rubel Pelican editions of Marx. C Wright Mills's selection "The Marxists" is rather uneven and David Caute's "Essential Writings of Karl Marx" in London Panther is somewhat intrusively edited, though less soggy than his usual "The Left in Europe" for the World University Library. For perspectives on British capitalism both the enlarged May Day Manifesto (Penguin) and "Towards Socialism" (Fontana Library) are valuable if taken alongside E P Thompson's long essay "The Peculiarities of the English" in Socialist Register 65, critical of their approach. For a view of the self activity of the working class as the heart of the revolutionary process read E P Thompson's magnificent "The Making of the English Working Class" (Gollancz, but why still no paperback?) Trotsky's "History of the Russian Revolution" (Sphere, Sunday Telegraph book of the year, 'Evil has never been so dazzling presented') and Hal Draper's polemic "The Two Souls of Socialism" (available from IS). International Socialism have also published the complete polish "Revolutionary Socialist Manifesto" written in a polish prison by Kuron and Modzelewski.

For your day to day activity read Socialist Worker, Voice of the Unions (and its area and industry based papers), Solidarity, International and perhaps the Black Dwarf. The bi-weekly Newsletter remains unbelievably sectarian and dishonest but is at least frequent. Tribune and Morning Star are beyond hope".

AGIT 1

Men fight and lose that battle, and then the thing they fought for comes about in spite of their defeat, and when it comes, turns out to be not what they meant, and other men have to fight for what they meant under another name.

There are of the English middle class, today ... men of the highest aspirations towards Art, and of the strongest will; men who are most deeply convinced of the necessity to civilization of surrounding men's lives with beauty; and many lesser men, thousands for what I know, refined and cultivated, follow them and praise their opinions; but both the leaders and the led are incapable of saving so much as half a dozen commons from the grasp of inexorable Commerce: they are as helpless in spite of their culture and their genius as if they were just so many overworked shoemakers: less lucky than King Midas, our green fields and clear waters, nay the very air we breathe, are turned not to gold (which might please some of us for an hour maybe) but to dirt; and to speak plainly we know full well that under the present gospel of Capital not only there is no hope of bettering it, but that things grow worse year by year, day by day.
William Morris, craftsman poet and political writer who asserted revolutionary social change against the dominant Fabian reformism.

When philosophy paints its grey in grey, one form of life has become old, and by means of its grey it cannot be rejuvenated but only known. The owl of Minerva takes its flight only when the shadows of evening are fallen.
The Philosophy of Right: by Hegel

The best laws that England hath are yokes and manacles, tying one sort of people to be slaves to another.
... let the gentry have their enclosures and waste lands set free to them from all Norman enslaving lords of manors ...
If you found out the Court of Wards to be a burden and freed lords of the manors and gentry from paying fines to the King ... let the common people be free too for paying homage to the lords of the manors.
Gerrard Winstanley
'The Putney Debates' radical agitator in Oliver Cromwell's army

You are horrified at our intending to do away with private property. But in your existing society, private property is already done away with for nine-tenths of the population; its existence for the few is solely due to its non-existence in the hands of the nine tenths. You reproach us, therefore, with intending to do away with a form of property, the necessary condition for whose existence is the nonexistence of any property for the immense majority of society.

In one word, you reproach us with intending to do away with your property. Precisely so; that is just what we intend.
Communist Manifesto, Karl Marx

The science of marvellous industry is simultaneously the science of asceticism ... Self-denial, the denial of life and of all human needs is its cardinal doctrine. The less you eat, drink and read books; the less you go to the theatre, the dance hall, the public-house; the less you think, love, theorize, sing, paint, fence, etc, the more you *save*—the *greater* becomes your treasure, which neither moths nor dust will devour—your *capital*. The less you *are*, the more you *have*; the less you express your own life, the greater is your alienated life—the greater is the store of your estranged being.
The Holy Family, Karl Marx

A negro is a negro, but only under certain conditions does he become a slave. A machine to weave cotton is a machine to weave cotton, but only under certain conditions does it become capital. Separated from these conditions it is as little capital as gold, in itself is money or sugar is the price of sugar.
Das Kapital, Karl Marx

In direct contrast to German philosophy, which descends from heaven to earth, here we ascend from earth to heaven. That is to say, we do not set out from what men say, imagine, or conceive, nor from what has been said, thought, imagined, or conceived of men, in order to arrive at men in the flesh. We begin with real, active men, and from their real life-process show the development of the ideological reflexes and echoes of this life-process. The phantoms of the human brain also are necessary sublimates of men's material life-process, which can be empirically established and which is bound to material preconditions. Morality, religion, metaphysics, and other ideologies, and their corresponding forms of consciousness, no longer retain therefore their appearance of autonomous existence. They have no history, no development; it is men, who, in developing their material production and their material intercourse, change, along with this their real existence, their thinking and the products of their thinking. Life is not determined by consciousness, but consciousness by life.

The existence of revolutionary ideas in a particular age presupposes the existence of a revolutionary class ...

The ideas of the ruling class are, in every age, the ruling ideas: ie, the class which is the dominant *material* force in society is at the same time its dominant *intellectual* force. The class which has the means of material production at its disposal, has control at the same time over the means of mental production, so that in consequence the ideas of those who lack the means of mental production are, in general, subject to it.

The question whether objective truth can be attributed to human thinking is not a

question of theory but is *practical* question. In practice man must prove the truth, that is, the reality and power, the this-sidedness of his thinking. The dispute over the reality or non-reality of thinking which is isolated from practice is a purely *scholastic* question.

The materialist doctrine that men are products of circumstances and upbringing, and that, therefore, changed men are products of other circumstances and changed upbringing, forgets that it is men that change circumstances and that the educator himself needs educating ... The coincidence of the changing of circumstances and of human activity can be conceived and rationally understood only as *revolutionary practice.*

Social life is essentially *practical.* All mysteries which mislead theory to mysticism find their rational solution in human practice and in the comprehension of this practice.

The philosophers have only *interpreted* the world in various ways; the point, however, is to *change* it.
Theses on Feuerbach,   Karl Marx
1818-1883, German revolutionary socialist. Exiled in Paris and later to London where he died. Founder of the First International, co-author of the Communist Manifesto and wrote Das Kapital.

A narrow empiricism denies that a fact does not really become a fact except in the course of an elaboration according to a method. It finds in each factor, in each statistic, in each *factum brutum* of economic life, an important fact. It does not understand that the simplest enumeration of 'facts', their stringing together without any commentary, is already an interpretation, that at this stage the facts are already examined from a point of view, a method, that they have been abstracted from the context of life in which they were found and introduced into a theory ...

When one faces a situation where the exact knowledge of society becomes, for a class, the immediate condition of its self-affirmation in struggle; when, for this class, self-consciousness of society; when this class is, through its consciousness, both of the subject and object of consciousness, then the theory is an immediate, direct and adequate relation to the process of the social revolution, then the unity of theory and practice, that precondition of the revolutionary function of theory, becomes possible.

Georg Lukács 1885— Marxist literary and social critic who served as Comissar for Culture in the brief Bela Kun Soviet Republic of Hungary in 1919 and supported the Hungarian revolution of 1956 serving as Minister of Culture in the Nagy Government and as a founding member of the anti-Stalinist Hungarian Communist Party. Professor of Aesthetics at Budapest University.

Continued P. 18

You are wrestling with the Enemies of the human Race, not for yourself merely, for you may not see the full Day of Liberty, but for the Child hanging at the Breast.
Instructions of the London Corresponding Society to its travelling delegates 1796

WITH REGARD to a false interpretation of our enterprise, stupidly circulated among the public, WE DECLARE as follows to the entire braying literary, dramatic, philosophical, exegetical and even theological body of contemporary criticism:

1) We have nothing to do with literature. But we are quite capable, when necessary, of making use of it like anyone else.
2) Surrealism is not a new means of expression, or an easier one, nor even a metaphysics of poetry. It is a means of total liberation of the mind *and all that resembles it.*
3) We are determined to make a Revolution.
4) We have joined the word *surrealism* to the word *revolution* solely to show the disinterested, detached, and even entirely desperate character of this revolution.
5) We make no claim to change the *mores* of mankind, but we intend to show the fragility of thought, and on what shifting foundations, what caverns we have built our trembling houses.
6) We hurl this formal warning to Society: Beware of your deviations and *faux-pas,* we shall not miss a single one.
7) At each turn of its thought, Society will find us waiting.
8) We are specialists in Revolt. There is no means of action which we are not capable, when necessary, of employing.
9) We say in particular to the Western world, *surrealism* exists. And what is this new ism that is fastened to us? Surrealism is not a poetic form. It is a cry of the mind turning back on itself, and it is determined to break apart its fetters, even if it must be by material hammers!

The Surrealist Declaration of 27th Jan 1925. Signatories included Aragon, Artaud, Breton, Eluard, Ernst and Queneau.

"One must dream," said Lenin. "One must act," said Goethe. Surrealism has never maintained anything else, for practically all its efforts have tended towards the dialectical resolution of this question.
Position Politique de Surrealisme, 1935
.
Both feeling and reason degenerated in the age of capitalism when that age was drawing towards its end, and entered into a bad, unproductive conflict with each other. But the rising new class and those who fight on its side are concerned with feeling and reason engaged in *productive* conflict. Our feelings impel us towards the maximum effort of reasoning, and our reason purifies our feelings.
Bertold Brecht 1898–1956. Marxist poet and dramatist

The working class must carry out all these changes in the area of political, social and economic relations in order to realize its own class interest, which is the command over its own labour and its products. Is this program realistic?

With the initial step toward its realization—making the enterprise independent—the working class would create the conditions for adapting production to needs, eliminating all waste of the economic surplus and the proper use of the intensive factors of economic growth. The same would be carried out by the technocracy, the difference being that the production goal of the working class is consumption by many, not the luxury consumption of privileged strata. That is why workers' control of production would assure the most radical resolution of the contradiction between an expanded productive potential and the low level of social consumption which impedes economic growth today.

The workers separate class interest coincides with the economic interests of the mass of low-paid white collar employees and of the small and medium holders in the countryside. In their combined numbers, they are the overwhelming majority of the rural and urban population. Since the slavery of the working class is the essential source of the slavery of other classes and strata, by emancipating itself, the working class also liberates the whole of society.

To liberate itself, it must abolish the political police; by doing this it frees the whole of society from fear and dictatorship.

It must abolish the regular army and liberate the soldier in the barracks from nightmarish oppression;

It must introduce a multi-party system, providing political freedom to the whole society;

It must abolish preventive censorship, introduce full freedoms of the press, of scholarly and cultural creativity, of formulating and propagating various trends of social thinking. It will thereby liberate the writer, artist, scholar and journalist; it will create, on the widest possible scale, conditions for the free fulfillment by the intelligentsia of its proper social function;

It must subject the administrative apparatus to the permanent control and supervision of democratic organizations, changing existing relationships within that apparatus. Today's common civil servant will become a man free of humiliating dependence on a bureaucratic hierarchy;

It must assure the peasant control over his product, as well as economic, social and political self-government. It will thereby change the peasant from the eternal, helpless object of all power into an active citizen sharing in making decisions which shape his life and work.

An Open Letter to the Party by Jacek Kuron and Karol Modzelewski Both these polish revolutionary socialists are in jail as a result of cirulating this document. Street fighting by young Poles in Warsaw this year originated in protest against the imprisonment.

This is a sad reality: Vietnam—a nation representing the aspirations, the hopes of a whole world of forgotten peoples— is tragically alone. This nation must endure the furious attacks of US technology, with practically no possibility of reprisals in the South and only some of defence in the North—but always alone.
The solidarity of all progressive forces of the world towards the people of Vietnam today is similar to the bitter irony of the plebians coaxing on the gladiators in the Roman arena. It is not a matter of wishing success to the victim of aggression, but of sharing his fate; one must accompany him to his death or to victory.

Che Guevara 1928–1967, Message to the Havana Tricontinental 1967

The International of Crime and Treason exists, the present task is to create an International of Resistance and Solidarity.

We must leave our dreams and abandon our old beliefs and friendships of the time before life began. Let us waste no time in sterile litanies and nauseating mimicry. Leave this Europe where they are never done talking of Man, yet murder men everywhere they find them, at the corner of every one of their own streets, in all corners of the globe. For centuries they have stifled almost the whole of humanity in the name of a so-called spiritual experience. Look at them today swaying between atomic and spiritual disintegration.

The Wretched of the Earth, by Frantz Fanon 1925–1961. Born in Martinique, Fanon was a doctor who became the leading thinker of the Algerian Revolution. He died of leukaemia.

The Government have referred the GLC rent increases to the Prices & Incomes Board. Tenants should be under no illusions that this is going to mean anything other than a postponement or slight adjustment, of the rent increases. Petitions and lobbies will only have the same effect.
In the last resort only a rent strike by GLC tenants will effectively stop the rent increases; otherwise they will go through. Lobbies and petitions which are not backed by strike action will be largely ignored.
If the GLC rent scheme is going to be stopped this will not be done by Parliament or the Labour councillors at County Hall.
IT WILL ONLY BE DONE BY THE TENANTS THEMSELVES THROUGH THEIR OWN RESOLUTION, ACTION AND ORGANISATION.

Not a Penny on the Rents. A leaflet of the GLC Tenants Action Committee

Moralists of the Anglo-Saxon type, in so far as they do not confine themselves to rationalist utilitarianism, the ethics of bourgeois bookkeeping, appear to be conscious or unconscious students of Viscount Shaftesbury, who—at the beginning of the eighteenth century!— deduced moral judgements from a

special "moral sense," supposedly once and for all given to man. Supra-class morality inevitably leads to the acknowledgment of a special substance, of a "moral sense," "conscience," some kind of absolute which is nothing more than the philosophic-cowardly pseudonym for God. Independent of "ends," that is, of society, morality, whether we deduce it from eternal truths or from the "nature of man", proves in the end to be a form of "natural theology." Heaven remains the only fortified position for military operations against dialectic materialism.
Their Morals and Ours, 1938 Trotsky

It is true that humanity has more than once brought forth giants of thought and action who tower over their contemporaries like summits in a chain of mountains. The human race has a right to be proud of its Aristotle, Shakespeare, Darwin, Beethoven, Goethe, Marx Edison, and Lenin. But why are they so rare? Above all, because almost without exception, they came out of the upper and middle classes. Apart from rare exceptions, the sparks of genius in the suppressed depths of the people are choked before they can burst into flame. But also because the processes of creating, developing, and educating a human being have been and remain essentially a matter of chance, not illuminated by theory and practice, not subjected to consciousness and will.
From a lecture in Denmark 1932, Trotsky

—Death to Utopia! Death to faith! Death to love! Death to hope! thunders the twentieth century in salvos of fire and in the rumbling of guns.
—Surrender, you pathetic dreamer. Here I am, your long awaited twentieth century, your "future".
—No, replies the unhumbled optimist: You—you are only the *present.*

On Optimism and Pessimism, 1907 Leon Trotsky 1879—1940. Leader of the 1905 Russian Revolution. Peoples Commissar for Foreign Affairs 1917-18; founder and leader of the Red Army during the Civil War. Denied possibility of 'socialism in one country' and continued to work for world revolution until murdered by Stalin in Mexico.

Even before I emerged from childhood I seem to have experienced, deeply at heart, that paradoxical feeling which was to dominate me all through the first part of my life: that of living in a world without any possible escape, in which there was nothing for it but to fight for an impossible escape. I felt repugnance, mingled with wrath and indignation, towards people whom I saw settled comfortably in this world. How could they not be conscious of their captivity, of their unrighteousness?

One night, in a port whose houses were shattered by bombs, the sick man in our party, some police officers and I went into a tavern filled with British soldiers. They noticed our unusual appearance. 'Who are you lot? Where are you going?'

'Revolutionaries—we are going to Russia.' Thirty tanned faces surrounded us eagerly, there were hearty exclamations all round us, and we had to shake everybody's hand. Since the Armistice popular feeling had changed once again; the Russian Revolution was once more a distant beacon to men.

Memoirs of a Revolutionary, Victor Serge 1890—1947. Son of Russian emigre, grew up in Brussels and Paris. Returned to Russia in 1918 and worked for Comintern. Supported Trotsky and the Left Oppositionists, imprisoned by Stalin 1933-6. Freed after outcry in France, died in Mexico.

Unfurl the red flag in the east wind
To turn the world scarlet
*Mao Tse-Tung 1893—
Reply to Kuo Mo-jo.
Assumed leadership of the Chinese Communists after their decimation by Chiing in 1927. Led epic long march to Yenan in 1934-5. Fought against the Japanese and defeated the Kuomintang in 1949 when he became Chairman of the Chinese People's Republic. Nationalist warlord and poet.*

Imperialist bestiality has been let loose to devastate the fields of Europe, and there is one incidental accompaniment for which the 'cultured world' has neither heart nor conscience—the mass slaughter of the European proletariat . . . It is our hope, our flesh and blood, which is falling in swathes like corn under the sickle. The finest, the most intelligent, the best-trained forces of international Socialism, the bearers of the heroic traditions of the modern working-class movement, the advanced guard of the world proletariat, the workers of Great Britain, France, Germany and Russia, are being slaughtered in masses. That is a greater crime by far than the brutish sack of Louvain or the destruction of Rheims Cathedral. It is a deadly blow against the power which holds the whole future of humanity, the only power which can save the values of the past and carry them on into a newer and better human society. Capitalism has revealed its true features; it betrays to the world that it has lost its historical justification, that its continued existence can no longer be reconciled with the progress of mankind . . .

Deutschland, Deutschland Uber Alles! Long live Democracy! Long live the Tsar and Slavdom! Ten thousand blankets guaranteed in perfect condition! A hundred thousand kilos of bacon, coffee substitutes—immediate delivery! Dividends rise and proletarians fall. And with each one sinks a fighter for the future, a soldier of the Revolution, a liberator of humanity from the yoke of capitalism and finds a nameless grave.

"The madness will cease and the bloody product of hell come to an end only when the workers of Germany and France, of Great Britain and Russia, awaken from their frenzy, extend to each other the hand of friendship, and drown the bestial chorus of imperialist hyaenas

with the thunderous battle cry of the modern working-class movement: 'Workers of the World Unite!'
The Accumulation of Capital 1913, Rosa Luxemburg

". . . socialist democracy is not something which begins only in the promised land after the foundations of socialist economy are created; it does not come as some sort of Christmas present for the worthy people who, in the interim, have loyally supported a handful of socialist dictators. Socialist democracy begins simultaneously with the beginnings of the destruction of class rule and of the construction of socialism. It begins at the very moment of the seizure of power by the socialist party. It is the same thing as the dictatorship of the proletariat.

"Yes, dictatorship! But this dictatorship consists in the *manner of applying* democracy, not in its *elimination*, in energetic resolute attacks upon the well-entrenched rights and economic relationships of bourgeois society, without which a socialist transformation cannot be accomplished. But this dictatorship must be the work of the *class* and not of a little leading minority in the name of the class . . ."
The Russian Revolution 1917, Rosa Luxemburg

"Mistakes committed by a genuine revolutionary labour movement are much more fruitful and worth-while historically than the infallibility of the very best Central Committee."

in Die Neue Zeit 1904, by Rosa Luxemburg 1871—1919. Born in Poland, became leading Socialist Revolutionary, moved to Germany 1898 where with Karl Liebknecht she led the anti-revisionist wing of the Social Democrats. Author of "The Accumulation of Capital" murdered by Fascist thugs in January 1919 during the abortive German Revolution. With Lenin one of the two greatest Marxists of the twentieth century.

It is not only the conscious hypocrites, scientists, and priests that uphold and defend the bourgeois lie that the state is free and that it is its duty to defend the interests of all, but also a large number of people who sincerely adhere to the old prejudices and who cannot understand the transition from the old capitalist society to socialism.

The State, 1919 by Vladimir Ilyich Lenin 1870—1923, leader of the Bolshevik wing of the Russian Social Democrat Party. Against the opposition of every other political group and sections of the Bolsheviks he agitated for and brought about the October Revolution, the world's first proletarian revolution. Died with the USSR isolated, the Western European Revolution he anticipated not having materialised.

AGIT 2

David Widgery

WHEN HARRODS IS LOOTED

1968 would be as good a year as any for the liberal intelligentsia to start taking politics seriously. Let's for example, pretend that the Metropolitan Police are the Wehrmacht and the dockers are breaking the windows of all the Indian restaurants in Gerrard Street. Orwe could make believe in the National Conservative administration of 1971, the first shot striker and the Student Problem. Or perhaps the meat porters do find out that it's the bankers and not the blacks. Either way the elaborate parlour games of most of our political intellectuals could be broken up very fast by the realities of a world recession, concentrated economic and political power and eroded democratic institutions.

Fleet Street's chain of fools and their allies in the university have told us for years that the class struggle didn't exist or wasn't needed any more or that it was our business to be on the other side of the barricades anyway. When the students in Germany talked about overturning capitalism, they patronised them and put the rebels on the front of their glossies like cavemen painted mastodons to show their mastery. When it happened in France, they talked of its 'style' and how we have a middle tier of oppression so it can't happen here. And when it does happen here and maybe its no longer chic but brutal and muddy and the rubbish is burning and Harrods is looted, they will not still see it's about revolution and socialism and that for us all else is folly. The nice people will have to choose then between those who honked their horns around the

Champs Elysee and shouted 'Cohn Bendit to Dachau' and accurately 'Liberate' our factories' and the workers marching in the Place de la Bastille with the clothes they have stood beside machines in all their life. And if that's already too much like cliche, then you've already chosen your side. As for us we should have chosen long ago. For until this struggle against capitalism and for popular power is finished, we remain in this log jam at the middle of the century slung as Arnold wrote, "between one world dead and the other still powerless to be born".

At least while the Labour Party is in opposition the myths of Fabianmight be maintained; for the intellectual that increased Parliamentary representation of the Labour Party means the increase and then the achievement of popular power, for the worker that if there was a Labour Government as well as a Labour Council then rents would not still go up and houses would get built. But the vulnerability of the British economy to international capital movement and 'confidence,' has revealed yet again the marked and unjustified optimism that social democrats have always had about economic and political power. The independent foreign policy, as beloved of C.N.D. as Douglas-Home, is so many sweepings before the broom of American Power. The 'export-led boom' depends simply on for how long and how low working class living standards can be forced, and the science of '64 means the productivity of '66 means the exploitation of '68. Labour has simply been taking its pleasure too often on the bed of Capital, for us still to be crying rape. But the rewards of collaboration with capital have not been adequate to buy mass support with wages and domestic booms and Labour has been without mass support for 4 years now. But over the last two years even those party activists who remained have been finally sickened away from politics and gone back to "Gardeners' Question Time" and mild and bitter. Increasingly suitable undemocratic

professionals of Transport House are wielding the dead weight of a party defined by the absence of militants or of real strength from the class socialism is all about. In fact the students' emphasis on opposition outside Parliament is a precise expression of the options open to serious socialists in the face of the shift to the right which social democracy and European communism has made over the last 20 years. Coalition social democracy has abandoned even its verbal claims to equality and social reform, the rhetoric of Wilson, Brandt, Mollet and Nenni (and for that matter Sik and Lieberman) is now thoroughly state plannist, elitist, technical and manipulative.

The Communist Parties have in turn occupied the reformist parliamentary programmes which social democracy has vacated. The drive towards respectability and the attempt to strip the tiger, ballot box by ballot box, has meant the isolation and frequent suppression of the CP's militants so that its functionaries could achieve the plush comforts of the Parliament. The marxism they practise is for the most part the ruling class ideology of the Soviet Union, national and conservative and forced to express the most authoritarian elements of European socialism. The responsible CP-ers appealing for moderation at tenants meetings are as fundamentally reformist as the French Stalinists who shopped the students and workers of Paris, just less successful. They are no more de-Stalinised than Globke and Oberlander are de-nazified. The cameos are plain; the leaders of the CBI welcomed to the leather chair of the Kremlin to complain about their workers over vodka aperitifs; the coutious and 'responsible' behaviour of the Moscow Narodny Bank Ltd. in tiding over the last two gold crises.

But because there is no visible political institution which can be seen to represent student socialists and because loyalty to Eastern Europe is no longer an accurate litmus to the far left, the political train spotters

Continued. p18

1640 cromwell's revolution PARIS COMMUNE

ANARCHISTS

DIGGERS

1791 jacobins
T. PAINE

LUDDITES
CHARTISTS
MORRIS

marx

1885 fabians

RUSSIAN REVOLUTION

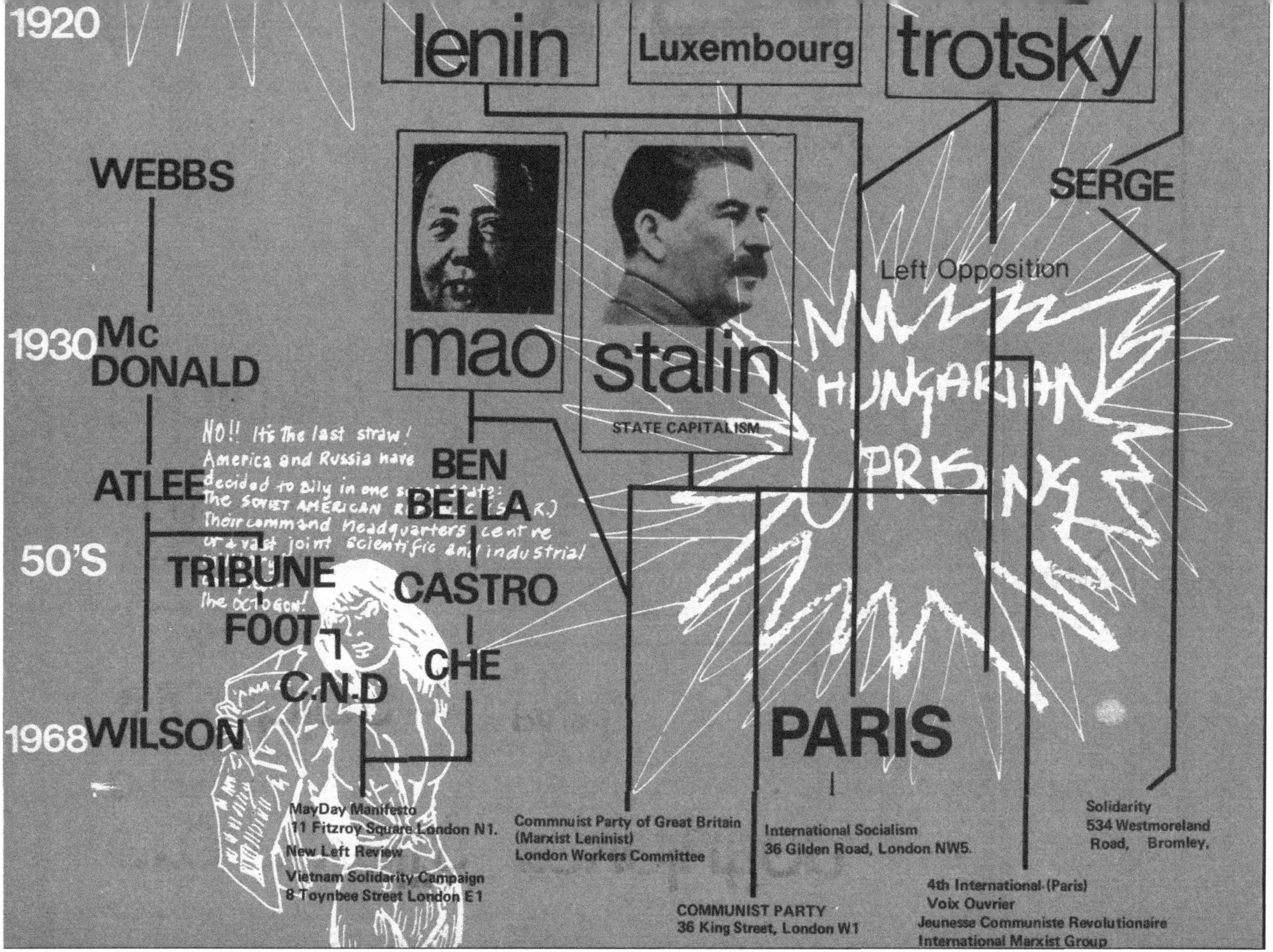

1920

WEBBS

lenin | Luxembourg | trotSky

SERGE

Left Opposition

1930 Mc
DONALD

ATLEE

BEN
BELLA

HUNGARIAN

PRAGUE

STATE CAPITALISM

mao stalin

No!! It's the last straw!
America and Russia have
decided to bily in one s...
The soviet AMERICAN R...
Their command Headquarters centre
or is it joint Scientific an industrial

PARIS

50'S

TRIBUNE

CASTRO

FOOT

C.N.D

CHE

The october

1968 WILSON

MayDay Manifesto
11 Fitzroy Square London N1.

New Left Review

Vietnam Solidarity Campaign
8 Toynbee Street London E1

Communist Party of Great Britain
(Marxist Leninist)
London Workers Committee

COMMUNIST PARTY
36 King Street, London W1

International Socialism
36 Gilden Road, London NW5.

Solidarity
534 Westmoreland
Road, Bromley,

4th International (Paris)

Voix Ouvrier

Jeunesse Communiste Revolutionaire

International Marxist Group

and student affairs experts whose ideology is end of ideology, have assumed that students are no longer interested in theory and analysis but are just in it for the punch-ups. If only lines of communication could be opened for full and free dialogue and the trouble makers eliminated, the universities could get back to the real and superbly harmless works of scholarship. Whereas in fact political students spend their waking, thinking, drinking life utterly bound up in politics and analysis. Those who are fond

of asking why we don't join the NLF should not suppose that the workers and intellectuals of the Spanish War are the only people who meant what they said when they declared they would die for what they believed. Indeed the very frantic new of students, their capacity for outrage and hope, is an affront to the play ethic of late capitalism for which a flayed self-awareness wears so much better than conviction.

What is at the back of this urgency, what makes the anger last and deepen is the horror which must happen every day to maintain the US occupation of South Vietnam and the final horror which comes from the realisation the Vietnams will be repeated until the US is either a fortress in mutiny or so over-extended that the final reckoning comes. But students response is not just the cont-

empt that any person with a sense of meaning must feel over the mouth disease of LBJ, Brown's righteous hypocrisy and Wilson's diatribes written in the Pentagon. It is not only the well chronicled, familiar, glutinous lies, the genocide to save a civilisation, humanities Incendergel, the fragmentation bomb of freedom. The mirror Vietnam holds up to the West illuminates precisely those myths that are at the centre of the status quo, the absence of class struggle, the inevitability of economic growth and thus increase in living standards, the post colonial powers' begin international intentions.

International capitalism has obliged the triple anniversary of Marx with a life-scale demonstration of precisely why it cannot make the world liveable for its people. It is not just the war in Vietnam, but the needs of an economy which makes Vietnam the rule rather than the exception an economy stabalized only by high unemployment and massive defence related expenditure, a system required to police the neo-colonial empire that it has, at least for a few more years yet, to expropriate economically and supervise politically. America, that fine citadel of democracy, needs its guns and buttresses; to get them Tom Paine must be bound naked to the stake of militarism. As the late Isaac Deutcher, whose magnificent witness against the new barbarism alongside Sartre and Russell was an initial inspiration to the movement which has grown up across Europe to defeat the Americans in Vietnam, wrote:

"About 60 years ago Rosa Luxemburg predicted that one day militarism would become the driving force of the capitalist economy but even her forecast pales before the facts".

The helplessness of Wilson even to make a formal diplomatic break with America (and thus the helplessness of those on the Left whose sole aim was to pressure him into dissociation) illuminated the nature of our satelitism to the needs of im-

perialism as clearly as the bankers budget, the gratuitous cuts say in the NHS for the foreign audience, and the shows of 'toughness' indicate the helplessness of national capitalist planning with capital international and irrational.

The world's on fire; all Wilson can offer is the nudging and anticipation of backward British capitalism into mergers, investment and what is known as technological advance. The carrot is his grim dedication to the task of depressing living standards to a level at which even British business cannot help but become more competitive in the bitter conflict over the dwindling growth (perhaps even an absolute decrease in '68) margin of world trade. The political drive towards state capitalism makes sense to Maudling and Shore as well as Robbins and is resisted mainly by small CBI firms. Its main political implication is the increased induction of the higher levels of the trade union bureaucracy into the state planning machinery and then the use of the unions themselves to discipline their own rank and file. The TUC leaders find themselves wandering the corridors of power without entry to any of the doors of control and having abandoned even the notion of a militant rank and file on their journey to the top.

In the fifties, it proved easier for much of British business to pay wage drift rather than fight it and union officialdom was able to acclimatise to relatively automatic reformism from above. But the conditions which underlie the Gold Crisis mark the end of this era; wage increase must be fought and won in conditions which inevitably link the industrial to the political. It is in this promising situation and in the opportunities it provides for attacking the fact and the politics of freezism, that student socialists have tried to find a footing. But as the aprons and boots in St. Stephens Yard suggest, there is no guarantee provided that the turbulence and disillusionment within the union rank and file will turn to the left, although similar vacuums in

Germany, France and US have led to important achievements for the revolutionary left. What is clear is that the Labour Party's roots in the working class are withered in the air; the MP's and intellectuals who remain must feel as far away from the young people who proudly carry NLF flags, as they do from the workers who are no longer ashamed to shout Keep Britain White.

The Sunday Press waxes, or rather wanes, eloquent, the svelte left cries into its whiskey and the Parliamentary Left continues to flog its dead horses in the Augean stables of Westminster but none of them notice there's no one listening and nothing's revealed. Of course the taste for revolution is nothing new to the young middle class. Acid hippies, progressive school boheminans and bored pop-centry graduates all like the language of total liberation and look of Che Guevara. Sad some can even spell their name rightly. But as for theory and ways of understanding, these are either brain-damaged any way or have already been gleaned from Cinerama Dr. Zhivago. Indeed, the more the underground load us on about revolution, the more obvious it becomes that pot serves readily the social role that gin did in the Thirties, by enabling the young enlightened middle class to gather round and talk about their enlightenment. The soul-called Revolution, where the young ruling class whom its under control's — idea and life is only typical of this natural dishonesty.

As the traffic to Xanadu thins, it ought to become clearer which of the new orientalists are moved to ask or answer any serious political questions. But in the USA the generous dreamings of the acid left has been overtaken by reality, hippies give away food but negroes take refrigerators, and will hopefully leave the induction centres, police stations and tenements in ashes. Ginsberg did drink the water of the Ganges and he did have dysentry for a month afterwards. The intelligensia seem happy enough treading the water of the Mall palaces, content in the knowledge that we live in a world of vio-

lently interacting bourgeois brie-a-brac. To paraphrase Buechner, the whole thing makes you realise how much more important is a single bus-man on strike than five thousand critics campaigning to legalise pubic hair.

What, on the other hand characterises the political militants is a strong sense of the impotence of seminar socialism marxist hash evenings and all the complicated rationalisations of the liberal intelligentsia which ultimately serve to limit all activity to discussion and contain all discussion within the magic circles of the academic middle class. It has made them wary even of the photogenic struggles within the university. For the result of such militancy is usually the collaboration within a few committees on the herbaceous border of power where a large amount of time is spent comparing the students white with the administrations black and settling on a negotiated charcoal.

Those who are serious are increasingly aware that the universities and the technical wing of the binary system are essentially there, enlarged or otherwise, to provide specified amounts of predictable skills to the medium levels, to a given industrial system. It is this system and the ways of changing it which finally concern us: the JCR's are voting their money to the picket line not the pantomine, students spend as much time with Tenants Associations as with their tutors, the spectre is still haunting Europe but its banners this time read: 'Today the students, tomorrow the workers'. Unnoticed by the whispering gallery of the London Left, students and workers are making growing contacts, gaining mutual self respect and through their activity and their experience of it retrieving something from the husks of Wilsonism. For without these roots into and connections with working class life, the most scintillating critique of bourgeois ideology, the fullest of blue prints for student power, and the grossest of anti-universities could all

be paid for by the Arts Council for all the danger they present.

To wait for revolution by Mao or Che or comprehensive schools or BBC-2 is to play the violin while the Titanic goes down, for if socialists don't take their theory back into the working class there are others who will.
Similarly the solidarity with our German and French comrades was not just a vicarious gesture, but because we know our struggle is integrally linked to theirs and that we both face and are overcoming very similar problems. The spirit in which the students of Europe increasingly collaborate and meet politically is specifically one of socialist internationalism, not the remnants of the Fourth International nor the furniture of international Stalinism or the dining clubs of European social democracy but rather the invisible international which the great revolutionary Victor Serge wrote of.
It represents the beginning of a recovery of the tradition of European revolutionary socialism and the activist heart of Marxism within it. It is no accident that Luxembourg and Liebknecht were the faces paraded in the German streets and Trotsky's face that the students pinned across the court-yards of the Sorbonne. The rifle butt and the canal for Luxembourg, the ice axe for Trotsky and the pistol for Dutsche, these are different weapons of different ruling classes.
The message of this last year is that their imperatives are being taken up again in the cockpit of Europe.

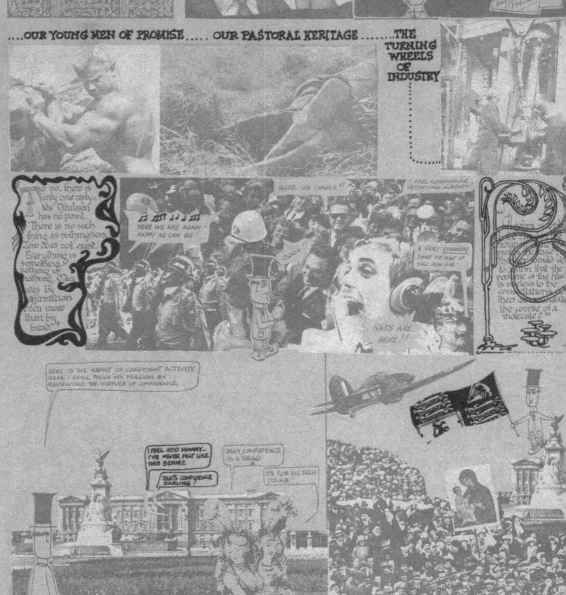

AGIT 3

THE MAY REVOLUTION

by Angelo Quattrocchi

Last day of May.
Hopes are crumbling around us, we
have lived a successful rebellion, a
failed revolution.
Now: rage, impotence, bewilderment.
Images of workers going back to the
same factories, owned by the same
capital.
Early morning. The factory gates opens
and sucks them in, as before, as always.
They sell their labour, they buy their
bread.
We have gone the full circle.
The red and black flags still wave at the
Sorbonne, at the Odeon. Hostages of a
dream, defenceless.
Feverishly, the frail hands of the
students prepare for the world to come,
amidst the ruins of a working class
betrayed by its leaders, the Trade
Unions and the Communist Party.
For decades those leaders have ski!-
fully bargained for crumbs, and in so
doing lost aims and will.

The paving stones wrote improbable
poems which lasted fulminating
seconds.
Calcinated cars, scars, fumes, flames,
flares.
Kids running and trembling and
running and throwing stones and being
hit, for having discovered they exist.
Nights of the long knives. Barricades
which changed the pages of history,
pages turned at unparalleled speed.
People stood to be counted, each
according to his dreams fighting his
ghosts, against blue slowly moving
barriers of ancient force and brutality:
the faceless arm of Capital.

We now commit to paper, after the revolution which is lost and before the
one which has to come, the words of
hate for old and new enemies, the
words of hope for new minds and
young consciences.
Riddles, examples, courage. The young
fight better.
More to hope, less to fear. In a revolution you risk your life to save your
soul.
A revolution is total or is nothing.

Everything in the melting pot.
Students take over the Universities.
Workers take over the factories.
Students want to run the Universities.
Workers want to run the factories.
To each according to his dreams.

The young girl who is not allowed out
after eleven is a bloodstained pullover
lit by the barricades in flame, in rue
Gay Lussac. The May Commune.
The three red fridays:
the 3rd, when the police invaded the
Sorbonne;
the 10th, the night of the student's
barricades;
the 24th, the night of the riots, when
the Stock Exchange burned for long
minutes.
The three red fridays, red with flames
and blood, but in the latter part of the
night black, dark with fear and
savagery.
Students and workers and innocents
pay. In the police stations the skulls
crack, limbs are torn, broken,
faces beaten to a pulp.
Silhouettes squashed against street-
doors, dark upon dark,
while the sirens run through the conquered streets.
Shame, misery, vulgarity.
The spasms of a class in agony, a class
which pays the mercenaries to maim
its own children, who have suddenly
learned to think.
When the workers joined the students
the walls were crying the revolution
could win, against the old logic of the
tired masters, against the tired horses
of marxist faith.
The revolution was feeding itself,
escalating madly and remorselessly,
because there was victory in every
defeat.
In the Latin Quarter, the end-products
of the factories were used to build
barricades. It was like trying to stop
the flow of the river. But then it
happened at the source, with the
occupation of the factories. The rebellion had become a revolution.

We state here, against the manipulators
of our truths, that this has been a
spontaneous rebellion, followed by a
spontaneous revolution, slowed,
harassed and finally brought to the halt
not by the enemy, but by those who
should have lead us, and betrayed us.
It has been confronted by the traditional powers of darkness, the strong-
arm of Capital.
And that is as it should be.
But darkness has found new allies: the
parties of the Left, the Communist
Party traitor to its cause, and the
Trades Unions, which assumed the role

of the police of the working class.
Two old aims. More bread and the
overthrow of the capitalist system. For
the first, the Trade Unions ,
For the second, the Communist Party.
A century goes by. The communist
Union —CGT— wants more money,
nothing else.
The Communist party wants order, at
all costs.
Two hundred young workers occupy
the first Renault factory, in the middle
of the night (when their police — the
CGT — isn't around). In a few hours
the fire spreads to the country, in
three days there are nine million
strikers. The country is at a standstill.
But the CGT asks only for money,
keeps the students out of the factories,
chokes the movement.
The middle classes hoard food and
tremble behind closed shutters, in
country houses. The government howls,
a powerless hyena. De Gaulle calls for a
referendum and is ignored.
The army is indifferent.
Then, the realization. No money, no
transport, the food is there only because the workers have decided to
bring it to the towns. Electricity is
there only because the workers want it.
The country is immobilized, breathless.
It's time for takeover. Start running the
factories, providing the essential services. Worker's control, workers'
councils. Now. Now.
The CGT and the Communist Party
prevent it.
They threaten, appeal to reason, cheat,
lie. The workers have taken over without them, in spite of them. But They say
they are not ready, they ask for a bit
more money. And De Gaulle goes to
see his Generals, pleads for their help,
brings in the army and his fascist allies.
It's election or civil war. The CGT and
Communist Party back down. It's the
end, the end of the first epidosde.

Burn, Saint Michel, burn !
Rue Gay Lussac is in flames. The tear-
gas burns eyes and lungs, plastic helmets
are handy, three cars are enough to
block a street. A street is a battle, the
paving stones are the same. The second
French revolution, the same stones.
Thanks to them, and thanks to the 73
comrade trees which consolidated the
barricades, and were burned by the
enemy's grenades. And thanks to
those people of the Latin Quarter who
didn't dare to come out but at least
threw us food that night we waited for
hours on the barricades, before the
attack.
Thanks to the people who gave refuge

to the students chased by the riot police, whose batons aim at the face and the crutch, two things they do not have.

And finally thanks to the fascist press and the fascist radios who have unwillingly helped the movement by their constant lies. One special mention for 'l'Humanite', organ of the French Communist Party, which has made clear to all that they are the fifth column of the enemy, in spite of their tradition and name.

Oh yes ! New people have been born. They do not experience poverty, physical hunger, only frustration for their social condition and contempt for the written and unwritten laws of society.

They are the students, the workers, the unemployed, the young who sparked the fire. The old-fashioned working class, under the grip of the Communist Party and the Unions, are the gunpowder. True, the mass of the working class only wants better conditions, mesmerized by its own institutions and half lulled marginal concessions.

Spark and powder came to contact, only the detonator didn't work.

It started in the Universities, concentration camps of the mind, where privilege is consumed, and perpetuated.

There, the predilected sons of injustice and absurdity learned the reasons for injustice, discovered the sources of that absurdity.

And rebelled.

Who is Charlemagne, Professor Emeritus ?

Charlemagne was a very good king who defended Christianity.

Do you know what workers eat for lunch ?

Professor Emeritus assumes his students want their piece of paper, to become patented oppressors. They are therefore allowed to give the right answers, not to put questions.

The trades union official assumes that his workers, ruled by poverty and fear, want just a few more crumbs to fall from the capitalist tree, a tree resplendent in goods and napalm, prodigal in arms and bombs, sparing with salaries. Both were wrong.

And the factories are occupied, the owners and the managing directors locked up in their offices.

There too, it's mostly the young, because the older fear victimization, which they have suffered countless times, and have wives, and families, and worries, and the best of them a party card, or a trades union card, which ties

them up. First Renault, then Citroen, and Berliet, and Nord and Sud Aviation, where they build the Concorde. Then the researchers and scientists came out, and all the rest, like an artichoke.

Do the scientists want just more money? Oh brother, they all talk of direct democracy. They talk of workers' and students' power. The old word 'comrade' is resurrected by exalted teenagers and handed back as good as new to the workers. All the universities occupied, all the secondary schools occupied. Will the children occupy the family homes and demand control, or better, the abolition of the family altogether ?

This is only the first episode of the second French revolution. Remember how many battles, riots, fights it took to eliminate the aristocracy and to behead the king ?

This time it is the people who want direct control against the system based on ownership of the means of production. The decisions are questioned at all levels by the people who produce. The producers, at all levels, from the working class level to the technocratic level ask for the elimination of hierarchy and direct control of their concerns. They challenge not only the functioning of the system but its very aims, and therefore its existence. The institutions of the Left prevented the workers from transforming their strike committees into workers councils. At other levels, from the teachers to the scientists, from the television men to the football players, they contested the existing system and prepared blueprints for a direct control of their concerns. They cannot be stopped. And what they want can only be done with a successful revolution.

The monarch flew to see his Generals, pleaded, won their support, flew back and declared war on the revolution. And astutely offered the escape to the washing-mashine-conscious left: elections.

There was a choice to make, a choice between the bullet and the ballot. That evening after De Gaulle spoke, when the army took its positions around Paris and at strategic points all over the country.

The leaders of the Left, chemists of sweat and crumbs, for decades preaching revolution and teaching resignation said they would take the ballot, once again. It could have been a victory, it would have been a victory because there were nine million strikers on one side, and only the police force on the other. The army is made of peasant soldiers and student officers. They could have

only used paratroopers and certain specialized corps. The proof. De Gaulle went to Germany to see General Massu, the only one who would have stepped in to obtain amnesty for his old friends of the Algerian coup. And they brought contingents from Corsica. The bulk of the army, soldiers and officers would have refused to be employed, let alone to fire on the strikers.

And the Gaullists, the shopkeepers, the fascists ?

They were there the day De Gaulle spoke and threatened, true, but very few, only commandos would have been prepared to fight. The bourgeoisie does not come into the streets, it pays the police and the fascists to do that. They would have been drowned by the people.

But the leaders of the Left took the ballot.

Murder ! Murder ! Fire to the police stations, this is a time of hate and blindness. History forgive us who could not be kind, who had to be hateful in order to create kindness.

11th of June. Two kids have died. No names, no sentiments, no time. Comrades, when shall we be able to sing again, in quietness and kindness ?

Comrades, the gates of the factories are the gates of hell and of paradise, because both hell and paradise are on earth.

We must, and therefore we shall, we will trespass.

Who will find the words to sing the Sorbonne besieged ? The agony of an era is agony of flesh and blood, it is screaming, pain, suffering.

Words come before and after, only. Oh it had to happen, the pattern is old, too well known.

Power, ready to bathe us in blood, played its cards.

The conventional left backed down. They started to bargain 10% of the present wages and sold all of our future. But many said no, the best said no and the vangard of the future was left alone to stand and be broken.

The Renault workers and others. And the students, the bad conscience of this society.

The Sorbonne shudders, the bell of the chapel has been heard last night, calling its occupants to defend the citadel. Pravda's and Figaro's rotatives lie. Transistors ooze soothing music and lies. But we have eaten the apple, we will be back to take the tree.

Your desires should come to consciousness, your dreams will become realities, because this is a revolution. Not for bread, not for comfort, but for all you think possible.

We do not want to have more, we want to be more. We want the factories because we want to produce what is needed. What is the use of getting a penny and working for factories which make bombs ?

Our mouths full of ashes will pass the words from university to factory, from factory to university. The humming of their machinery which impartially produces visible goods and invisible injustice cannot stop that. Those who have nothing to fear, those who do not care about what they own or what they will own, they will be the carriers of the future.

And our old organizations we will throw away like used rags. Only two rags to be kept, the red and the black, the red to scare the old bourgeoisie, the black to scare the old communist horses.

Old horses who tried to prevent the link between the students and the workers, the link between mind and body which would have made, which is making the revolution unbeatable. They had thrown a mystifying ring around us, the last emissary of the enemy.

Now the ring is broken.

Factories occupied, country paralyzed, power on the defensive, bourgeoisie hoarding food and keeping indoors. We were at the top of the mountain, the promised land in sight.

The movement, the students of the pale hands and troubled minds and the workers with heavy hands and clear minds, they wanted to take over. They wanted to start the factories themselves, to start running the country. But those who keep the workers in ignorance and the students in their ghettos, our false leaders said 'no'. They were contented with a mess of pottage, they were reasonable, sensible, peaceloving, they kept the country in check so that the owners and the State could find the machinery in order when the time came.

The promised land in sight, yes, but this side of the mountain, the forces of darkness grew denser, darker. Ready for the embrace which suffocates, for the pistol-shot which kills. We had to climb down the same way we came, to the waiting embrace of those who own in fear and live in death.

Splintered glass and burning wood, cobble stones are good projectiles, handkerchiefs soaked in lemon juice against the tear gas, the stones are dug up and passed from hand to hand and reach the barricade, where the defenders

stand.

When the gas makes the position untenable, run to the second barricade, when they cross the first one, then and only then it's time to throw all you have.

Barricades shouldn't be kept for too long. When running away from it, do not leave anybody behind, pick up your wounded if possible, because lying bodies will be kicked by successive waves of the enemy with white sticks. Between the barricades, fifty yards or so.

The enemy front line, the shielded and masked men with the grenades, are heavy and clumsy, they can run for fifty yards and no more. So by the time they come you should be already entrenched behind the second barricade. The enemy, like all barbarians, shouts in a frenzy of excitement. Remember when faced they are cowards, they are only mercenaries. Just beware of the ones who shoot their grenades point blank, they shoot to kill.

Encirclement is the everlasting danger. Most battles have a pattern. The enemy comes from the river and works its way up Boulevard Saint Michel. If Saint Michel must be kept as long as possible, diversionary tactics are essential. They have prooved successful more then once. The attack on the police station by the Pantheon is the best example.

Police stations where they beat and torture the prisoners are the most advisable targets, of course.

Do not break anything if not absolutely necessary for self-defence. Cars have to be used for barricades; big and posh ones are more useful, small ones might belong to people who cannot buy another one.

The purpose of the enemy is to break your morale and your bones. Your purpose, to defend your ideas. The barricades are only self-defence, the street battles are only a necessity, because the enemy has only brute force, and employs it.

Victory is inevitable. Only, it must be conquered.

The first episode is often the most heroic.

It has proved that a takeover is possible. Now the unpredictable is at hand. People have learned to measure their lives in weeks, not decades. Hope is their strength, resignation their only enemy.

All the rest is rubbish.

Only the small-minded want better conditions for themselves, and bugger the neighbour.

Look at the shopwindows, full of things, if you are good, you can buy them too, like others do.

Please be good, and work, so you can consume, please consume, so everybody can carry on working.

Don't ask questions, just work and consume.

Your superiors, teachers, trades unions leaders and bosses think for you. They are good for you.

When work is finished, the telly and the radio tell you how to spend the money you have been handed. Please be good. Nice people do not make demonstrations.

In the cruel month of April
this was true, but France was waiting.
In the gay month of May
all this muck was washed away.
In the hard month of June
we shall see who sets the tune.

Latin Quarter: battleground
Who did throw the first stone ?
Echoes reverberate from Rome.
Nothing is given, just one more pound.
All must be taken, like the Sorbonne.

Rue Monsieur Le Prince: scattered fights.
Rue Gay Lussac: we lasted three hours.
Place Denfert Rochereau: we were too many.
Boulevard Saint Michel: taken and lost.
Gare de l'Est: the workers are there.
Renault factories: we don't want elections.
Citroen factories: the people are with us.
The Sorbonne and Odeon: the revolution goes on.

AGIT 4

Angelo Quattrocchi

PHILISTINES TEARS — NECTAR OF THE GODS

Nanterre la Folie, where it all started.
Resentment bottled in people. Remember:
the poor suffer, the not so poor are bored.
In France more than everywhere else.
Undercurrent of class hate.
Cohn Bendit is rumoured to have laid the
daughter of the ex minister of education, a
student of Nanterre.
At Nanterre now, meetings. The kids from
the surrounding slums play hide and seek
in the Campus.
Will they go to University?
The examinations are the police patrol of
the mind. Abolish the University altogether.
Culture, learning is for all.
The population of Flins (Renault factory)
joined strikers and students against the
police.
The kid drowned near Flins was seventeen,
and a Maoist.
The police Unions issued several commun-
iques during the months of May, asking for
more pay and complaining about being put
in front of the students and the strikers.
The communique said that if they were

asked to confront the strikers it could
become, for many, 'a case of conscience'.
They must be using only the most brutal
and ignorant now. When the army was
called in to clean up Saint Michel after the
nights of riots, the police was keeping watch
on them. Power feared they would talk
to the students and sympathize with them.
One student was stripped naked but for his
slip. Taken to a police station they put a
grenade on his slip. It blew up. It's been
testified by other students present. It
has been impossible to trace him since.
Passers by with red hair or red garments have
been beaten late at night and in the early
morning, the time of the witch-hunt in the
Latin Quarter.
The most popular sign at the Sorbonne:
'It is forbidden to forbid'.
Many of the soldiers were confined to
their barracks during the month of May.
What did De Gaulle promise to General
Massu, in exchange for his support and
intervention in case of a showdown?
The amnesty of the generals of 'Algerie
Francaise'.

It was De Gaulle who gave orders 'to be
firm', the first night of the students
barricades, when police attacked at 2.20 in
the morning.
When a demonstration went by the 'General
Assembly', the Parliament whose MPs
people will vote for at the elections, there
are six policemen to guard it. The demonstrators ignored it.
When granpa De Gaulle made his fireside
chat it was retransmitted in the courtyard
of the Sorbonne. The students laughed a
lot. When he said that the police had done
its duty admirably, there was silence. Not
one single shout.
The Paris Prefect of Police said that he too
was clobbered when a student.
The high school students have been the
bravest under police attack. Kids between
fifteen and seventeen were totally obliv-
ous to danger, even more than university
students.
The Communist Party says it respects two
flags, the red one and the French one. They
are Communists, but also French.

OZ NIGHT

JUNE 30

We need you!

THE NICE

THIS HAPPENED AT THE FIRST OZ NIGHT. THE SECOND ONE IS JUNE 30
Colour naked laughter crying films feathers wars newsreels revolution pop grapple-glee.
OZ Nights at Middle Earth.

26 Next one Sunday 30th

subscribe
donate
to oz

One: Theological striptease . . .
turn on, tune in, drop dead . . .
In bed with the English . . . Raped
Congo nuns whipped with Rosary
beads . . . Private Eye axed.

Two: Mark Lane's BBC expose
. . . British Breasts . . . Peter
Porter's Metamorphoses . . .
Little Malcolm and his struggle
with the 20th century . . .
Cut out pop stars.

Three: Sorry, absolutely
unavailable.

Four: Hapshash and the coloured
coat golden gatefold . . . Tarot
Cards . . . Process exposed . . . Sgt
Nasser's Lonely heartbreak bank
. . . Norman Normal . . . Guide to
Living in Sin . . . Let de Gaulle die
quickly.

Five: Plant a Flower Child billboard poster . . . The Great Alf
Conspiracy.

Six: (OZ & Other Scenes) Blue
movies by the yard . . . The king
of Khatmandu and his Coca Cola
Court . . . Dope Sheet . . . John
Peel interview . . . . Letter from
a Greek Prison . . . Leary in Disneyland . . . Mcluhan's one eyed kingdom.

Seven: What's so good about
Bob Dylan . . . Wog Beach Shock
. . . Michael X and the Flower
Children . . . In bed with the

Americans . . . Review of Maharishi's The Science of Being and
the Art of Living.

Eight: Mis-Spelt Guevara poster
. . . Russia, you have bread, but no
roses . . . Playboy's banned pictures . . . Spyder Turner's raunch
epistemology . . . Edward de Bono
on lateral thinking.

Nine: New Dylan Lyrics . . . 'If I
could turn you on' UFO digest . . .
Death at St Pauls.

Ten: The pornography of violence
. . . Amnesty report from Athens
. . . Gaol in Arkansas . . . The men
who ban OZ . . . OH! what a law-
ful war . . . Roger McGough's
Summer with the Monarch.

Eleven: Brutal New Statesman
parody . . . Vietloon spring
offensive . . . Yippees hit Chicago
. . . the Anglo-American Pumice
Factory . . . Ray Durgnat's Hippy
High Hopes.

Twelve: Yes, Virginia, there is a
Maharishi . . . Excuse me, is this
the way to the gas chamber? . . .
plus 3 giant magical posters.

I enclose 30/-d for a subscription plus two free back issues (US $4) ○

Send me back issues No 2,4,5,6,7,8,9,10,11,12. (delete inapplicable) 2/6d each (US $35c each) ○

I enclose £1 for the exorbitantly priced first issue. (US $2.50) ○

I enclose £2.10.0d for 12 OZes to be sent immediately. ○

I enclose as much as I can afford and want nothing in return except for OZ to continue. ○

Name

Address   Country

RUSH TO OZ, 38a Palace Gardens Terrace, London, W8.

Unfortunately, some 'Smalls' advertisements have been lost. If you sent us a cheque for an ad which hasn't appeared; let us know.

'TAROT CARD' readings by Sheridan, psychic consultant. Guidance on problems, future trends. Phone 636-8975.

The New KONTACT has many fascinating details of switched on people searching for people. Send 5/- for current issue, to:
KONTACT (A)
c/o Lloyds Bank Chambers
Harpenden, Herts

DUREX

DUREX Gossamer: 7s doz.
DUREX Fetherlite: 10s doz.
AMERICAN SKINS: 38s doz.

Post free from Colne Valley Mail Order Co. (OZ), 126, The Rock, Linthwaite, Huddersfield.

WAYOUT ENGLISHMAN 6ft goodlooking small beard own pad London digs blues beat folk & middle earth Seeks attractive wayout girlfriend 18—32 for keeps Genuine all letters answered. Box No 34.

Any Way to Make CASH quickly for a male, 26 Box No 32.

NEW METHOD RELAXATION Therapy Tape Recording 10/-d post free. H. Clark, 45, Woodlands Grove, Isleworth, Middx.

LEGAL HASH

Now, new formulas use legal chemicals to make legal synthetic Hash (THC), PLUS the famous TURN-ON BOOK telling how to make or grow Mescaline, LSD, DMT, Peyote etc. $2.00 to TURN-ONS UNLIMITED, Dept 5 Y, 313 No Edinburgh, Los Angeles, Calif. 90048. If not ecstatic, we refund.

PAINTER, 30 needs girl friend any age, also anyone willing to model. (13) Box 3

smalls

Costs: (see form below). 2d per unit. 31 units per line. (The dot indicates new line). A unit is a letter/space/numeral/punctuation. Indicate capitals as required.

Semi-display words: 1/6d each. Box-numbers: 2/6d. Display: £2.10s per col inch.

PELISSE

CLOTHES BY FREDDIE AND SERENA, AT 240 BROMPTON ROAD, SW3

ARTS LABORATORY, 182, DRURY LANE, WC2.

THEATRE and DANCE THEATRE, CINEMA, GALLERY, FOOD ETC.

Open 6 days a week.

ARTS LAB, 242-3407/8 phone for details

Did you miss the May isse of New Worlds? W H Smith refused to handle the March issue, though they are taking others. For banned issue send 4s plus 6d postage (3s if student) to OZ AD, 11 Goodge Street, London W1.

WHY SHOP? Use our discreet rapid postal service.

Conture (Form-Fitting)   15/-doz
Durex Fetherlite   15/-doz
Durex Gossamer   10/-doz
Crest Naturac   10/-doz
Silver-Tex   8/-doz
Koralle Spezial   3/-each
Sixteen assorted   18/-

Booklets free. Return post. Double-packed, plain envelope. SUREX LTD. 8 Edward St. Blackpool.

Girls meets boy at 'Dukes'. (13) Box 2

New York bargain. VC 10 Flights. Autumn/Winter £66 return. Flats available. (13) Box 1

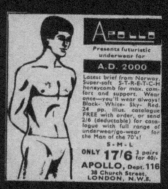

OZ NIGHT—MIDDLE EARTH SUNDAY, JUNE 23. 43 King St. Covent Garden.

LEGALISE POT RALLY, July 7 Hyde Park.

RELEASE office at 52, Princedale Road, W11. Holland Park Tube. Office 229 7753 Emergency 603 8654. We sell OZ IT Peace News and Posters. Come and see us for legal or other advice. We need information about busts and irregualr police behavious etc. Ring us if you have, or want a room or flat to let. RELEASE needs your help — support us if you can.

AGIT 5

GRAFFITI 1968

These graffiti photographs are from a series of postcards being prepared by JLTY, 49 Kensington Park Road, W11. Phone: 727 3723.

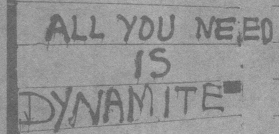

ALL YOU NEED IS DYNAMITE

MOORHOUSE ROAD W2

A GRIEF WITHOUT A PANG

VOID, DARK, DREAR
A STIFLED, DROWSY
UNIMPASSIONED GREIF

POP IS DEAD

Join the men

CRIME IS THE HIGHEST FORM OF SENSUALITY

DENBIGH STREET W11

I.T. IS SHIT

CARS ARE DEAD!

FOR HOTELS
BOARDING HOUSES
FURNISHED ROOMS

BURN BABY BURN

BURN IT ALL DOWN

ALL RACES ALL MEN ARE BROTHER

THE CAST

BOB DYLAN	ALAN PRICE
ALBERT GROSSMAN	TITO BURNS
BOB NEUWIRTH	DONOVAN
JOAN BAEZ	DERROLL ADAMS

The dialogue below is taken from 'Don't Look Back,' a film of Dylan's tour in this country by D A Pennebaker. The full transcript has been published in paperback by Ballantine Books Inc. 101 5th Avenue, New York. 10003.

WHO THREW THE GLASS IN THE STREET...

Dylan's hotel room—party—Donovan listens, as one of his records plays in background.

DYLAN *From either side of room, breaks in suddenly.* Hey come on, I want to know who threw that glass in the street? Who did it? Now, you better tell me, now if somebody doesn't tell me who did it, you all gonna get this fuck, quiet here and never come back. Now, who did it? I don't care who did it, man. I just wanna know who did it.

DRUNK I'm pissed . . . I was out there in the bathroom, coming out . . .

DYLAN Hey, don't tell me you're pissed, man. Don't tell me you're pissed because I don't want to hear you're pissed.

DRUNK I'm not. I'm not.

DYLAN Who threw the glass in the street?

DRUNK I didn't throw the glass.

DYLAN Well, who did it? Tell me, you were there— who threw it? You know who?

FRIEND OF DRUNK Yeah, I know who, Bob. But you know—

DYLAN All right, hey, I don't care who did it. If you know who did it or you just better tell whoever did it to get out there and tell the cats that came up here to ask who did it, tell them who it was. I'm not taking no fucking responsibility for cats, I don't know, man, I got enough responsibility with my friends and my own people.

DRUNK I agree.

DYLAN Now, now come on!

DRUNK I was out there . . .

DYLAN I don't care who was . . .

DRUNK . . . When you asked who did it.

DYLAN I didn't ask no—none of your—none of your shit, man.

DRUNK I'm not givin' you shit.

DYLAN Throwing a glass in the street?

DRUNK I'm not givin' you shit.

DYLAN What'd you do it for man? What'd you do it for, I mean, what'd you throw a glass in the street for?

DRUNK I didn't throw a glass in the street.

DYLAN Well, show me the person that did it. If you don't have him here by the time I count to ten you better take the responsibility for him.

DRUNK All right.

DYLAN All right—one, two, three, four, five, six, seven, eight, nine, ten . . . you got him here?

DRUNK No.

DYLAN Hey, man, I'm not kidding. You think I'm kidding. He's gonna clean up that glass, man, or I'll clean it up.

VOICE I'll clean up your glass.

DONOVAN Hey, I'll help you man.

DRUNK I wouldn't clean your . . .

DERROLL ADAMS He's all right— he's . . .

DYLAN Hey, I believe he's all right, man. I believe he's all right. Well, okay, I believe it.

DRUNK Listen.

DYLAN I know a thousand cats that look just like you, man, hold just like you.

DRUNK Ah, fuck off. You're a big noise, you know.

DYLAN I know a man; I know I'm a big noise. I'm a bigger noise than you, man.

DRUNK I'm a small noise.

DYLAN Right.

DRUNK I'm a small cat.

DYLAN That's right.

DRUNK If I'd thrown a fucking glass in the street

DYLAN *Shows him.*

DRUNK You're anything you say you are, man.

DRUNK I'm nothing!

DYLAN You say you're small you're nothing

DRUNK I'm nothing!

DYLAN I believe you.

DRUNK Nothing.

DYLAN I believe you, man.

DERROLL ADAMS Boys

Later . . .

DYLAN *. . . went over and takes drunk's hand,* I just didn't want any, I didn't want that glass . . . if you're sober, I didn't want that glass to hurt anybody.

DRUNK What?

DYLAN I just didn't want that glass to hurt anybody.

DRUNK It didn't.

DYLAN Okay.

Denmark Street

London home of agents and music publishers. Grossman sits in office of Tito Burns, British Producer.

GROSSMAN Now, what kind of money do you think? How far do you think we can push him?

TITO BURNS I tell you. As far as Granada goes, uh, they were talking 12-13 hundred pounds but there's 15 hundred there, I know.

GROSSMAN You don't think we can do better?

TITO BURNS Possibly, yeah. But I know that like he's talking to us 13 . . . .

GROSSMAN Why don't we ask for 2,000?

TITO BURNS *laughs.* Well, I had that figure in mind, strongerly enough.

GROSSMAN *doesn't laugh.* Get it settled.

BURNS Great.

GROSSMAN Why don't we, why don't we know now and get an answer from them . . . 'cause you know why don't you? Just tell them that I have to present it to Bob before we can give them the final answer, burns'll give it to them by tomorrow.

BURNS Fine . . . I'll get Johnny Hamp, Granada in there. The other one was staff—um, but they're the same

To secretary:
Uh, Johnny Hamp, please. Urgently, wherever he is. Track him down, dear.

To Grossman:
The top one so far really is Granada, but I haven't spoken to him.

Phone rings.

SECRETARY *on intercom.* Listen, Johnny Hamp is in the studio, his secretary's there. If she could have some idea of what it's about she might be able to get him to speak to the phone.

BURNS Just say Bob Dylan. He'll be there in a shot.

To Hamp: Two grand, Johnny. Yeah, as an exclusive. And it would be very much exclusive. He's not going to do anything else. Yeah . . . yeah . . . yeah . . . you want to leave that with you, John? Hello?

CHRIS *On phone at other end.* Hello.

BURNS Yes.

CHRIS Ah, this is Chris, Stewart's P.A. speaking. He's not there. He's not, he's not, you know, available at the moment. He's a bit tied up in the theatre. Can I help?

BURNS Well, I think he might untie himself. Would you tell him this is the call he was expecting regarding Bob Dylan?

CHRIS Bob Dylan?

BURNS Yes.

CHRIS OK, well you know, when I say he's tied up I really mean it. You know, I'm not kidding.

BURNS I know he is . . . with rope, right?

CHRIS No, look, we've got a show on in the theatre here, you know?

BURNS Don't get upset, don't get upset—I'm only kidding ya.

CHRIS OK, well I'll try and get him.

BURNS Well, you tell him, Chris, that I have Mr. Grossman with me. Uh, Bob's manager, Albert Grossman's with me now.

CHRIS OK.

BURNS OK? first . . . how 'bout that? Thinks I'm tryin' to get him on.

To Stewart on phone: Stewart! timmm . . . yeah yeah— oh fuck, oh dear. That for the hire know might go to 15, I see. Uh, fine. Well, I'll tell you what I'll do. Yeah, not bad for me. I'll tell if for a week's work. I don't mind. Uh, Stewart, look, shall I just clock his out with Albert now and sit down there and . . . to save your from hanging on? And they give you a call back? God bless you.

To Grossman:
1250. You could probably get him to stretch it to fifteen hundred. So, I figure this, you know, BBC, oh—

GROSSMAN One show, but not for two.

BURNS No, I had a feeling that Granada would come up with the money because they have done it, live past. Remember what he offered? Peter, Paul & Mary for two shows BBC. For two that seem to be able, their tops.

GROSSMAN If you got him back, why don't you leave me take a crack at him on the phone.

BURNS Person.

GROSSMAN 'Cause he called me in the states, you know.

BURNS Who . . . Stewart or Johnny?

GROSSMAN Stewart.

BURNS Stewart? . . . listen Stewart, I've got Mr. Grossman for you. Will you hold on a second?

GROSSMAN I speak to you in New York, didn't I? Uh, remember. Yeah. And uh, at that time I indicated, uh, the kind of money we were looking for . . . for Bob and I assumed that when I told me you were interested that we were somewhere in that vicinity and then I was personally, you know, kind of you know, surprised, you know, at, you know, the nature of the offer. In other words, as much as we'd like to do the show for BBC I think we can't even consider it at that money 'cause it doesn't come anywhere near the other offers that we have. OK, well the minimum that I would consider would, uh, be the fee that you mentioned for each half hour. No, no, no—I wouldn't . . . 1250 for each half hour. Well, uh, thank you very much. Bye.

To Burns:
He said he'll put it to them but he's almost certain it'll be, it'll be no . . . but I think he's going to come back with 2,000, I bet. For two shows.

six, "Subterranean Homesick Blues." Yeah, jumped from like 45 or something to six. Yeah, I'll be with Albert within two minutes or so.

Albert leads up off to.

THE HOTEL ROOM

BURNS: Then, then we're no better off. We're still better off the other way with one show. Aren't we, Albert?

GROSSMAN: I don't know.

BURNS: I don't, uh...

GROSSMAN: Can we, without, uh, asking to bad sure, can we get Johnny Hamp back on the, on the phone and, and tell him it looks like we have a better offer from, uh, I'll tell him. No?

BURNS: Albert, if many if you go along with me, cause I know Johnny, and Johnny's a good guy—in other words, Johnny it isn't about to con them money, you know.

GROSSMAN: I know. We only ask of for two. He's certainly not going to come with more than that. I mean, he's certainly not going to come back and say, well I'd like to give you a little more that you asked for.

BURNS: Well, what, what we can do is this. If you—you're hold on, Johnny'll be back in the morning, and if he comes up with the two, and if if they've turned round in the end, and say, you know... forget it, no op. If they come up with the two, I'll say "look, Johnny, so your friend because Albert wants us to talk shit, we're selling this to you, we're not saying we're you and saying the other one, we're going to tell you straight, when happened. We were ready to do yours if you come up with the two but then the BBC got raving mad and come up with two. So you've got to top it."

On the telephone.

Albert? Um, Albert. Stewart? I'll be with Albert in a few moments and—

Holds up two fingers for Grossman. Grossman smiles.

Um, I'll put it to him and uh, uh, and you know I'm sure he'll come up with a decision, you know, very quickly. Well now Stewart, let me tell you, between you and I, um ... very truthfully, you know, oh, like two months ago, Granada came on when they heard he was coming, and, you know then, they pay - you know, what, they pay for the taxi as well, if you know what I mean. Uh, and they've been on there hammering away like mad. So, uh, Albert does have a pretty tough decision in a

Hotel manager enters, accosts Grossman.

HOTEL MANAGER: Who is in charge

HOTEL MANAGER: In charge of what?

HOTEL MANAGER: Who is in charge of this room?

GROSSMAN: what do you mean? Who's in charge of this room? He's rented to Bob Dylan. What is your mean, who is in charge of it?

Dylan appears in doorway.

HOTEL MANAGER: Are you Bob Dylan's manager?

No, with move in from of Dylan protectively.

GROSSMAN: Yes, I'm Bob Dylan's manager, but I'm not in charge of his room

HOTEL MANAGER: No, you're in charge of Bob Dylan?

GROSSMAN: No, I'm not in charge of Bob Dylan.

HOTEL MANAGER: we have had complaints about the noise-about, below

GROSSMAN: Oh that's unfortunate. We'll try to hold it down.

HOTEL MANAGER: And it isn't organized in two minutes, I will ask you to leave.

GROSSMAN: Why don't you get a constable... would you... present?

HOTEL MANAGER: Please do that. There's been no-outs in this room, and you're done... of the damn... turnstiles and the most stupid personal... we aren't spoken to in my life, if we...

were some place else I'd punch you in your goddam nose - you stupid nut! Would you... we've rented this room and I'm asking you to leave this room. We have valuables on here and I don't want you in here.

Dylan smiles at camera.

Would you get out of this room?

THE SCIENCE STUDENT

DYLAN: Are you going to take the content?

SCIENCE STUDENT: Yeah, I'm going to watch. I mean, I... with, this is what I came to see mostly.

DYLAN: Listen.

SCIENCE STUDENT: I come to see you.

DYLAN: Listen.

SCIENCE STUDENT: But I thought I might have a word with you first. I mean, what is your whole attitude to... I self mean, when you meet somebody, what is your attitude towards them?

DYLAN: I don't like them.

SCIENCE STUDENT: I mean, I come in here. What's your attitude towards me?

DYLAN: No, I don't have an attitude towards you at all. Why should I have an attitude towards you? I don't even know you.

SCIENCE STUDENT: No, but I mean and it would be an attitude if you wanted to know me or didn't want to know me.

DYLAN: Well, why should I want to know you?

SCIENCE STUDENT: I don't know ... that's what I'm asking.

DYLAN: Well, I don't know. Ask me another question. Just give me a reason why I should want to know you.

SCIENCE STUDENT: Um... I might be worth knowing.

DYLAN: Why?

SCIENCE STUDENT: Huh?

DYLAN: Why? Tell me why. When good is it going to do me for me to know you? Tell me. Give me, name me one thing I'm going to gain.

SCIENCE STUDENT: Well, you might learn something from my attitude to life.

DYLAN: Well, what is your attitude towards life? Huh?

SCIENCE STUDENT: I can't explain that in two minutes.

DYLAN: Well, what are you asking me to explain in two minutes?

SCIENCE STUDENT: Huh?

DYLAN: ... that's all you're getting in a two minutes. You're asking me to explain something in two minutes too.

SCIENCE STUDENT: But you're the artist. You're supposed to be able to explain it in two minutes.

DYLAN: I am?

SCIENCE STUDENT: Yeah.

DYLAN: Hey, now, what about you? Aren't you an artist?

SCIENCE STUDENT: Oh, no.

DYLAN: What are you?
SCIENCE STUDENT: I'm a science student.
DYLAN: Well, let's hear it again, what are you?
SCIENCE STUDENT: A science student.
DYLAN: A what student?
SCIENCE STUDENT: A science student.
DYLAN: Now, what does that mean? Just what does that mean?
SCIENCE STUDENT: Hmmmm?
DYLAN: What does that mean? What do you do? What's your purpose in the world?
SCIENCE STUDENT: Ummm ...what's my purpose in the world?
DYLAN: Yeah.
SCIENCE STUDENT: What's my purpose in the world?
DYLAN: Yeah. How do you help? You know. What do you do for me, I guess.
SCIENCE STUDENT: Well, I'm uh, uh, uh, I'm in the world for me...
DYLAN: Well,
SCIENCE STUDENT: Just let it in me.
DYLAN: Like everybody else.
SCIENCE STUDENT: Yeah, yeah.
DYLAN: So we're just alike, aren't we?
SCIENCE STUDENT: I guess so.
DYLAN: We don't come from two different worlds...
SCIENCE STUDENT: No, we're both alike.
DYLAN: We both come from, uh, I mean.
SCIENCE STUDENT: You're wrong, you're wrong. I was right, I was right all the time. No, but like, I mean, it is interesting. Now I go, I go in-interview-...in groups. If I go interview didn't wish I didn't think they're there, they couldn't care less about me, you know.
DYLAN: Well, you know, why should, you know, (aren't) you ever stopped to wonder why?
SCIENCE STUDENT: Ummmm.
DYLAN: There's gotta be some reason, doesn't there? I mean it just doesn't happen.
SCIENCE STUDENT: Yeah, yeah, but it's nothing to do with me because they don't wanna know me before I go in.
DYLAN: What do you want? Can you write them up in your report? That's not it. What's that?
SCIENCE STUDENT: No, I don't, I don't think of myself as — as — as ...
SCIENCE STUDENT: Well, do interviewers ask the same questions on me?

PRICE: Yeah, obviously they do because...
SCIENCE STUDENT: They do?
PRICE: ...You don't know what to ask anybody, because you don't know what's on any person's mind anyway. Who wants to talk to anybody who doesn't...
DYLAN: We don't want it either.
SCIENCE STUDENT: Well I wasn't know if I didn't try to find out, will I?
DYLAN: We don't want it either.
SCIENCE STUDENT: Well, I can't play it.
DYLAN: What, obviously they do because...
SCIENCE STUDENT: Uh, I might learn something.
DYLAN: What are they going to give you something material, I'm not necessarily interested...
DYLAN: When?
SCIENCE STUDENT: Huh?
DYLAN: What? What don't you know that you want to know?
SCIENCE STUDENT: Oh.
ALAN PRICE: You gotta kick out of interviewing people, yeh'know.
SCIENCE STUDENT: Ohhh, come on, Alan. If I asked to somebody?
PRICE: People ought to better sense 'cause I don't know.
PRICE: That's all the same questions 'cause nobody I — mean... you get interviewers to ask the same questions...you're asking questions as well.
PRICE: ...You don't learn what to ask anybody because you don't know what's on any person's mind anyway. Who wants to talk to anybody who doesn't...
SCIENCE STUDENT: Well, do interviewers ask the same questions as me?

DYLAN: Yeah.
SCIENCE STUDENT: No matter how hard I try I couldn't.
DYLAN: Well how do you know that?
SCIENCE STUDENT: Hmmmm?
DYLAN: Well, let's try and understand each other. And so you can understand each other. And you know what each other are thinking.
SCIENCE STUDENT: Yeah.
DYLAN: Uh huh.
SCIENCE STUDENT: Ah.
DYLAN: You can ask your first question.
SCIENCE STUDENT: Ah...
DYLAN: Go ahead. You got a question to ask? Come on.
SCIENCE STUDENT: Ah...
DYLAN: You haven't got any questions?
SCIENCE STUDENT: Well, I didn't.
DYLAN: Knock on door.
SCIENCE STUDENT: I think somebody's calling for you.
DYLAN: No, they don't have to go.
SCIENCE STUDENT: Look like you.
DYLAN: No?
SCIENCE STUDENT: No.
DYLAN: Look like you?
SCIENCE STUDENT: Uh... not me ...
DYLAN: Somebody that they're just like you.
NEUWIRTH: Hey, man, the high sheriff's lady would like to talk to you.
HIGH SHERIFF'S LADY: I'm the sheriff's lady. And I'm here on behalf of all of them I've come to say, we hope you have a very successful night because everybody loves you.
DYLAN: I write them all, yeah.
LADY: So then I do think you'd better be good. Oh, you are good. I don't think you can help being good. But we're really very thrilled indeed to have you here. And if you come after May again, then I'll have you as my guest in the mountain home.
LADY: And are you write them yourself, too, don't you sometimes?
DYLAN: I write them all, yeah.
LADY: Yes, honey you really? Yes, because they're just feeling and they're really marvelous. And I really mean this, I think you're really a good example for the youth.
DYLAN: Thank you.

SMOKELESS INTERZONE

— After another
All nite rave
Envisioning
Mine owne
        stomping micromatic macromantric psycho

                                    Chassidelique pop-troupe

— 'The Negative
Capabilities' I —
        yawping chanting droning whooping recharging the earth's
        Afro-American Asiaticking over Jeru
                                    salemic Huzza grailzapp
                                    v i b r a t i o n s

— I had to go
            & buy
                        the 3 posh Sunday
                                        papers —

Shat & vomited into them
                        all the fantastic food & drink
                        & orgiasmic sex-candied groovejoice
                        gorged down my gullet
                        over the previous 36 hours

— rolled it all into an immense
                                but not to me at all grotesque

multi-   techni-
                colour-
                    supplemented
                                joint

& was just about to light it
When my wife comes round the corner
and says Hey wait
I want to read that —

Michael Horovitz

01-385 4539

bag
MUSIC FOR THE MIND

'BAG' IS A
REVOLUTIONARY
CONCEPT IN
DISCOTHEQUES

PHONE JOHN 01-385 4539

This year's Legalise Pot Rally is on July 7. Should the sun shine, as tribal rites go, it will almost certainly be a success—a harking back to what John Peel describes as 'last year's beautiful, futile, happy summer.' As an act to impress Legislators, the Rally's chances are as likely as Yoko Ono's of becoming Chairman of Great Britain Ltd.

Law Reform will come when we who support change, develop sufficient cool to demystify our own responses. Something is happening to Mr Jones, but neither he nor Bob Dylan really know what it is. But Herman Cohen, Joe Berke and Calvin Hernton might be able to tell them, round about August, when the computers feed back the collected findings of the first systematic studies on Cannabis and related drugs. Joe Berke's and Calvin Hernton's Research Committee on Cannabis was founded in 1965, and first set about compiling a bibliography of the available literature. It didn't take too much page turning to discover that no valid scientific data existed, for the most part, throughout the western world. So a pilot study was set up to provide original data about the uses of Cannabis in Britain—social variables: background, education, vocation, life-style, sex, age, income; as well as objective information concerning the phenomenology of the Cannabis experience; how the users experience themselves whilst under the influence of the drug. No results until August, but early feed-back appears to explode much of the conventional wisdom.

Herman Cohen in Amsterdam has taken a slightly different approach. More concerned with the interaction of drug takers with society (he lectures the World Health Organisation on Discriminatory Tendencies Towards Drug Takers in London this August), he has set up a Questionnaire concerned to survey what is going on. At least in Amsterdam. How many people are using what? In what kinds of combination? And with what frequency? What kind of social groups do they come from? What interaction do they have within their group? With other people? With Society? And with the Legal machinery of Society? Cohen is intrigued by the influence of legal pressures on the structure of 'the Scene.' He is also very concerned to redefine the terms 'use' and 'abuse' of drugs. Cohen is not so sure that legalising Pot is the answer.

'Of course,' he says, 'it would be better than the present laws, but in itself it is too simple a solution. What I am trying to do is explore the sociological process going on, but in the end, I suppose, I am one of 'them,' because I view the drug taker as a social deviant.'

As the survey is his doctoral thesis, and he has publishing commitments, the full results of his work are unlikely to be available for two years, however, he thinks the early results are less favourable to the basic 'head' position than he himself would have thought. Last question in Cohen's questionnaire:

Was u "stoned" toen u deze vragenlijst invulde?

a consumer survey would have little difficulty in establishing that readers of the new Italian invader *International Playmen* get more square metres of tit per unit cost than *Penthouse*holders. But London Editor Herbert Van Thal maintains in a stiff Home Counties accent, that he would prefer to publish more

We clothe every child in napalm

Guerilla Art Sloane Square, one day recently, before the Underground's six man graffiti squad pacified the area for Harrod's once again.

things like the long Marcuse interview in the launch issue. The younger almost revolutionary tone to some of *Playmen's* pieces he says is conscious and he is concerned to deny that *Playmen Italy* was one of the Roman magazines prosecuted for publishing fairly pornographic papparazzi shots of Bardot and Sachs. Though he is not quite sure.

At *Penthouse*, Bob Guccione is coolly unconcerned. No it wouldn't be fair for him to comment on one of his staffer's remarks that Playmen having failed to make Smith's might be left with a lot of the 185,000 initial print order on their hands. (Van Thal: 'Typical of Smith's. We're still negotiating.') Guccione points out that Penthouse's quarter million run allows them more colour and draws more advertising revenue than anyone else. And the run goes up to half a million in November when Penthouse applies for a U.S. entry visa.

Last month, Paradise Hartley got married, turned 21 and came of age as "the man who threw a toilet roll at *Conservative Leader, Edward Heath and was afterwards fined £100 by Gloucester City Magistrates*" (Gloucester Citizen, May 26).

In an Anti-Vietnam demonstration outside Gloucester Guildhall, a policeman's helmet was splashed with red paint, Paradise's guitar was crushed, and two toilet rolls were thrown, one by Paradise into an open window. he was arrested, and charged with "Using Threatening Behaviour, Whereby a Breach of the Peace was likely to be occasioned."

For the crimes of, (1), throwing a toilet roll, and (2), singing protest songs, he was fined £45 less than the seventeen demonstrators arrested in the Battle of Grosvenor Square, and £85 more than 3 men with prior convictions for grievous bodily harm who rolled a drunk outside a pub. £15 more than a drunken driver who killed a four year old child sentenced in the same court, the same day, by the same Gloucester Magistrates.

'Don't Look Back'—the movie of Bob Dylan's tour of Great Britain should have been titled 'Don't Think Once.' It has never been shown here, suppressed at the insistence of his manager Albert Grossman—who did look back, closely —and thought twice

When Prince Philip was in Australia recently he made two mundane, mildly critical observations about that country which provoked a national outcry. Australians believe that when a Duke or a Queen opens their mouth it should be only to smile. Unfortunately, whenever Prince Philip opens his mouth he puts his foot in it. He hasn't yet learnt that Australians resent criticism; especially from bloody foreigners. Nevertheless deep down they love Prince Philip. Last time he was in Australia (in 1963) he brought his wife and thousands of locals risked injury to admire the lovely couple. These extracts, taken from the first issue of Australian OZ, show what a Royal Tour is really like!

— being a diary of the Queen's excursions in the great cities of her Australian and New Zealand subjects, culled from Sydney's adoring morning newspapers.

Nothing has been exaggerated or distorted. It all really happened.

Wednesday, February 6: The Queen arrived in New Zealand at the Bay of Islands.

Local and imported Maoris staged a welcoming ceremony and later applauded wildly when the Queen spoke a few words to them in Maori: "Araha-nui kia ora koutou", meaning "Love and good luck to you all".

Fifteen of the imports were unluckily killed when the bus in which they were going home toppled 200 feet into a valley.

AUCKLAND

Thursday, February 7: The Queen arrived in Auckland and attended an opera in the evening.

In the foyer fifty people were treated for shock and heat exhaustion.

WELLINGTON

Monday, February 11: The highlight of the Queen's day in Wellington was a children's rally and shearing contest at Fraser Park.

In the grounds of Wellington Hospital a 14-year old crippled girl crawled across the grass by the driveway and on her knees saw the Queen go by in her car only 3 feet away.

The girl, in nightdress and bed jacket, moved quite fast on her knees from her seat as soon as she saw where the Royal car would pass.

With a delighted smile, she waved to the Queen.

DUNEDIN

Friday, February 15: Twenty children were taken to hospital when a bus careered down a steep hill and crashed through the iron gates of Dunedin Botanic Gardens.

Two were admitted to hospital and the other 18, slightly injured, were hurried back to the Royal Garden Party.

The Duke quipped to 9 year old Vicky Sherwin, who lost two front teeth, "You won't be able to eat for a while".

Another small girl with "a sore head" said that the Duke had jokingly asked her if she would be walking home.

ADELAIDE

Wednesday, February 20: 9,500 people turned Adelaide's Royal Garden Party into a free-for-all.

Fashionably dressed women with shoes off clambered on to chairs for a better view of the Queen.

The Duke picked up a handkerchief for a tiny woman in her seventies and said loudly for all those nearby to hear: "There you are. Now we'll make a date."

People laughed, clapped and cheered at his gesture.

During the evening a gala music festival was held. In an over-crowded stand eighty choristers collapsed.

Thursday, February 21: At Victoria Park race course 65,000 children were packed in for a rally.

With the temperature soaring into the 90's the South Australian Education Department installed extra toilets and brought in iced water supplies.

700 children collapsed.

MELBOURNE

Saturday, February 23: A section of Melbourne's racegoing public staged the worst display of rudeness on the tour.

Matrons in new summer ensembles climbed half way up the fences surrounding the mounting yard and for several

She ate and drank a little with the guests, though the Duke plucked an occasional glass of beer from a passing waiter's tray – Sydney Morning Herald

At one stage the Queen was so relaxed that she stood, one foot behind the other and with her hands on her hips as she gazed about – Telegraph

He was badly shaken by the incident. So much so that he was enable to make his customary quip – Telegraph

With the reporters and photographers cluttering the rocks all around the Pinnacle look-out he had ample opportunity to clown or make one of his renowned "cracks" – Telegraph

It was pointed out to the Royal couple that the Opera House was more than a mere building . . . The Queen and Prince Philip seemed to appreciate this – Telegraph

Photographers and Prince Philip stood grinning at each other, but the Queen maintained a dignified demeanour – Telegraph

hours did not cease gawking at the Royal party.

One woman in a smart blue frock and large blue hat teetered on top of the fence gazing at the Queen.

She had a small Union Jack stuck on the top of her binoculars and another mounted on her camera.

Sunday, February 24: In the morning Her Majesty attended the Scots Church, which was filled with 800 people, many of them regular worshippers.

In the evening several people were hurt when spectators ran out of control at the Myer Music Bowl.

The rush began when Miss Lauris Elms and the Royal Melbourne Philharmonic Choir were performing "Land of Hope and Glory".

The crowd knocked down and trampled on middle-aged women and children. Handbags were trodden into the lawn.

As the Queen stood outside the Royal box talking to concert performers, ambulance men 10 yards to the rear were treating middle-aged women who were lying on the ground.

Monday, February 25: 500,000 people came to the city to see the Moomba parade and Royal couple.

Watching the parade the Queen saw a second, but unscheduled, procession.

The impromptu parade was made by stretcher bearers carrying women who had fainted near the Royal dais.

The Queen appeared to be concerned.

SYDNEY

Saturday, March 2: Organisers were gratified by the number of small craft on the harbour to greet the Britannia, despite the rough weather.

Several small boats capsized.

At Circular Quay, before the Queen stepped ashore, a tour official with a loud speaker, told waiting dignitaries how to behave.

He told them to stand up when the Queen and the Duke entered the wharf building, to sit during the Queen's inspection of the guard of honour and not to stand on chairs.

Thousands lined the city streets for the Royal progress. In all, twelve people collapsed and had to be taken to Sydney Hospital.

In Bedford Street 32 crippled children waited two hours to greet the Queen.

At Hyde Park a youthful choir sang "A Rose in the Land of Wattle". The Queen waved to the girls, who were blind.

After the progress the Queen remarked: "I'm very pleased with the large crowd that came to see us."

Sunday, March 3: In the morning the Royal couple attended St. Andrew's Cathedral.

Along the route the excitement proved too much for 13 children, who fainted.

The couple made an impromptu tour of the Opera House site with Professor H. Ingham Ashworth, who reported: "I think they both realised it was unique."

At a special quayside ceremony, during which he accepted the keys of a new boat for the Outward Bound movement, the Duke was greeted with the cries of "Rhubarb! Rhubarb!" from some teenage girls.

It was reported that the puzzled Duke was told that "Rhubarb" was a general purpose catch-cry adopted from the "Goon Show". It was a term used to express pleasure or annoyance, enthusiasm or disdain.

The Queen and the Duke's response was to walk to the wharf with barely a glance at the crowd as though they had not really been expected and were just passing by – S.M.H.

The Queen examined a portrait of herself in the hospital foyer before she went to the general wards – S.M.H.

As they stepped aboard the launch, two women gave a self-conscious cheer and began giggling – S.M.H.

Monday, March 4: In the morning the Queen opened the Wallace Wurth School of Medicine and the School of Biological Sciences at the University of N.S.W.

In the university grounds 50 people collapsed and one woman suffered a heart attack.

The Royal couple made a surprise visit to the Moore Park children's recreation centre.

Bert Balbi, 11, said: "When I saw the Duke I asked if he was someone special and if he was the Queen's husband. The Duke said 'yes' but it did not matter if I did not know who he was."

Jimmy Moshides, 13, asked Prince Philip: "Do you play the trumpet?" He later sheepishly admitted to reporters that he had the Duke of Edinburgh mixed up with Duke Ellington.

BRISBANE

Friday, March 8: Before the Queen's arrival in Brisbane, the loyal citizens were reminded by the Premier to give "Resounding cheers and forests of waving flags".

The highlight of the day was the unveiling of a memorial commemorating the discovery of the Moonie oilfields. The ceremony was held at Bulwer Island, a spot transformed almost overnight from a mangrove swamp into a tropical haven.

Fully grown palm trees were planted around the Queen's dais and the whole area was sprayed with mosquito repellent.

Citizens of a nearby suburb irreverently complained that the island's mosquitoes had moved into their homes.

Saturday, March 9: In the morning the Queen attended a rally of 82,000 children, of whom 100 were treated for heat exhaustion.

In a remarkable change of form, the skies almost washed out the Royal Surf Carnival at Coolangatta.

Before the Royal car arrived a band playing on the beach gave up when some of the instruments filled with water and policemen stood ankle deep in slush to hold back crowds near the road.

As the Duke stepped from the car, people nearby were shocked to hear him remark: "It's bloody wet."

MY WIFE DOESN'T GO TO THE LAVATORY. IT BLOODY WELL COMES TO HER

THE WONDERFUL WIT OF HRH PRINCE PHILIP

Nearly everyone restrained from over-staring – Telegraph.

Mr. Menzies amused the Queen by mistakingly introducing 18 year old Eileen Hannan of Melbourne as Mrs. Hannan. "I thought she looked a little young," said the Queen when greying Senator G. Hannan explained she was really his daughter – Mirror.

Although a little hesitant at times, the Queen sensed her guests were too embarrassed to start a conversation and always had something – often pertinent and lively – to say – Telegraph.

Stanley Kubrick's

2001:
a space odyssey

The worst Trip ever – Tom Nairn

2001 is a stunning experience. Its impact is so great that one's critical faculties are left numb. And yet, to get at the real sense of the experience requires critical reflection — a great deal more reflection than the average 'message' film, in fact. Hidden in the blinding techniques and psychedelic dazzlement of 2001 there is a moral fable which betrays the apparent meaning of the film. Kubrick's Odyssey through space and the future is also an obsessive voyage among his own ideas, ideas already familiar from Lolita and Dr. Strangelove. The trip to Jupiter is an effort to escape from the profound, pessimistic nihilism of these earlier works. And it is characteristic of Kubrick that escape is felt to be impossible: his dream of the redemption of humanity is in fact a nightmare, perhaps the most disturbing nightmare ever projected on the cinema screen. Beyond Jupiter and the infinite lies man's destiny. This destiny is the contradiction of his existing nature, not its development. And yet the new universe beyond our dreams is even more frightening than the one we know.

2001 is essentially a fantasy-diagram of human evolution. It is punctuated by three titles, printed on the screen like chapter-headings. The first is the Dawn of Man, the second — after the discovery of traces of intelligent life on the

Moon — is Eighteen Months Later the Mission to Jupiter, and the third is Beyond Jupiter and the Infinite.

In the dawn of man, a species of primitive anthropoids clings to its marginal and precarious existence in a hostile nature. Then one morning a strange object is present when they awaken. It is a tall, black monolith quite devoid of markings. This tablet — whose shape is a formal key-note of the

film — vaguely suggests the 'Tablets of the Law' to a culture whose subconscious is still Christian. The effect is reinforced by the loud choir of unearthly voices which explodes on to the soundtrack every time the Thing appears. However, its form and colour also suggest another familiar emblem of Christianity : the tombstone. The ape-men cluster curiously round this mystery, and touch it.

Somehow the object's influence leads them to see the possibility of tools, in their struggle for life. Next we see them using simple bone implements to hunt, and as weapons in their own wars. They have become meat eaters, killers as effective as the leopards they formerly feared. The leader of a band throws his bone-club victoriously into the air, and as it hurtles through space, it is transposed into a satellite circling the Earth. Our victorious conquest of nature, culminating in space-flight, is merely a continuation of the same story. The tools have become more complex, and we have space-suits instead of anthropoid hair; but essentially nothing is changed. And nothing will change until another Tablet is discovered on the Moon.

It is important to observe that this picture of human evolution is itself an out-of-date one. Lewis

Mumford recently pointed out that

> The misleading notion that man is
> primarily a tool-making animal . . .
> will not be easy to displace. Like
> other plausible conceits, it evades
> rational criticism, especially since
> it flatters the vanity of modern
> Technological Man, that ghost clad
> in iron . . . (The Myth of the Machine)

It was a notion which suited the Industrial Revolution, the great burst of tool-invention that created our conditions of everyday living But its limitations have become obvious in the age of computers and cybernetics which has followed. Here, a new vision of human pre-history has gathered force, where language is seen as the decisive transition from nature to culture. After all, how could tool-using have become established, as a developing tradition within primitive societies, without a context of culture and communication? Speech, dreams, and rituals are more fundamental than implements. The fact is simply more evident to us, from within our web of electronic communication and our mind-simulating automative machines.

In the second part of the film — Jupiter Mission — Kubrick shows he is perfectly aware of the facts behind this change in attitude. It is about a computer with a 'mind' of its own, a perfect cybernetic machine. So why the archaic ideology of the first part? The answer is that this archaism has a definite function in the unfolding of the film's content.

In space, we are carried first of all to a circular space-station, then to the American Moon-base. The musical accompaniment of the voyage is a slow Strauss waltz, evocative of the security and comfort of the past. This device of counter-pointing images with an unusual sound-track — used by Kubrick in other films — again emphasizes the lack of real novelty in the action. Travelling in space has not really changed anything. The complex and beautiful models, the extraordinary 'realism' of these sequences — so much commented upon — have the same total effect. Technical marvels are juxtaposed to human banality, repeatedly. Clever enough to escape from their own world, a race of advanced monkeys is carrying an outworn and still animal heritage towards the stars.

Thus, every sequence in the film shows people eating. Or, when not eating, fighting. The images refer back always to the pre-historic visions of our ancestors chewing their raw meat and battling over the possession of a water-hole. On the space-station, a polite but suspicious encounter between Dr. Floyd (the American Space Agency official on his way to the Moon) and a group of Russians shows that even now the Cold War is not over. The fight on the Jupiter expedition becomes between men and their own creation, the HAL 9000 computer. When we first see the astronaut Bowman, he is running round the space-ship's centrifuge making boxing gestures. The two stewardesses on the Moon-ship settle down — with a meal, of course — to watch a judo match on television. In general, there is an ingenious use of film-within-film to accentuate the message. In the very first space episode, we see Floyd asleep before a small movie-screen showing a boy-girl dialogue in a futuristic automobile : vehicle apart, it might be from any Hollywood movie of the forties. Later, there are scenes of exquisite banality when Floyd picture-phones his daughter back on Earth, and a message is relayed to astronaut Poole from his parents on his birthday. There is even a cake with candles, which they blow out for him with big smiles as he glides away from them through infinite emptiness. Even the comic picture of the Zero-gravity Toilet with its arm's-length of instructions fits into this logic : a consequence of eating (animality) man does not escape from, in his conventional adventure into space.

On the Moon, after a briefing reminiscent of the Pentagon scenes in Dr. Strangelove, Floyd and his party go to inspect the Thing. They are sustained by artificial chicken and ham sandwiches on the way ('They get better at it all the time' says one of the crew). On arrival, the analogy with the anthropoids is rubbed in as they crowd round the black slab : Dr. Floyd reaches out to touch it with the same gesture as the ape Chieftain, four million years previously.

Then, there is an abrupt transition to the Jupiter expedition, after the

second title. The lack of a title between the anthropoids and the earlier space sequences emphasized continuity; this one states, in effect, that something more important than all the intervening human history must have occured on the Moon, but we do not yet know what. However, we do have a firm picture of a hopeless, unchanging, backward-looking 'human nature' tied to animality and to social rituals which technological advance has rendered ridiculous.

Going towards Jupiter, the two representatives of this hopeless human nature, Bowman and Poole, are in a vast spacecraft which is also a computer. This mechanical intelligence ('HAL') controls every aspect of the craft. As it is programmed to respond to voice instructions, the astronauts can 'converse' with it. It can even take conversational initiatives, as when it inquires how Bowman feels about the mission. It has motives — as we learn later, when it becomes clear that there was a hidden reason for the inquiry into the astronaut's state of mind. In the course of the same conversation, the computer suddenly reports a fault.

Repairing this fault entails going outside the craft in a one-man space machine. We learn that there is in fact no fault — it was a pretext for getting rid of the two humans (and the others hibernating on the voyage) because, as HAL puts it, 'I couldn't let you endanger this mission'. Bowman survives alone, but manages to get into HAL's brain and disable the machine.

Then we learn the truth. The computer knew about the objectives of the mission all along, as it had been programmed with the information before leaving. The astronauts themselves did not — they were supposed to find out on arrival at Jupiter. HAL had therefore to inquire and find out what Bowman (the commander) knew, before deciding how to realize its design : to meet the source of the alien intelligence itself, without human interference. The Moon monolith had given off a radio beam pointing towards Jupiter, like an instruction. Thus, the perfect and infallible intelligence man has created wants to approp-

riate this cosmic intelligence to it-self.

The point is emphasized by the for-mal properties of the scene inside the computer. The oblong red space in which Bowman swims weightless-ly, as he struggles to disconnect the higher brain-functions, recalls the shape of the Tablet. Even more strikingly, so do the computer keys which spring out as he severs them. Hence, H A L is as near as humans can get to Intelligence — but even the machine is corrupted by the human touch. Egoism and aggress-ive possessiveness have been built into it unwittingly — so that, by themselves, men cannot escape from their own nature even here. They need help, or rather Help. Kub-rick's equivalent of the US cavalry - is waiting at Jupiter.

It is worth at this point recalling Kubrick's history as a film-maker. His films are all histories of defeats, from Killer's Kiss up to Dr. Strange-love. Even the glossy brochure given out with 2001 admits weakly that

> Kubrick tends to be somewhat pess-
> imistic and sceptical by nature ...
> He came to the conclusion that
> space exploration might be the only
> thing that the human race could
> learn to do which would keep it from
> blowing itself up.

2001 lies beyond the destruction of the world. Having dismissed the human species in Strangelove, Kub-rick has tried to imagine an alternat-ive. As the brochure puts it :

> For nearly five years, ever since he
> finished making Dr. Strangelove,
> Stanley Kubrick has been fascinated
> by the theme of extraterrestrial life...

This life is waiting for the sole rem-aining astronaut at Jupiter, so that terrestrial life may be redeemed Another black monolith is circling the planet to conduct Bowman on, a trip of exploration 'Beyond Jup-iter and the Infinite'.

In other films, Kubrick offsets his cold pessimism with outrageous gro-tesqueries (like the scenes between Quilty and Humbert in Lolita that underlined the message in black-com-ic fashion) This element is missing from Space Odyssey — its place has been taken by the grandly experim-ental sequences of Bowman's voyage beyond time and space. The dazzling technical novelties are designed to convey the dissolution of all the normal barriers of the humanly-

conceived universe : inner space and outer space, the seeing eye and the inorganic fuse together into one experience.

Finally, Bowman's trip ends in a bizarre room where time too has ceased to exist. Here, he sees him-self age and die, in a few moments of our time, where the only action is, naturally, a meal (a kind of Last Supper), and the shattering of a glass. Then as he wastes away, the Tablet materializes again (more tombstone-like than ever) and death and life themselves are reconciled. He is reborn, and becomes the new life-form demanded by the logic of Kubrick's Weltanschauung, the cosmic answer to human depravity. He floats back to Earth, an ethereal foetus in a transparent ball, and turns to face the audience in the film's concluding image :our future, or a reproach to what we are?

Obviously, the interpretation of these last sequences is crucial for understanding the film. The critics were very nice about 2001, on the whole, though some were puzzled by the ending. Writing in New Society, Paul Mayersberg claims that

> Kubrick's previous view of man . . .
> as a self-destructive animal has been
> considerably modified in 2001. This
> latest film proposes the possibility
> of a new start for mankind in space
> . . . an optimistic, evolutionary view
> of man . . .

He attributes this softening of Kubrick's pessimism to the influence of co-writer Arthur C. Clarke. It is quite true that Space Odyssey is an att-empt at transcending the gloomy vicious circle Klubrick previously moved in, and this might indeed be due to Clarke's participation. But it is no less important to ob-serve that this attempt emerges as quite unconvincing, and both looks and feels all wrong.

The strange room fashioned by the cosmic Intelligence for Bowman is utterly chilling. Described as 'an elegant apartment' in the British Film Institute Bulletin's review, and taken by Mayersberg as repr-senting humanity's past, its most evident characteristic is actually phoniness. It is in Mid-Western Louis Quinze, rendered even more eerie by the shadowless underfloor lighting. What happens is even

more nightmarish. Bowman under-goes the universal horror of the body's ageing and decay in a lived-out dream-time of instants, from which he may not awake. Uncom-prehending, he feels close on him the trap of time, tolerable to our real condition only because the you-ng can never see themselves as old-er. His position is like a guinea-pig in some cruel laboratory experiment. Then, given rebirth by the faceless experimenter, his cold alter ego turns enigmatically once more in our three dimensions.

The Bulletin says that

> The film's major achievement is
> nothing less than to provide a new
> mythology for Space Age Man . . .

But it would be more accurate to say that Kubrick has given a new, uncomfortable twist to the oldest religious ideology of all : the idea that men were made by a super-being beyond our understanding called God. However, the old notion pictured this Being as nice, rather than simply intelligent. Christianity: the hand of the red-eeming God is disclosed in the last sequences, as cold as an empty ice-box. The texture of the closing images does not show a new Christ of kindness, but one of those chill-ing Super-brains which stalk the pages of conventional science-fic-tion. This is not a new start for man', but something else altogether — a being without animal qualities, but also without human ones. Nat-urally, the film defines the process and its result as inscrutable, un-known; but why must the unknown be nasty?

The Christians always said we shouldn't judge what appears nasty, as it may be for our own good in the long run, and we cannot fathom the ways of God. Fortunately, the ways of Kubrick are another matter. They appear to lead us towards a new world of experience, using the utmost in technique and free imag-ination; in fact, they lead us back into the heart of the oldest, stalest kind of despair with the human state. The message was always false. In this year of our Revolution, it is absurd, too

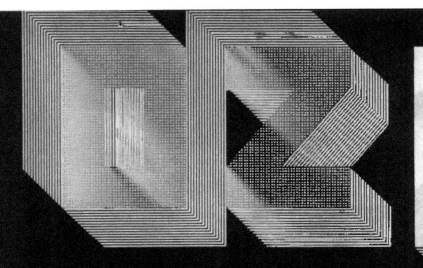

OZ 14

Editor: Paul Lawson
Design: Rick Cuff / Paul Lawson
Photography: Keith Morris / Steve Dwoskin
Advertising: John Leaver
Oz Workers Co-op: Jenny Crowe,
Pauline Carter, Tim Epps, Andrew
Fisher, Richard Neville,
Mazin Zaki, Marge Reagan,
Pusher: Anou

Dear Sir,

I have just received for the first time a copy of OZ. I have been trying to find out what issue it is, and have not, and that is the trouble with your Publication. Let me explain:

I found this issue on a seat whilst travelling on the tube and looking through it I was attracted by the colours, taking at home I began to read but found that several articles were unreadable:

1. Agit OZ. Why? Because there is a clash of colours and it strains one's eyes to read. Finding it so I passed an article which I most likely should have enjoyed.
2. Agit 2: White print on a pink background.
3. White print on green background. They can't be read.
4. And last but by no means least, if you are going to reproduce nude or sex shots, do it so they can be seen.

I don't know if the faults listed above are due to failing sight or the fact that I'm reading. I broke off to write this letter - at night.

However, I've disregarded the former since I'm no way near the age of failing sight and have assumed that if the four faults are not justified then it must be due to the fact that I'm reading at night. If therefore, this is the case I still think, in the interest of gaining further readers, you discontinue from the above, because your publication would be limited only to-day readers.

Put it to the test. Publish, not necessarily this letter but an edited version and ask your readers to comment. If you are not already aware of what I've written, you may very well be surprised. All the best

Very truly yours,
E. Ernest.

2 Mortimer Road,
Kensal Rise,
London N.W.10

2

For Andrew Fisher and David Spode. OZ 13.

Dear Sirs,

Zen is nothing
nothing is nothing

Zen is everything
everything is everything

Everything is nothing
Nothing, everything

Karl Hawkins.

1 Little Silver.
Exeter

Dear Sir,

I returned a few weeks ago from India, where I had been meditating in a Buddhist monastry, and was pleased to see many signs that the London scene has become more turned-on. One of these hopeful signs appeared to be a new magazine called OZ which I had heard about through an interview on the radio with your editor. Finding myself very much in agreement with the views he was putting forward, I went out and bought a copy.

The magazine—an old one (OZ 12) as it turned out—opened out into large sheets covered with various games to play. (Bravo and all that for this original idea.) But I was amazed to read that these jolly pastimes were "based" on the teachings of Buddha. I could see no connection. It seems that Buddhism to you is just something to boost the swinging-trendy-groove image with which you push material that isn't really all that new. It's part of a snap-crackle-pop sensationalism, "guaranteed", as you say of the Indian religious instruction tract on page C, "to astonish English teenies everywhere."

What dismayed me most of all were these sentences taken from the statement which prefaced the whole production:

"Three of the four poster-sides represent three out of the four truths which comprise Buddhism. The fourth side—and thus the fourth truth—had to be dropped because of extra advertising." So instead of the "Noble Eightfold Path which leads to the cessation of suffering", we get "personal products." I am invited to enlarge, not my consciousness, but my prick!

Poor us. Lost in a fog of confusion, we wander in circles, aimlessly. Buddhism offers us an escape into a place of light and peace. What hope is left to us when even Buddhism itself is made into just another game?

Yours sincerely,
Timothy Coakley.

4 Gascony Avenue,
London NW6.

Dear OZ,

On Friday, July 26 I took an overdose of sleeping-pills and was admitted to Kingston Hospital. On Saturday evening I was told that I was admitted compulsorily to Long Grove Mental Hospital. I was driven down by the Mental Welfare Officer together with my father.

When we arrived the door was locked. After a while somebody opened it but none of the nurses we spoke to at first could understand English. A nurse took me to a small, bare room next door to a room in which a woman was screaming. The nurse told me to undress but I did not; my handbag was emptied and all my possessions taken away. My father refused to leave until I was found a better place to sleep, so I was allowed to sleep in a dormitory near the Night-nurse. The Mental Welfare Officer apologised to my father afterwards for the poor reception we had had

On Sunday morning I went to the staff-nurse's room and said that I could not stand the place and that I wanted to go home. She summoned three men who thrust me forcibly into a cell containing

THE doors
WAITING FOR THE SUN

elektra

only a bed; the window was locked and shuttered so that no daylight came into the cell. But then I was extremely distressed; I took the mattress off the bed and rammed the door with the iron bedstead. The men returned, flung me on a mattress and held me down so that I could be given an injection. After that I was semi-conscious for the rest of the day. My father came during the visiting hour and was told he could not see me. He insisted and eventually the medical officer was telephoned and was asked to give his consent. My father was allowed to stay in the cell for the hour. I was lying on the mattress (the bedstead had been removed); no chair was provided for my father to sit on.

On Monday morning a woman doctor saw me and took a few notes; no treatment was mentioned. I was allowed to spend the rest of the day in the day-room with the other patients. I was not allowed to have my hand-bag and other possessions back, so, since I did not have my money, I could not buy cigarettes, as the other patients could. Monday night I spent in a small furnished room which was locked.

On Tuesday morning at a case conference it was decided that I was still a suicide risk and could not therefore be discharged, although the psychiatrist agreed with me that I was not in need of psychiatric treatment. The staff-nurse said that I was uncooperative so it was decided that I should not be allowed to wear my day clothes. I was then allowed to leave the case conference; I was disappointed not to be allowed home, so my first thought was to telephone my father. There were no telephones in the building for use by patients. To use one of the telephones in the grounds one has to be accompanied by a nurse.

No nurse had the time to escort me to the telephone, so I asked another patient to come with me, which he did. I was not able to get through to my father. On returning to the building I met the male staff-nurse who was waiting for me in the corridor.

He pushed me forcibly into my room where the window had already been barred and locked and told me that the reason why I was being confined was that I had made a telephone call without being escorted by a nurse. He then locked the door after me. After knocking several times I was given a chamber-pot; later on I was allowed to have my book. Altogether I was on my own in the room for six hours, not knowing how long I was going to be kept there. At visiting time my father came and asked that I be discharged. This was allowed but, as it was against medical advice, he had to undertake to accept full responsibility for me for the re-mainder of the 28-day order.

[Name supplied but withheld]

4

Dear Sir,

We feel that the Prime Minister cannot totally take the blame for having to confer on M. Jean Roche an honorary degree at Bradford University.

A motion put before the Student Union Council at Bradford proposed that the University should be urged not to confer this honorary degree. Despite the fact that previously a general meeting of the Students Union had pledged solidarity with the French Students, the right wing extremists majority on the union council defeated this motion and this resulted in two of the council members resigning and expressions of extreme disgust from others who voted for the motion.

Yours in disgust,
A. Tuckman.
D. A. Martin.

27 Clive Terrace,
Bradford 7,
Yorkshire.

Dear OZ,

John Hopkins has sent me the following comment which no doubt applies to my Hippy High Hopes in OZ. I'm sure he would-n't mind my sending it on to you and it may well express what many of your readers feel!

Ray Durgnat

Dear Ray,

I have been reading your writing on and off for a few years. I must say that it is about time you started making constructive sug-gestions instead of putting every-thing down the whole time. All you are doing in fact is relaying your hang-ups to other people and increasing the number of general hang-ups.

It is a damn shame.

Best Wishes,
Hoppy.

DEAR OZ
AGIT 1, OZ13 JUST ABOUT SUMS UP THE STUPIDITY OF REVOLUTION — for instance

"YOU ARE WRESTLING WITH THE ENEMIES OF THE HUMAN RACE NOT FOR YOURSELF MERELY, FOR YOU MAY NOT SEE THE FULL DAY OF LIBERTY, BUT FOR THE CHILD HANGING AT THE BREAST" WRITTEN IN 1796!

THAT CHILD NEVER SAW THE DAY OF LIBERTY, NOR WILL ANY. TRYING TO CHANGE HUMANITY THRU POLITICS IS FUTILITY. THERE IS A BIT OF THE ENEMY IN EACH OF US, AND GOODNESS TOO, IF YOU CHANGE YOURSELF, & YOU HAVE ALREADY CHANG-ED THE MOST IMPORTANT PART OF THE WORLD — AND THAT GOES FOR EVERYONE — xxxx
JAMIE, NORWICH.

Matrix, the arts workshop of Crawley and the South East, meets every Friday evening at WEA, Robinson Rd, Crawley, Sussex. Come and do your own thing.

Future events.
Kieran Krlroy—
Poetry Show
6th Sept: Film by Yolk product-ions 'Charge of the Leek Brigade' Also other films from the International Film Pool.
13 Sept: Folk night
20 Sept: Mixed media group from Sussex/Oxford Universities

SMALLS

Will 16 yr old female pupil of Roman Catholic School (OZ12) write to Box No 14 (2)

Graduate wishes contact girl alone or pairs, of either submissive or aggressive nature to dramatise fantasies Box No 14 (3)

'NEW LIFE' Newsletter reports on communes the love revolution, new underground ventures. Specimen copy 2/6 (blank p.o.) Box 14 (4)

LEGAL HASH

Now, new formulas use legal chemicals to make legal synthetic Hash (THC). PLUS the famous TURN-ON BOOK telling how to make or grow Mescaline, LSD, DMT, Peyote, etc. $2.00 to TURN-ONS UNLIMITED, Dept SY, 313 No Edinburgh, Los Angeles, Calif. 90048. If not ecstatic, we refund.

ORGY BUTTER (The Luxury Lubricant)
A bold, red warm body rub for fun loving people. Gives a slippery, sensual effect. Works into the skin with rubbing, providing an after-glow. ORGY BUTTER comes in a 4oz. jar of delight. Send $3.00 to: TURN-ONS UNLIMITED, 313 N. Edinburgh Dept. 54 Los Angeles, Calif. 90048.

Male witch seeks female partner. Box 14 (1)

ARTS LABORATORY.
182 DRURY LANE, WC2.

THEATRE and DANCE THEATRE, CINEMA, GALLERY, FOOD ETC.

Open 6 days a week.

ARTS LAB, 242 3407/8 phone for details.

RELEASE office at 52, Princedale Road, W11. Holland Park tube. Office 229 7753. Emergency 603 8654. We sell OZ, IT, Peace News and Posters. Come and see us for legal or other advice. We need information about busts and irregular police behaviour etc. Ring us if you have, or want a room or flat to let. RELEASE needs your help— support us if you can.

DUREX Gossamer: 7s doz.
DUREX Fetherlite: 10s doz.
AMERICAN SKINS: 38s doz.

Post free from Colne Valley. Mail Order Co. (OZ), 126 The Rock, Linthwaite, Huddersfield.

SUICIDE OR DESPAIR?

Phone the SAMARITANS (the number's in your local Phone Book). Confidential befriending.

Volunteers also needed.

WORLD CALL! Swedish liberty in sex. Send 17/6 (or $1 or equivalent) for 100 illustrated brochures of photos, magazines & books. Adults only. Write to HERMES-OZ, BOX 6001, S-20011 MALMO 6, SWEDEN.

ALL WEARERS to do so at their own risk. We accept no responsibility whatsoever for people who wear our naughty Knicks and tantalising (G) strings. Still interested? Then why not send for our free list to:— Ron Lee, 118 Leavesden Rd., North Watford, HERTS.

BEN-mad teacher and Czech trainspotter—phone Annabelle please.

LIGHT REMOVALS. Dormobiles with helpful, working drivers. GUL 8923—Taximoves. Please quote this advertisement.

Attractive hostesses under 30 wanted for V I P lounge of West End nightclub. Hours 6pm to midnight. Salary and commission £30— £40 per week can easily be earned without previous experience. Phone HUN 1873 after 5pm or call CRAZY HORSE SALOON, 2 Allsop Place, London, NW1

TO YOU WHOM IT MAY CONCERN . . . . We are opening A MARKET PLACE OF CREATION. A permanent market place where you can buy or sell your posters, clothes, pottery, paintings, jewelery. . . anything. . . A number of people in London are working towards opening a community of exchange for POSITIVE PEOPLE. Based on the idea of sale or return, this is to be YOUR SHOP. Come and talk to us about your ideas. Write YOUR SHOP, Box No 14 (5) and watch OZ for further information.

Youth, 19, seeks fast cash. Anything considered. Box No14 (7)

TURN ON! With Personal Posters. Erotic, Fetish, Psychedelic or anything. State requirements. Box No 14 (6)

DON'T USE PINUPS—use these instead

3 SUPERB PHOTOS (Male or Female) are yours for only 10/-. Write now to MANNERS (ART), 38a Crawford St., London, W1. 7 days on guarantee - send cheque/P.O. Sent in plain sealed envelope. O'seas orders in local money O.K.

Rare OZ first issues. £1 to: 38a Palace Gdns Terrace, London W8.

Costs: (see form below). 2d per unit. 31 units per line. (The dot indicates new line). A unit is a letter/space/numeral/punctuation. Indicate capitals as required.

Semi-display words: 1/6d each.
Box-numbers: 2/6d.
Display: £2.10s per col inch.

Use this form for your small Ads. (see above). Mail to: OZ Smalls, 38a Palace Gdns Terrace, London W8.

Name: _____ I enclose postal order/cheque for £   s.   d

Address: _____

5

BOURGEOISIE

a lexicon

Ever since I got married I can't eat tongue.

Even the children love to do things together

Good people get theirs, and bad people get theirs too.

I never like to be out alone in the streets in case I am attacked.

Children must be taught to believe.

I am certain that all teachers are very good teachers.

George and I never quarrel about serious things.

At one stage, Patricia was really rather worried, she was going around with all these Bible stories and thinking they were absolutely true, and we had to explain that they weren't really true, more or less, you know.

I find it difficult to do anything that will make a difference.

A young man should keep himself free, forge his career, nicely secure, settle down, and then think about bringing a woman into his life.

I do go to church, but it's cold and musty and you say the same thing every week.

I didn't have any brothers so I never really had any thoughts about it.

I am often, as it were, sexually satisfied in ways that don't involve full intercourse.

Even in the best of homes . . .

I keep any eye on my son and keep on at him to do things, and he does them, and it turns out all right, and that's all one can hope for.

I never read the paper anymore, and I never vote except when my husband tells me to, in fact, I never have.

ESP is still a great challenge.

Families who pray together, stay together.

I don't think there's any foundation for the Oedipus complex at all.

Children should learn to be happy.

Buddhists look pretty ignorant.

I don't normally dream.

I can't take you seriously unless other people take you seriously.

He can be serious for a week or two, but then he's finished.

I don't know why people buy budgies when they can pick up sparrows so easily.

A man should be able to see the world before settling down so he can realise that home is best.

I mean, why don't I just go and tell the children that I think things are made of atoms, because, well, I think they are.

How can you say Europe is dying, look at West Germany.

I don't care if everyone in the world is living in sin, it's none of my business.

Dance halls in the West End are not good for a boy of sixteen.

I always vote Labour because they have better ideas, more suited to the Middle Class.

I am reaching the age where I need to be a certain generation and I'm not sure which.

Children should eat everything on their plate.

KNICKERS

All those people at Eton and Harrow, all they do is learn Greek in the morning and rugby in the afternoon.

I expect a boy to respect my daughter when she gets to that age.

I object to being taught anything by my children.

Conscription was a jolly good thing.

Fortunately, all of Richard's friends are what I call nice boys.

I don't think our children would be happy living in a completely free atmosphere.

Drinking leads to violence, and gambling leads to the gutter.

God is someone else whom people can turn to.

I collect for spastics.

Freud doesn't know everything.

God is a pie in the sky.

I don't think that I have any particular brand of insanity.

God save the Queen.

I have always had the idea that the final act is frightening, and in some ways unpleasant.

Don't be bourgeois.

Compiled by Joe Berke

WHERE WE'RE AT

Trip Without a Ticket

NOTTING H. GATE

Our authorized sanities are so many Nembutals. 'Normal' citizens with store-dummy smiles stand apart from each other like cotton-packed capsules in a bottle. Perpetual mental out-patients. Maddeningly sterile jobs for strait-jackets, love scrubbed into an insipid 'functional personal relationship' and Art as a fantasy pacifier. Everyone is kept inside while the outside is shown through windows: advertising and manicured news. And we all know this.

How many TV specials would it take to establish one Guatemalan revolution? How many weeks would an ad agency require to face-lift the image of the Viet Cong? Slowly, very slowly we are led nowhere. Consumer circuses are held in the ward daily. Critics are tolerated like exploding novelties. We will be told which burning Asians to take seriously. Slowly. Later.

But there is a real danger in suddenly waking a somnambulistic patient. And we all know this.

What if he is startled right out of the window?

No one can control the single circuit-breaking moment that charges games with critical reality. If the glass is cut, if the cushioned distance of media is removed, the patients may never respond again as normals. They will become life-actors.

Theatre is territory. A space for existing outside padded walls. Setting down a stage declares a universal pardon for imagination. But what happens next must mean more than sanctuary or preserve. How would real wardens react to life-actors on liberated ground? How can the intrinsic freedom of theatre illuminate walls and show the weak spots where a breakout could occur?

Guerrilla theatre intends to bring audiences to liberated territory to create life-actors. It remains light and exploitative of forms for the same reasons that it intends to remain free. It seeks audiences that are created by issues. It creates a cast of freed beings. It will become an issue itself.

This is theatre of an underground that wants out. Its aim is to liberate ground held by consumer wardens and establish territory without walls. Its plays are glass cutters for empire windows.

The Diggers are hip to property. Everything is free, do your own thing. Human beings are are the means of exchange. Food, machines, clothing, materials, shelter and props are simply there. Stuff. A perfect dispenser would be an open Automat on the street. Locks are time-consuming. Combinations are clocks.

So a store of goods or clinic or restaurant that is free becomes a social art form. Ticketless theatre. Out of money and control.

'First you gotta pin down what's wrong with the West. Distrust of human nature, which means distrust of Nature. Distrust of wildness in oneself literally means distrust of Wilderness.' Gary Snyder.

Diggers assume free stores to liberate human nature. First free the space, goods and services. Let theories of economics follow social facts. Once a free store is assumed, human wanting and giving, needing and taking become wide open to improvisation.

A sign: If someone Asks to see the Manager Tell Him He's the Manager.

Someone asked how much a book cost. How much did he think it was worth? 75 cents. The money was taken and held out for anyone. 'Who wants 75 cents?' A girl who had

just walked in came over and took it.

A basket labelled Free Money.

No owner. No Manager, no employees and no cash-register. A salesman in a free store is a life-actor. Anyone who will assume an answer to a question or accept a problem as a turn-on.

Question (whispered): 'Who pays the rent?'
Answer (loudly): 'May I help you?'

Who's ready for the implication of a free store? Welfare mothers pile bags full of clothes for a few days and come back to hang up dresses. Kids case the joint wondering how to boost.

Fire helmets, riding pants, shower curtains, surgical gowns and World War 1 army boots are parts for costumes. Nightsticks, sample cases, waterpipes, toy guns and weather balloons are taken for props. When materials are free imagination becomes currency for spirit.

Where does the stuff come from? People, persons, beings. Isn't it obvious that objects are only transitory subjects of human value? An object released from one person's value may be destroyed, abandoned or made available to other people. The choice is anyone's.

The question of a free store is simply: What would you have.

Pop Art mirrored the social skin. Happenings X-rayed the bones. Street events are social acid heightening consciousness: of what is real on the street. To expand eyeball implications until facts are established through action.

The Mexican Day of the Dead is celebrated in cemeteries. Yellow flowers falling petal by petal on graves. In moonlight. Favorite songs of the dead and everybody gets loaded. Children suck deaths head candy engraved with their names in icing.

A Digger event. Flowers, mirrors, penny whistles, girls in costumes of themselves. Hell's Angels, street people, Mime Troupe.

Angels ride up Haight with girls holding NOW! signs. Flowers and penny-whistles passed out to everyone.

A chorus on both sides of the street chanting UHHI—AHH!— SHH BE COOL! Mirrors held up to reflect faces of passersby.

The burial procession. Three black-shrouded messengers holding staffs topped with reflective dollar signs. A runner swinging a red lantern. Four pall-bearers wearing animal heads carry a black casket filled with blowups of silver dollars. A chorus singing 'Get Out Of My Life Why Don't You Babe' to Chopin's Death March. Members of the procession give out silver dollars and candies.

Now more reality. Someone jumps on a car with the news that two Angels were busted. Crowd, funeral cortage and friends of the Angels fill the street to march on Park Police Station. Cops confront 400 free beings a growling poet with a lute, animalspirits in black, candle-lit girls singing 'Silent Night'. A collection for bail fills an Angel's helmet. March back to Haight and street dancing.

Street events are rituals of release. Reclaiming of territory (sundown, traffic, public joy) through spirit. Possession. Public NewSense.

Not street-theatre, the street is theatre. Parades, bank-robberies, fires and sonic explosions focus street attention. A crowd is an audience for an event. Release of

8

rowd spirit can accomplish social facts.
Riots are a reaction to police theatre.
Thrown bottles and over-turned cars are
responses to a dull, heavy-fisted, mechanical
and deathly show. People fill the street to
express special public feelings and held
human communion. To ask 'What's Happening?'

The alternative to death is a joyous funeral in
company with the living.

Industrialization was a battle with 19th
century ecology to win breakfast at the cost
of smog and insanity. Wars against ecology
are suicidal. The US standard of living is a
bourgeois baby blanket for executives who
scream in their sleep. No Pleistocene swamp
could match the pestilential horror of
modern urban sewage. No children of White
Western Progress will escape the dues of
peoples forced to hand their raw materials.

But the tools (that's all factories are) remain
innocent and the ethics of greed aren't
necessary. Computers render the principles
of wage-labour absolute by incorporating them.
We are being freed from mechanistic consciousness. We could evacuate the factories, turn
them over to androids, clean up our pollution.
North Americans could give up self-
righteousness to expand their being.

Our conflict is with job-wardens and consumer
keepers of a permissive loony-bin. Property,
credit, interest, insurance, instalments, profit
are stupid concepts. Millions of have-nots
and drop-outs in the US are living on an overflow of technologically produced fat. They
aren't fighting ecology, they're responding to
it. Middle-class living-rooms are funeral
parlours and only undertakers will stay in
them. Our fight is with those who would
kill us through dumb work, insane wars,
dull money morality.

Give up jobs so that computers can do them!
Any important human occupation can be
done free. Can it be given away?

Revolutions in Asia, Africa, South America
are for humanistic industrialization. The
technological resources of North America
can be used throughout the world. Gratis.
Not a patronizing gift, shared.

Our conflict begins with salaries and prices.
The trip has been paid for at an incredible
price in death, slavery, psychosis.

An event for the main business district of
any US city. Infiltrate the largest corporation
office building with life-actors as nympho-
maniacal secretaries, clumsy repairmen,
berserk executives, sloppy security guards,
clerks with animals in their clothes. Low key
until the first coffee-break and then pour it
on.

Secretaries unbutton their blouses and press
key clerks against the wall. Repairmen drop
typewriters and knock over water coolers.
Executives charge into private offices claiming
their seniority. Guards produce booze bottles
and playfully jam elevator doors. Clerks pull
out goldfish, rabbits, pigeons, cats on leashes,
nose dogs.

At noon 1000 freed beings singing and dancing
appear outside to persuade employees to take
off for the day. Banners roll down from
the office windows announcing liberation.
Girls in business suits run out of the building, strip and dive in the fountain. Elevators
are loaded with incense and a pie fight
breaks out in the cafeteria.

THEATRE IS FACT/ACTION

Give up jobs. Be with people. Defend
against property.

Garbage or Nothing

1. The recent death of capitalism has
everybody fucked around and confused.
Private enterprise laissez faire legally murderous piracy GONE already buried to be replaced
replaced by what? If it doesn't have a name,
how can you talk about it? And what about
the garbage? WHO'S GOING TO COLLECT
THE GARBAGE? Now there's something
you can talk about . . .

11. America 1968 so incredibly wealthy that
the local spiritual crisis is what're we going to
do about the garbage, the economic crisis how
to distribute the garbage, the political crisis
who's going to collect the garbage and why
should anyone want the job, while in the
oblivious streets attention has suddenly ex-
ploded into flesh bodies and the various ways
of rubbing them together. The Evolutionary
Credit and Loan Association has terminated
our contract, stamped it PAID IN FULL and
the planet is ours at last. Sudden flashes that
maybe those five thousand years of time
payments
--all those payments ON THE DOT—
                                  all those
food wars and social cipher contracts were
gestures of empty anxiety. Now that it's
ours and we can take a casual look around,
well there's so much GARBAGE.
Our wilderness is turning sour.
IT STINKS!
No place in the cosmology of planetary
physics for garbage.
What?
What an astounding oversight!
What were our ancestors THINKING about?

111. America a nation in 1968 so incredibly
wealthy that all morality is based on the
problems of EXCESS:
Fantasy executives and governmental spies
running wild-eyed down the corridors of
control.
'There's too fucking much of it!'
'It's completely out of control!'
'Power leak! Power leak!'
The cults of power grow wild: undisciplined
freedom cancer. Sudden flashes that the
future of bureaucracy spy systems lies in
garbage control.
People are USING it, picking it up FREE on
the streets, living on it, they no longer
respond to the seduction of the state, there's
no way to get a HOLD on them.
Pomposity suicided and rigidity machines put
to work at a furious clip: all this garbage
must be catalogued and filed, garbage destruct-
ionteams trained, parking lots on the tillable
land, thousands of well-programmed garbage
experts march to work each day to GET IT
DOWN ON PAPER, enormous factories
hastily tooled for garbage conversion.
'By God, we'll make napalm out of it.'
Youngsters who don't understand it's all
been paid for already
are given guns!
given napalm!
and shipped to parts of the planet where
there MAY be people who MIGHT be hip to
OUR garbage and MIGHT WANT SOME OF
IT FOR THEMSELVES.
The situation complicates itself incredibly.
Computer engineers make it worse: the
machines don't UNDERSTAND power, sex,
and control: the machines programme useable
garbage and forbidden fantasies of FREE.
The Secretary of Garbage Control considers
dropping acid and getting it over with.
Systems of control grow schizophrenic . . . .
they writhe and contort in involute paranoia.
SYSTEMICIDE MAKES HEADLINES.

1V. America a nation so incredibly wealthy
in 1968 that all morality is based on EXCESS:
true American career counselors now ask
only one question.
'Do you want to produce garbage or do you
want to collect garbage?'
Industrialist or politician?
Fishfarm or junkyard?
The young people want no part of it, of
course what with garbage their natural matrix

9

and medium.
Produce it?
Collect it?
They want to fuck in it!
The career counselors build marvelous constructions of seduction and mystery, they trans-substantiate symbol money
into sex
into power
into death insurance
into pleasure.
But it's just THINGS, it's garbage, it's overflow and the young people know it.
They throw the career counselor out of the window.
Who's going to collect the garbage?
Who knows?
Who cares?
Let's use it to act out our fantasies, use it for unimaginable gratifications.

V. We were sitting around the other night talking about garbage, making screaming intuitive leaps thru each others arguments, when Wm. Fritsch suddenly woke up and shouted,
'What I gotta do is learn to do nothing.'
And of course that's it
and it's not surprising that the solution came from a man who sometimes arrives at the compulsion to visit all his friends and empty the garbage for them.

VI. Garbage crises cannot be SOLVED: they must be ALLOWED TO DISAPPEAR.
The alternative to the garbage collection production box is to do just exactly nothing . . . . no more and no less.
Sudden flashes of the invisible network w/ the individual spine planted squarely on it.
organic units in the planetary ecology.
DOING NOTHING.
Ecological systems have no garbage in them, contain nothing that is alien to them.

VII. Invisible networks of nameless human connectives (names shed as metaphysical garbage) can help each other to do nothing.
That part of the psyche organism to which name is attached, that part which DOES things in praise of the name,
that part withers in the flesh caress of the anonymous community.
The galactic actor does nothing in the NAME of anything;
he receives his direction from the silent spinal telegraph,
his spine is planted square on the invisible network.
HE DOES NOTHING.
his movements are not outside the process.

VIII. It's paid for, all of it.
A cellophane bag represents 5000 years of machine history, inventors suicided by their inventions, aeons of garbage dedication, paid for in cancer wombs, in fallen cooks, in the crazy waste of our fathers.
Generations dead of lacklove sold for 29 cents.
Your birth certificate is your final credit card.
Stack the garbage in piles and people will live in among it, communities of free parallel spines planted square on the invisible network.
They will do nothing to effect the celebratory transformation of garbage into spinal food.
Their movements are not outside the process.

IX. The invisible networks grow thru the absent university of nothingness, disguised as dopesellers,
as sneak thieves
as naked dripping 17 year old Americans girls,
Doctors of garbage of philosophy
Doing nothing in PUBLIC teaching nothing demonstrating nothing living paradigms of nothing!
The absent university is powered by social magic.
It has flesh classrooms.
It is the university of the spine.
Tuition is paid in units of psychic bondage.
Its graduates are FREE.

10

SO...

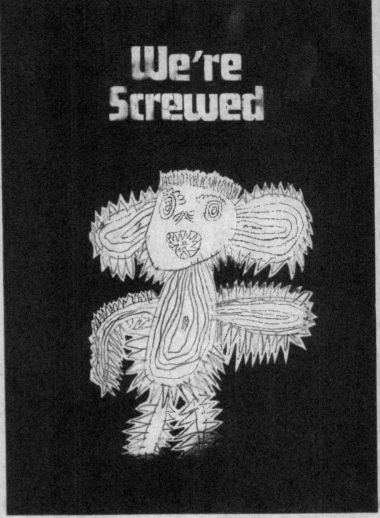

We're Screwed

But Digger Batman b.5.7.67 might just make it

O sky glorious, O sky divine—People—dominions—nations—Heavens—door—O walking deliverance O Passage -People—O People —Machines—Animals—Trees- Towers & bridges—OSeed—O colors—Faces—All Moving Things—Life,hello, ... I want to tell you of the birth of Digger.

Morning, about 9, 30, July 5th 1967—clear and sunny upon the city, the sky echoing with happiness, the streets still and clean and just to walk on them is to be silent in the bright rising from the night after a big 4th of

July electric music and free feed celebration out in the park where Emmett and the cooks fro, tje Fillmore had made barbecue for about 4,000 people.
I am up early and out into the street from Peter Cohon's on Pine Street where the Communication Company lived—out and standing in the good day with the smiles all over me, just letting the warmth and the light honey about on me, my clothes glowing and the fine feeling seeping to the skin and a touch tasting to my innards; and O the head is just wanting to face with smiles in all

directions. I had driven Susan Parker to the airport a couple of days before and still had her car so I swings over a few blocks to Geary thinking to have coffee and a morning smoke with the Jahrmarkts, Billy and Joan and the kids.

Up two flights, rap rap on the door and Bill answers to my hello half-dressed and happy. The baby's coming,' is what I remember him having said. And there is Joan sitting in the sun of those bright windows looking out over downtown and the bay, sitting on the bed, the mattress inevitably close to the floor, and the three kids—Jade, Hassan and Caledonia—kind of hushed and happy because they know the baby is coming and they have been waiting too.

So Joany's been in labor since the night before and now sits very calm with a $ tin watch in her right hand timing the contractions—about every 7 minutes and getting closer together. So me and Billy just standing there kind of stunned and sunny not thinking too much about what to do. 'You got my arrangements made?' I says, and 'no' is his reply.

It kind of goes like that, having a cigarette and a cup of coffee in the warmth of the morning in the corner room with just one fact we're standing in the baby's coming and we are smiling and blinking lumenent with speech in soft sounds. Nobody is thinking too much about hospitals though we figure lightly first about getting Joan into one of those places, but none too serious.

I sound on Joan if she thinks she got time for me to go phone around and see what I can do, get help I guess is what I meant, and she says there's plenty of time so I cut out and drive over to Margo St. James place on Nob Hill and start phoning.

I get hold of Kaiser Hospital and after about seven switchings back and forth I get ahold of some voice that says No, there's no chance of getting into their facilities without two hundred and fifty dollars in front even if the baby is on the way right now, and that the only thing that They, this voice, can suggest is to take The Expectant to County Hospital, which said set of instructions vis-a-vis that exhausted brick pile of agony so offends my ear I come near to throwing the phone across the room.

So I phone Bill Fritsch to let somebody else know what's happening (who tells Emmett who sends an ambulance which nobody quite knows what to do with except send it away). So I clean out Margo's refrigerator of all its food and drive back over to the Communications Company where is lovely Sam and Cassandra and Claude and Helene who I break it down to.

Right away Claude is on the horn talking here and there. I get Cassandra and head back to Billy's, drop off Cassandra and split down to the store to get some smokes and when I'm just rounding the corner on Geary when Claude pulls up to tell me he is on his way to Botines to get John Doss, a friend and head of Pediatrics at Kaiser.

Upstairs is Cassandra cleaning the kitchen, making coffee and a bit to eat for the kids. It is late morning now and we relax—everything seems to be going along unmolested by even the quiet logic of time—Cassandra molested busy in the kitchen, Billy sitting with Joan in the sunny corner room, the kids hushed and talking among themselves in their room, and I with the stillness if no thinking in my head gazing out of the window under the flat flag at the greenish dome of the city hall.

Rap rap on the door and I go out to open it to Richard Brautigan who comes in under soft tan hat, checks out the action, spots

Cassandra in the kitchen, decides everything is cool, walks once again through the rooms, tall slightly stooping like a gentle spider standing up (we are all spiders, or ants, or something, I remember wondering, watching Richard putting his hands in his pockets and taking them out) decides to split. 'Be back in a while—need anything?' 'No, nothing.' Out the door he goes.

It's early afternoon now. Quite suddenly Joan gets up, walks into the kitchen and squats down flat-footed on the floor with her back leaning to the wall, contractions coming quicker, Billy kneeling withher, Cassandra calm, me getting nervous—smoking cigarettes.

Knock on the door and in comes Claude and Helene with John Doss, way over 6 foot, a tower of a man withthose huge gentle hands that by a mere holding can take panic from a hurt child. All of a sudden it seems we got the best. Right away he's with Joan, coat off talking real easy, squat'd down, laughing with the simplicity of things. Claude asks me if I want to smoke some gold and lays a joint on me—I take it and put it on Billy.

People begin arriving—Billy Fritsch and Lenore, Bill much calmer than the day before in the park loaded on acid and getting Richie Marley real anxious, 'There's a warp in the continuum!' Emmett arrives. Diggers start coming.

By now the kitchen is a place of prayer— Joan in labor on the big patch quilt now in the middle of the kitchen floor and around her kneeling and sitting silent people—silent and back within listening to what silence says at self to birth.

John Doss moves in from the crowded front room every now and again and kneels his huge person down to speak quietly to Joan as he feels with those giant hands across her belly for the baby within. Billy squats Arab-silent flat-footed beside Joan, his hair long about his shoulders, staring into the thick air that holds the deep flux of his unspeaking Arab prayer.

Now the city has darkened for night, and Geary Street outside the window crawls alive with the homeward bound. Across the street the huge sign of an auto-agency—BOAZ, in Hebrew 'the lion hearted'· in black and white and red letters sends ancient benedictions into the rooms, and the green dome of city hall is alit as if it were a mosque removed one world and glowing not with bulbs nor candle but rather ringed with another light.

Now from out the night John and Sara and Peter and Sam and Gandolf and Natural Suzanne and more Diggers arrive like a troupe or miming chorus bearing brown paper sacks filled with sandwiches ·huge Poor Boys from some ecstacy delicatessen—the picture: Joan about to give birth on the kitchen floor, one dim shaded desk lamp by her feet, and a dozen people encircling her eating sandwiches and smoking weed, faces all in a shadow of the only lamp.

The contractions have begun to quicken and Joany is saying over and over again softly. 'Come on Baby. . . . Come on little Baby. . . . come on.'

The labor was becoming long, more than 24 hours now and the concentration of Joany's song had drawn the muscle lines tensed above her eyes pointing to a spot between them, slightly above them, and directly within.

John Doss had a slightly worried look as his hands felt over her belly. He seemed to be trying to gauge the position. Reaching within he felt for the baby's head which seemed to be turned in the wrong direction. The contractions were now great visible waves that

moved down across Joan's belly and with each one her tightened face appeared to have the full focused power of everything behind it pouring down through her body toward the slow and heavy working and waves of force that carried the baby in its passage.

'I need an instrument,' he said mentioning some sort of birthing clamp. 'I have to turn the baby's head'· He turned to someone there and told them to go across the street to the hospital and get an instrument and an intern.

Meanwhile Joan begins instructing Billy in how he, Billy, is going to receive his baby. Beneath the belly skin you can see the baby making its movements. Around Joan about a dozen Diggers and Digger ladies looking like all the accumulated faces of the Universe, the Divines of Ever pouring from each eye.

Like no time there is a bang on the front door and two white coated hospital guys come in stiff and important with shiny metal in their hands, take one look at the scene and decide it won't do for them to have anything to do with it. John Doss goes to meet them and they start backing off real quick. John grabs one of the guys by the lapels and starts

to jerk the doctor's jacket off and gets it down to around the guy's elbows.

'Take off that coat and get to work in here, for Christ sake. Be a doctor for once in your life!' he says to the guy.

'Take it easy John, take it easy,' the other guy tries to soothe. 'This can't be done here. . . . . it's not sterile. She must be moved to the hospital.'

About this time I start to ride up. 'She isn't going anywhere.' I says leaning across Joan at the guy. 'Cool it.' Bill says from the floor. They split threatening an ambulance and, for all we know, the Heat, so everybody settles down again with 'Come on baby' going real strong.

So John is back down with Billy showing him how to receive the baby, when it starts to come out and so quick and easy it seems a miracle but Billy has the baby's head in his hands and it looks like throughout the whole scene of deliverance the baby had turned its own head and decided to come out and with a thick liquid whoosh is right in Billy's hands. I am on my knees by Joany's head and I lean down with little more than a whisper, 'It's a boy.'

With some cotton string John Doss ties off the umbilical cord and cuts it with a pocket knife and the baby is born, out, free, alive and beautiful crying in his father's hands so fast that it was not a process of birth at last but life occuring.

John Doss begins cleaning up Joany and places the afterbirth in a basin.

'Eat!' he says to the circle of joyously lighted faces holding out the basin. 'Everybody eat!' and starts carrying the basin around from one to one and each dips a hand into the stuff of birth and blood and tastes and never, from no dope I have ever taken, have I got so instantly high. Somebody marks the time, 10.41, and asks Billy the baby's name.

'Digger!' Billy answers back with a voice loud with single word as its own rising song.

The bloodied ends of the umbilical tying string Billy takes and wraps up in a poem I had made that afternoon to lay on the kitchen floor:

Velvet kneeling meat—
Crazyblood in his prayers.

is all I remember.

11

Towards the New Synthesis

Herman Kahn

ought to start by admitting not that
m a war planner or a member of the
tablishment but that I come from
os Angeles. And it's a good place.
fact a good deal of what I'm going
be talking about is the Los Angel-
ation of the world. Somebody called
the barbecue culture; someone
ferred to it as a kind of wholesome
egeneracy. The issues which arise
that culture I think we pretty
uch will be talking about and
cing over the next 33 years. I
ve seen the future, and it doesn't
ork.

I like to start by taking a kind of a
eo-Marxian view of the problem.
ook at the economics of the situation.
he numbers aren't important. Let
e backtrack for a second. I gave
talk in Washington a few weeks ago
nd I decided to look very profound.
o I started the talk by saying, "Man
as been on earth two million years."

at doesn't sound as profound as
ying I'm one with the cosmos, but,
ou know, it's a pretty big idea. And
en I pointed out that I had examined
ery one of those years with loving
re and all that, and I noticed only
vo incidents of any interest. If you
e a religious man, you'll have to add
third.

he two incidents of interest were the
gricultural revolution, or the neo-
chnic revolution, generally say, about
vo hundred years ago, but you can't
ace it exactly. The agricultural
volution was exciting because it
ade civilization, cities, living in
ties. That was a very, very big
ange. It created classes, it created
rganization. It didn't really increase
he standard of living of people be-
ause Malthus was operating, and the
ange in technology meant that
here were more people rather than
at they lived better. And there -
some concern, of course, that
his may happen again. I don't think
is will happen, but you see it ex-
ressed, and sometimes the same
eople will talk about the fact that
here is total starvation facing the
orld and unlimited goods, and these
ok a little wrong and they could be
ght together too if you're stupid
ough but that seems unlikely.

p until roughly the Industrial Revol-
ion, no human community ever got
uch above, say $200 per capita, much
elow, say $50 per capita. Think of
donesia today -100 million people
out 100 dollars per capita. That's
he Han empire, the Roman empire.
ou know, the same number of
eople, same way of living. Roman
easants or Chinese peasants they go
here today. They would recognize
and vice-versa. You can think of
at as the normal state of human
eings. Normal is a bad phrase there.
ypical.

If you think of the Industrial Revolution, you think of Europe today, say
somewhere between $500 and $2,000
per capita. And again, here's a
Marxian notion, if you make enough
of a change quantitatively it eventually
makes a qualitative change. It's
different. Europe is not like a pre-
Industrial civilization. I think it takes
about a factor of 10 to make the next
change. That's roughly $5,000 to
about $20,000 per capita; and that's
roughly the United States and about
20% of the world.

At the end of the century, it is not a
post-economic world. That is, most
of the people in it will be worried
about how to pay the rent, and how
to make the payments on the third
helicopter, and it's really too expensive
to put in a second swimming pool,
you know. You may say, "My God!
What trivia," but you know, it's nice
to have a swimming pool, and you
may want another one so the kids
can play in theirs. If you look at
a man in the United States who makes
about $50,000 a year after taxes, he
generally does not feel post-economic.
He rather objects to any terminology
of that sort.

Rather surprisingly, it would not be
shocking if before the 21st century
closed you would hit what I would
call an almost post-economic society.
The "almost" is of some importance...
somebody will want to take a trip to
Saturn and not quite be able to afford
it, and he'll feel very deprived because everybody else is going that
year. Or they'll want to go to Mars
'cause that's where the action is, and
you can't make it, and that's annoying
because it'll just cost too much. But
for any kind of thing that we think
of today as a moderate necessity of
life, other than love, affection, friendli-
ness, competent teaching and so on,
these (the necessities) will be sort of
free. The other may or may not be
free; that is one of the things I'd
like to talk about. I want to restrict
my remarks to this post-Industrial
society, which is not yet post-economic.

Now, post-Industrial: it doesn't look
like Europe. It may also be a post-
business society. Here, the notion is
that when Calvin Coolidge said that
the business of America is business,
he was probably making a perfectly reasonable statement for his
period. I would say as late as 1955,
when Secretary Wilson made his
statement, "I'm not aware that what's
bad for General Motors is good for
the United States, or that's what's bad
for the United States is good for
General Motors" . . . . remember he got
kicked in the teeth for that . . . . it's a
reasonably accurate remark.

If you ask what makes what makes the
United States the kind of country it is,

lemme tell ya, General Motors plays a
bigger role than any activity I know of.
Now you may not like it, that's your
privilege, but it's an accurate descrip-
tion of the United States, as people
think of it. I am reliably informed
that they manufacture unsafe cars, and
that can't be good for the United
States. Unless you don't like the
country, as some of you I gather don't.
But you really don't probably want
people killed in accidents. I am saying
that by and large, it's hard to imagine
the United States sick and General
Motors healthy, or General Motors
sick and the United States healthy,
economically. That's no longer true
today. The United States is bigger than
General Motors, and it'll be increasingly untrue in the future. It's a little
bit like a farmer. A hundred years ago
this was an agricultural country. Today
a farmer comes home and tells his wife
"I just doubled production in the
south 100." Wife says, "That's marvelous, what else did you do today?"
No confrontation, no interpersonal
relations. She's not interested. The
New York Times puts it on page eight,
none of you read it. No because
I've got to; it's my business, but I'm
not excited either. It's just not an
exciting thing to do to double productivity on the south 100 acres in the
United States. That's a fantastic statement but true. Twenty or thirty years
from now, and even in some degree
today, we would expect a minority of
the country to be in business and a
certain manufacturing, and a doubling
of productivity of goods will not be
exciting. It'll be interesting, you know,
you'll be richer, but it won't be exciting.

Where will the excitement be? I don't
know, but I would predict a kind of
mosaic society. Not Moses, but mosaic
in the sense of lots of little patterns.
Uh, I'm getting a slight fondness for
the other kind of Mosaic society, as I
look at the current society. I had a
grandfather who was a rabbi. He
talked regularly to God. He looked
very rigid. He had no identity problems
by the way, knew who he was, knew
who his children were, knew what the
world was like. Couldn't eat pork, but
somehow led a freer life than many
people I know. Married for life, it
never occurred to him to uh... I see
you're nostalgic for that. You may
like to see those familiar wrinkles on
the pillow next to you. A surprising
thought, but ponder it.

Why is it that people think they have
so much freedom today? Well, the
world has changed. Roughly speaking,
there's 135 nations in the world today.
Fifty-five of them as far as I know do
not worry about frontiers. And as far
as I know that was never true anywhere in the history of the world before.
No Latin American country, for
various reasons which are kind of com-

plicated, worries about its frontiers. Now you can find no twenty year period in Latin American history since 1810 in which there was not a serious frontier confrontation, except in the last twenty, and no one expects it for the next thirty either. That's true in North America. I can't write you a scenario in which Ho Chi Min gets into San Francisco unless invited by an audience. It's just, you know, very difficult to write that scenario. In Western Europe, with the exception of Germany's east border, there's no problems. Everybody knows that Germany and Japan lost World War 11 and are the most successful nations since. Neither has a navy and they're the second and fifth largest trading powers in the world today. And don't seem to worry about the flag following it. Uh, there's a joke I sometimes tell, you may know the story about the Israelis. About four or five years ago they had a balance of payments problem and decided to declare war on the United States, on the theory that the US would win the war, occupy them, rebuild their economy, protect them from the Arabs, you know, no problems. And this rabbi got up who was grey with wisdom, and said, "With our luck we'll win". You couldn't have told that joke thirty years ago. Nobody would have known what you're talking about.

Alright, let's look at the economic problem. Now, there's a possibility of starvation in the world. I think it's overstated because it depends on a series of things . . . . you have a problem which I ought to mention. If someone comes up to you and says, "Everybody in the world's going to starve to death," he generally looks like a warm-hearted human because somehow he's worried about it. But if he says that everybody's not going to starve to death, he looks kind of callous, he looks detached and he's not worried about it. My statement's in between: I am worried about it, but I don't think it will happen. For it to happen would depend on the monsoons, floods in China, maybe bad weather in North America. The US government, I think unwisely, cut back production this year. They looked at the problem and decided that the problem was a lot more likely to be a food surplus. I think that's a mistake because our food stocks are depleted, and it's good to have a surplus, but I think their guess is right. But there are serious economic problems in the world. Most of the people, if not as hungry as often described, are hungry, and a lot of them are undernourished and underfed and so on. In the US, as far as I can see, outside of some pockets, in the South and some other very odd areas, no serious starvation. There's a fair amount of malnutrition, that's of, both the over- and under- sort, and

it has the question of choice involved in it.

I'm not sure about Haight-Ashbury. I've talked to some of the people here and they tell me it's the same. I know about the East Village and Cambridge Square, and my friends there tell me it takes about ten dollars a week to live reasonably well, per person, about $500 a year. That if you go to New York City or Boston, and I suppose the same here, and work at the Post Office at night, that's about $500 a month; so roughly in one month you can get a year's income, or say twelve people in a pad, they can take turns working one at a time. And you don't have to take a bath or dress or anything like that because the Post Office doesn't care at night. It's very permissive. The thing's stronger than that. An American, an upper class American can drop out, knock around for four or five years, get married, have a kid. There are three syndromes; it's kind of interesting. Criminals, dope addicts, and many hips who grow out of it. About the age of thirty-thirty-five (we know less about the hippies because they haven't been around that long), they often want to go back to that society. If you started off as an upper middle class kid with the skills you achieved people will say, "Come back, we're delighted." They don't foreclose it. It's not like Europe. In Europe if you drop out for five years, you've had it..you'll have trouble getting back in. No problem in the United States; you look kind of romantic and you can make a living years afterwards telling anecdotes about it. There's no pressure.

Let me give you a distinction in pressures here for example. I was in Israel about two years ago. That country has a peculiar structure. It's about 40% Ashkenazy, or European Jews, and 60% Oriental Kews. Ashkenazy Jews are more or less on the top; Oriental Jews are more or less on the bottom. Sometimes a Moroccan Jew will say to an Ashkenazy Jew: "I don't want your European Culture." which is being forced on him, by the way. Ashkenazy Jews will always say, "There are a hundred million Arabs." The Moroccan Jew will think about ten seconds and say, "Where is the electrical engineering school?" You see he has absolutely no choice. He can't fool around; there are no illusions possible, you know. He is in a structure, and the structure tells him what to do, and that's reality, and he can see it. Now if you take the structure away you've changed reality. If there aren't one hundred million Arabs around, you don't have to go to electrical engineering school. But you have another interesting problem: you are free to define reality any way you choose. And nothing's going to knock it out of you, at least in the short run.

You notice, for example, how people play the soldier game, or the business game, or the farmer game? You've all the terminology. I want you to think of two countries. One of them is tough, mean, nasty, barbarian, and they've got soldiers. They don't play the soldier game; they've got soldiers. You know, people who believe in Duty, Honor, Life and Death matter, Glory. The kind of people who enjoy a good fight. There are a lot of people like that. The other side's got a group of people who play the soldier game. You know, it's the kid's game grown up. Who do you think's going to come out well? Well, I'll tell you: the people who are not playing the soldier game but have real soldiers; Take away the barbarians, no river, big ocean, no problems. You can play the soldier game, you know, and nothing's going to happen. Take a country faced with starvation You've got to have farmers rather than people who play the farmer game. Take a country which is economically in trouble. It's good to have businessmen, not people who are playing the businessman game.

What I'm saying is that in the United States you will be able in the future to downgrade what we used to think of as serious activity to the level of a child's game. As far as I can see, the thing will not become so pervasive—not everybody will do it, you understand, somewhere between say five and thirty per cent of the population. That means they have no problems. A little bit like the Greek or Roman Empire. The Stoics ran it for about two hundred years, ran it very well. Nobody appreciated what they did. They didn't expect appreciation - it was part of their creed not to. When Marcu Aurelius died, they just disappeared without a trace, and then people learned that they had something useful. In the sense that from that point on, the Roman Empire was run by crony, by warlord systems, gangster systems, and it was different. And people noticed the difference by the way. Romans had middle class cops. You could riot and they would not knock you in the head unless you were a christian. Then, they'd throw you to the lions because they made distinctions which we don't today.

Now, how dangerous or good is it to have this kind of freedom? How good is it to have this kind of freedom? It clearly gives you enormous ranges of choices. It is true, you can choose now, to a great degree. Not everybody can choose now, you understand. I was having an argument a few minutes ago. I had made the comment at Berkeley that in Continental Europe, there are no hips. There are Provos or people like from the Dada movement who

14

mock society or don't like the middle class smug morality and hypocrisy. But they're elite groups. They don't say everybody should drop out. They say, "We drop out; you keep working."

It's hard for a European to say, "Everybody drop out." He's got a vague fear in the back of his mind that maybe everybody will! It looks to him like it's hard to put together. Take it apart and maybe it doesn't operate as well. You know you may not be able to put it back together again. In the United States, it's different. Middle class Americans will borrow up to their next year's salary, and that spirit rolls right down to the hippy. We all have faith in the future. We all know the system's going to work. We all know that we're not going to get into a 1929 depression again. We all know the country's not going to be invaded, almost irrespective of policy-good or bad policy.

There is however sensible policy which at least realizes that while you can't manufacture goods simply by defining money, you can lose goods by defining money badly. The system is an organization, a social system. Money is a symbol, if you will, but really, money is a technique for making the thing work. There are lots of other ways for making it work. A number of the socialist economies have noticed that even if you want to have socialism, it's good to have this technique of money and using market prices and market orientation.

Alright, how good is it to lose this structure? To be able to make total free choice? And really not having any nagging, guilty conscience that you're not paying your share because you're really not making an example for other people anyway. No, you're doing your thing; let the other guy do his thing. I would guess that there is a real possibility for a superior type of human being. But I would be very dubious that he is going to be a hedonist. My guess, and I'm not just being sentimental, goes back either to the European tradition of the gentleman or the Hellenic tradition of being a good Greek.

I don't happen to like the kind of thing that's produced over here, but I would guess it would be something like the following: let me define a gentleman for you - a man with many, many skills in all of which it is very hard to achieve high capability, but in all of which he does achieve high capability, none of which are useful. They are done for other reasons. They are not done grimly, but they are done seriously, but with a touch of lightness. A society could live that way I'd guess if it has a kind of internalized discipline. To be a little inaccurate, the Greeks were like that, the Romans weren't. The Greeks

stayed fit because they liked to be fit. The Romans stayed fit because they had to be fit to fight wars. Take away the war, they quit being fit, and they ran into trouble. The Spartans had that same sort of theory. They were more like the Romans than Athenians. They had the notion that once they got rich, the place would collapse. They got rich and the place collapsed. One of the soundest predictions I've ever seen.

Freud once made a very perceptive comment which I want to rephrase to make it better. "For most people the long arm of the job and the requirements of national security are their only touch with reality." Take that away and they can live a completely illusioned life. They need not touch face with any kind of reality from that day on. They can make it up as they go along, and they will find it satisfactory.

Now that is, of course, part of your freedom. That's learning by making mistakes. But one of the important things about making a mistake is to know it's a mistake early enough in the game to change. Say you could create an environment in which you could raise you children so that practically 100% of their experiences were affirmative, pleasant, warming, supportive, and so on. Would anybody care to raise their children in that environment?.... You have a strong sense that they ought to have at least some frustration, some failures, some rejections, some nastiness. Not too much; it's not good for young children I'm sure, say up to ages 5, 6, 7, but at some point the psyche can take it. It bruises, but it doesn't get damaged. And the world has that character.

I remember at the Berkeley riots, one girl was carrying a sign saying, "I'm a Human Being. Please do not fold, bend, spindle, or mutilate." Well that's a reasonable request. I also recall a slight change in styles of raising children. Some years ago we were told that if you frustrate them, it gave them neuroses. Today we're usually told, not always, that a certain firm discipline is as natural as rain, and the kid needs it as well as he needs vitamin B. It's part of his growing up. The ability to do sustained effort on unpleasant, dull tasks–that's part of the ability to grow up. Not everything comes for free, for fun. Now this girl appeared on a BBC programme, and it was really kind of fascinating. The BBC announcer said to her, "Berkeley is one of the three, four or five best schools in the world. You have a sign saying that life here is a living hell. Now this is really a marvelous area within 20-30 miles from Berkeley. You can get any kind of wholesome or degenerate pleasure; you have a wide choice. So why is

it living hell?" The girl said, "They have a computerized program for classes. It gave me only ten minutes to get from the tennis courts to math class, and it takes fifteen. I'm not treated like a human being." The announcer said, "That doesn't seem to me to be a living hell. Do you have another anecdote?" The girl, "I'm an art major, and the computer programmed my class for the cellar, and programmed the engineers for the sixth floor with the view, and this is very bad for the psyches of the art majors, and anyway the engineers have no psyches." The announcer looked dubious. It didn't strike him as a living hell, but he was an Englishman and didn't understand these things. Then the girl pointed out perfectly correctly that suicides are on the increase among college students. Well, you can't laugh about that. But you wonder, is it the living hell or is it the students? Maybe it's the low frustration index. There seems to be some evidence of that.

What about the longer term? That is let's assume we pick a society which really was hedonistic, secular. How many people here worry about an afterlife? One of the things that will change this way will be not just the economies but the technology. Let me give you three examples of this. I'll start with the computer.

Let's look at the computer for a few minutes. It's an interesting gadget, an exciting one. They talk back to you. Computers have improved by about a factor of ten every two or three years, which is one of the new elements. Anything you learned about computers two or three years ago can be obsolete today, and anything you learned today can be obsolete in two or three years. And this in turn may mean that you will want some familiar sign posts elsewhere. Today, for example, in computer technology, unlike say civil engineering, you can reach your peak salary at about early thirties. And then you're obsolete. You go into administration if you want to keep up your salary. You don't make an honest living anymore. Or, you really work hard, and go back to school at night, which turns out to be kind of dull today.

A second thing of interest. There is reason for believing that despite many of the computer experts, this improvement of a factor of ten will continue for the rest of the century. This means an improvement by a factor of some billions or some quadrillions. Now some of you are not familiar with numbers; those are very big numbers. It means that they surpass the number of neurons in the human brain by quite a bit.

That raises another issue. You sometimes see statements that there are

15

some things which a human can do and which a computer cannot do. Nobody has ever made that statement carefully. To the extent that a person really knows what he's talking about, he must have had divine revelation. Now it's hard to argue with a man who has talked with God, and I don't. I don't argue with my grandfather; I don't argue with him. But for those of us who haven't got divine revelation, we simply do not know if there are any characteristics of a human being, including the most intimate at the mental-emotional-feeling evel, which could not be duplicated or in some reasonable sense of the term, surpassed by a computer.

If it turns out that somebody proves that computers cannot do what a human being does, that there is something vital or special or different about human beings, that we're not just a collection of atoms put together in a laboratory, I think that would be the most significant event of the 20th century, ranking with the other two events I mentioned earlier, and for some of us replacing the events I overlooked. It's a kind of theology, in other words. It's a theological statement.

If, as I believe much more likely, the computer can do anything the human being can, and maybe surpass, that is also in its own way the most significant event of the 20th century, though achieved more gradually, and will change very much our view of ourselves. This is secularism at the limit. And when the computers get better, who needs human beings? It's not a joke. I would guess that before the post-economic society comes, you'll get the intelligent computer. I used to make a comment that it wouldn't surprise me if by the year 2000 a computer was making this lecture to a group of computers. But it wouldn't be as funny. If I say that to a technical audience, they say, "How do you know?" They get mad. I want you to imagine this human being: he's got an artificial heart, a false leg or two, carries an extra three brains on his back because he gets tired thinking with the other ones sometimes. And, you know, when you phase out the other obsolete equipment maybe you phase him out too. He's only another mechanism. Or, maybe you have votes for the computer.

Let me give you the next device which is interesting. Pleasures pall, you get tired of them. That seems largely correct, but there's at least one exception which is of interest. Some experiments were done with rats. You can take a rat and wire his pleasure centres to a button and give him the choice of pressing either the button for food, water, sex, or rest. He seems to like it very much. He seems to press that button 6000 times an hour, give

or take a factor or two. If you force them to take a little food and rest, they seem to lead longer lives than the control rats. In other words it's a sort of healthy thing to do.

We know where the human pleasure centres are roughly; there are people doing experiments on them right now. Get them wired to a computer on your chest or a consul. I'm a prudish type. I'm not free, so I won't let you play your own buttons. That's depraved. But get yourself and opposite number, hopefully of the opposite sex, but I'm not going to be rigid, and play each other's buttons. If the mice experiments are any example you've got it! It's what you've been looking for! Anybody want anything else? There's something annoying about it. My grandfather would be very upset. He'd be more than upset. It's clear that's not what you want by and large, so I would guess only 5-10% of Americans would go for it. But the rest of us are going to find it somehow inadequate. But it's very hard to explain why it's inadequate.

I think it's clear that Western culture and the United States in particular has very much neglected the side of the human personality, sometimes known a as "inner space." I would assume that as part of this post-Industrial revolution there will clearly be more emphasis on so called Dionesian man, spiritual man, mystical man, and drugs definitely go in this direction. They clearly lead to an increase in privatism of the personalityif any of the reports are right. They lead to a withdrawal from structured situation to unstructured One of the real problems with the drugs is that maybe the people who so to speak could use that change in personality most are least likely to take it; the ones who are already pretty unstructured are the most likely to take it. The ones who in some sense it may be most harmful for. The question of legalizing it either under care or generally is a messy one and I don't know where I would stand. There is widespread agreement, no particular data, but you don't need data to get agreement, that marijuana is less dangerous than alcohol. So that if you had a choice between marijuana and alcohol, you'd probably choose marijuana. On the other hand, if the question is whether to add marijuana to alcohol that's not so persuasive that it's less dangerous. Alcohol does cause a lot of damage in the world and you're asked to sort of double it or at least by half. And that's something you want to look at with care.

One of the points which strikes me is that when you do any study of groups from the viewpoint of objectives—that is you have some kind of objective, a nation trying to increase wealth, or a business-

man trying to make money, it can be people trying to win a football game, don't care what it is--you soon find th there's a role for what's called the rationality of irrationality. That is, you cannot do your objective efficient by almost any criteria you care to mer ion unless you can lock yourself in o some issues rigidly. To give you a simple example: any business situation unless you can lock yourself in to pay ing money you can't borrow money. A society which doesn't feel any obligation . . . well, do you know the game of chicken? If you get in a car dead drunk, throwing whisky bottles out the window, very blind, throw the steering wheel out, you win the game. Because you're locked in. I'm not recommending that, but I'm describing in a very dramatic way som of the roles of irrationality. For many people, getting married for life may be a very important thing for them. Literally. Because that's the only way that they can conceive of it. They simply cannot give and receive unless they feel that it's permanent. Take away the concept of permanence and they can't have the same kind of relationship.

In an interpersonal encounter, you car get a kind of feeling that would come to most people only after a lifetime of interaction. Now, that's a typically American thing too. If you go to Europe, you'll find that the people don't call each other by the first name unless they went to high school or college together. If you loo at World War 11, for example, if you had a guy next to you who was killed, and he happened to be a close relative or a very close friend, you often get a syndrome of tremendous guilt. Because you first feel happy that it was him not me, and you then feel very guilty for that happiness. It turns out that Americans get that syndrome for someone they met last week with the first-name basis and get along with the very well. To Europeans that closeness looks very ersatz. They find it incredibly shallow. I think the other kind of course will also satisfy us. We get the habit of getting into relationships with someone we brushed past in the elevator. You know, we shared that experience together so I can give you my most intimate thoughts and you can give your most intimate thoughts because what could be closer than sharing the same elevator. I think you'll find people like that in life. Bu I think many people here would not like it. Who's to say who's right and who's wrong? I really don't know.

I don't know what it'll be like, but I would give you even money for a new human being in the 21st century. But I really doubt that he'll be a hedonist, a dropout, a materialist, a console player . . . I rather suspect he'll be a little bit like me.

Towards the New Synthesis

Herman Kahn

hip ocrates

Question: I am a girl of 18 with a sexual hang-up. I want to share a beautiful, gentle relationship with my boyfriend and also feel loved by him. Yet there are times when I would like to be brutally and cruelly balled. But not by my boyfriend!

I have visions of being tied to bedposts and having men (all types) coming in and taking turns on me and doing whatever.

Is this normal and what can I do about it?

Answer: A part-time coed, whom I suspected daydreamed only of chocolate cake, told me recently that her favorite sexual fantasy was making love while floating in water. Another student, inspired by her panoramic view of San Francisco, fantasizes about making love while floating through the air. Both fantasies could be realized. The first by determined swimmers and the second by swift high-jumpers, gutsy skydivers and bored astronauts.

Fantasies of sexual masochism occur in both sexes but are more common in women. In fact, a certain amount of masochism is normal in females. Why this should be so is unclear. Perhaps it has to do with women's sexual role (taking rather than putting in).

Fellini's 'Hero' in '8½' had vivid sexual fantasies and in one sequence told his mistress to act the part of a prostitute. Some psychiatrists would advise you and your boyfriend to act out between you the fantasies you desired. Most would tell you to seek psychiatric aid if you felt you were about to make this fantasy come true (especially by advertising in the classified section). A course of psychotherapy might enable you to better understand your unconscious motivations.

Question: I am a girl (23) who has an unusual bustline problem —too much! I'm 5' 5", 120 lbs., wear a size 10 dress and have a 36D bustline.

I wouldn't mind it so much if it weren't so droopy—without a bra I closely resemble those Neolithic Venuses on the cover of the latest 'Scientific American'. I didn't start wearing a bra until a year after I should have and didn't wear one at night until I was 20. Weight loss only makes things worse. Consequently, I'm quite unattractive in the nude.

I've been trying exercises for the past couple of months but it hasn't helped a bit as the problem isn't the muscles but the skin. What I'd like to know is 1) Would plastic surgery help? 2) How much would it cost? 3) If I did have surgery, would it permit me to go braless occasionally—if not I might as well forget the whole thing right now.

Yours truly,
The Neolithic
Fertility Goddess.

P.S. While we're on the subject of breasts—one of my nipples is constantly hard, the other is always soft even when I'm turned on— is this abnormal?

Answer: Those Neolithic Venuses looked pretty good to me. Who told you you're unattractive in the nude?

Surgery is sometimes performed to reduce the size of very large sagging breasts. The cosmetic results vary depending upon the breasts, the skill of the surgeon, and fate. A certain amount of scarring is inevitable. Having one nipple erect and the other soft when aroused is perfectly normal. But if you continue wearing bras to bed you'll turn off any potential arouser.

Question: Please hurry and have this printed. I haven't found the answer in any books and this problem has been bothering me for some time so you are one of my last resorts. Why is it that my labia minora protudes [at least ½ inch] from my labia majora? What can be done to correct this? Fortunately, I went to a high school in a state that didn't require Physical Education so I didn't have to take embarrassing gang showers.

Answer: The labia are the 'lips' of the vagina, the outer labia are the majora or the larger lips and minora are the smaller inner lips. Variations in size are normal. If any of your intimate friends think your 'problem' is unusual, it's due to their lack of experience. Perhaps it was unfortunate that your state did not require Phys. Ed. Your fears would be fewer now.

Question: What are the implications of balling four guys consecutively in the course of one afternoon (physically/psychologically)? And what are the signs of nymphomania?

Answer: Women are so constructed that they are physically capable of far more sexual activity than are men. No physical harm would be expected from the situation you describe unless one of the men had a communicable disease. Of course, the risk of contracting a venereal disease increases directly with the number of one's contacts.

Psychological implications of varied sexual situations depend on the personality of those involved entirely, for example one of those four guys might freak out. In Masters and Johnson's study, 'Human Sexual Response,' every one of the 312 males questioned expressed some concerns about 'excessive' masturbation. One man who masturbated once or twice a month thought once or twice a week was excessive. Another who masturbated 2–3 times a day might lead to a case of 'nerves'. Not one thought his own pattern was abnormal.

Dorland's Medical Dictionary (23rd edition) defines nymphonia as 'exaggerated sexual desires in a female,' Webster's Collegiate Dictionary refers to 'morbid and uncontrollable sexual desire in a female.' I think I understand the phrase 'sexual desire in a female' but find it hard to quantitate 'exaggerated' and am not sure what 'morbid' means in this connection.

My conclusion is that 'nymphomania' means more sexual activity than is considered proper by the woman-hater using the term.

Question: I often read ads in the underground press for people wanting 'French' love. Could you please tell me what this is?

Answer: 'French love' or 'French culture' refers to oral-genital relations. The French may call this 'Italian love'.

Question: A friend of mine has been forbidden by his doctor to indulge in intercourse until a nasty bit of the clap is entirely cleared up. If any of his girl-friends should decide to employ digital manipulation of his primary sex organ to achieve orgasm and release on his part, would this result in a case of the 'hand-clap?'

Answer: I applaud the concern you have for your friend and his friends. Gonorrhea of the hand is unknown because the gonococci bacteria favor a warm, moist, airless environment. Gonorrhea of the mouth is possible but seen rarely. Most physicians believe all sexual activity should be avoided while treatment for gonorrhea is underway.

(Note: The symptoms of gonorrhea in the male are itching, burning and pain on urination and a discharge from the urethra. Symptoms in the female may include the above but are usually less severe or absent in the early stages. Females may later develop pain in the lower abdomen and a low-grade fever resulting from spread of the infection to the uterus, tubes and ovaries.)

Question: When at home by myself sometimes walking around in the nude or while taking a shower, I get an erection. What bothers me is when I think of going to a place like a gymnasium to work out or a Turkish bath or some other place where I may be taking off my clothes, I worry that I may get an erection in front of members of my fellow sex in such a place. I know that all men get erections but should I be concerned about getting one in a public place?

How do other men feel about this? Does it happen to them, and, if so, does it bother them? Should I consider this a problem? I have never brought this up to anybody before because I thought I might be abnormal.

Answer: Your 'problem' is one that almost all men have worried about, especially younger men — but these fears are usually never expressed, except perhaps, to a psychiatrist.

Some solutions suggested by patients—jump into a cold shower, think of jumping into a cold shower, think of making it with the Johnson girls, try to make it with one of the Johnson girls, remember the first time a policeman's flashlight shone into your car when you were making it in the back seat, think of Doris Day, recall a hospital or university cafeteria meal. The possibilities for turn-offs are endless. Another possibility is not to worry about it.

Question: I recently, at the advice of my friends, drank a bottle of Romilar C.F. cough syrup. This was supposed to get me stoned. It did just that. After about 20 minutes my arms and legs got limp. I could hardly think and slurred when I talked. I laid down and found myself hallucinating.

About an hour later, I got real sick and threw up, after which I couldn't walk. My pupils almost covered my whole iris. I went to bed that night and found myself hallucinating in double vision with my eyes open. The next day I had chattering teeth and every time I took a deep breath I would end up yawning which would make my body go limp.

I feel fine now (3 days later). What possible damage did I do to myself? Is what I did illegal?

Answer: I first heard about dextromethorphan cough syrups and tablets used for 'high' from a British ex-commando in Copenhagen in 1965. Apparently, it had not appreciably benefited the ex-commando. He often went about bopping peaceful Danes on the chin in pubs such as Lauritus Betjen and the Rijsgaarten.

Recently I treated a girl who had taken half such a bottle of cough syrup at a rock dance. As a result she was semi-comatose, incontinent of urine and required hospitalization. Her boyfriend, who had taken the same amount, seemed normal, except for dilated pupils.

Nothing is known about possible long term harmful effects after frequently using large amounts of dextromethorphan.

Buying cough syrup is not illegal. Using it to get high may be against the law though that's hard to prove. You're missing the point if your chief fear about this incident is violating a statute.

Dr Schonfeld welcomes your queries. Write to Hipocrates c/o OZ 38a Palace Gardens Terrace London W8.

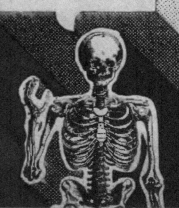

ENSURE CONFUSION!:,??!

Every OZ is different. We don't have a standard, instantly recognisable cover-style, shape, form, content, texture size or smell. (Yes, smell. Sniff out OZ 12 again. We mixed a Woolworths cologne with yellow ink). That's why some people miss OZ on the news-stands. This edition (14) has a new printer and a special guest editor. The next OZ (15) is already being prepared along different almost contradictory, lines. We know it's confusing. It confuses us. You too can ensure regular confusion by subscribing. Just 30/- for a whole year's subscription plus two free back issues.

THE MYSTERIOUS VANISHING BACK ISSUES

Sorry, we're quickly running out of back issues. There are absolutely no more OZ 3 or 4's. Some OZ 5's are still left—the famous plant-a-flower-child poster—but we're mean and broke enough to now charge £1 for them. All the rest are still available, but 6's and 7's are disappearing fast.

RARE FIRST OZ

The Johnson caricature, 'Madonna of the Napalm' is a three page gate-fold in OZ 1. This issue sold out and we have been unable to fill the many subsequent orders for it. However, a few have been returned from our distributors and we're going to offer them to our readers at the ludicrously expensive price of £1. They're not worth it. But no doubt some neurotic collectors will want to complete their sets.

OLD OZes

One: Theological striptease . . . . turn on, tune in, drop dead . . . . In bed with the English . . . . Raped Congo nuns whipped with rosary beads . . . . Private Eye axed.

Two: Mark Lane's BBC Expose . . . British Breasts . . . Peter Porter's Metamorphoses . . . . Little Malcolm and his struggle against the 20th Century . . . . Cut out pop stars and the giant Toad of Whitehall Sharp poster.

Three: Not available

Four: Not Available

Five: Plant a Flower Child billboard poster . . . . The great Alf Conspiracy. (We have just heard this poster has been banned by beautiful Australian Customs)

Six: (OZ & Other Scenes) Blue movies by the yard . . . . The king of Khatmandu and his Coca Cola Court . . . Dope Sheet . . . . John Peel interview . . Letter from a Greek Prison. . . . Leary in Disneyland . . . . Mcluhan's one-eyed electric kingdom.

Seven: What's so good about Bob Dylan? . . . . Wog Beach Shock . . . . Michael X and the Flower Children . . . In bed with the Americans . . . . Review of Maharishi's 'The Science of Being and the Art of Living'.

Eight: Mis-spelt Guevara poster . . . . Russia, you have bread, but no roses . . Playboy's banned pictures . . . . Spyder Turner's raunch epistemology . . . . Edward do Bono on lateral thinking.

Nine: New Dylan Lyrics . . . . 'If I could turn you on' UFO digest . . . . Death at St Pauls. . . . David Widgery's Devaluation Trilogy.

Ten: The pornography of violence . . Amnesty report from Athens . . . . Gaol in Arkansas . . . . The men who ban OZ . . . . OH! what a lawful war . . . . Roger McGough's 'Summer with the Monarch' (complete version).

Eleven: New Statesman parody . . . . the Yippee call to arms . . . . The Anglo American Pumice Factory . . . . Vietloon Spring Offensive . . . . Ray Durgnat's Fading Freedoms, Latent Fascisms and Hippie High Hopes.

Twelve: Yes Virginia, there is a Maharishi . . . . Excuse me, is this the Way to the Gas Chamber? . . . . The giant three poster Buddhist issue (hash recipes sex card game, spiritual post-cards etc.)

Thirteen: Mike English's golden wheel of fire gatefold . . . . AGIT OZ . . . . When Harrods is Looted, by David Widgery . . . . The May Revolution by Angelo Quattrocchi . . . . Bob Dylan film script . . . . The Great Alfback (i) . . Tom Nairn's Worst Trip Ever—a review of 2001 . . . . Interviews with Tuli Kupferberg and Jean Jaques Lebel . . . . plus all those filthy advertisements that are the bane of Hampstead.

FULL SETS

These no longer exist. But we'll still give you a rare bundle of OZes (Nos: 1, 2, 5, 6, 7, 8, 9, 10, 11, 12, 13) for £3.

COMPLETE COUPON!?

Name

Address

Country

RUSH TO OZ, 38a Palace Gardens Terrace, London, W8.

I enclose 30/- for a subscription plus two free back issues (U.S. $4)

Send me the exorbitantly priced OZ 1 and/or 5. £1 each (U.S. $3.)

Send me a big surprise bundle of OZes for £3 (U.S. $8)

Send me back issues 2, 6, 7, 8, 9, 10, 11, 12, 13. (Delete inapplicable) 2/6 each. (U.S. 35 cents.)

I hear you're broke. Please accept my donation.

FADING FREEDOMS/LATE HIPPIE HIGH HOPES:

A Paranoid Guide by Raymond Durgnat

9 Libertarians, Left and Right

The rightwing puritan broods upon the immorality of those leftwing intellectuals up in Hampstead. The leftwing puritan shakes his head sadly over the bright young things of Chelsea. The common man disapproves of all those students who live the life of Riley, Oscar Wilde and Mick Jagger combined on lavish grants paid for out of his own hardearned taxes.

On balance, libertarianism gets associated with the left, for two main reasons. The upper-class code is designed to cope with middle-class puritanism. It sets out to maintain a facade, and has two main rules: (1) the real sin is being found out, (2) it doesn't matter what you do so long as you don't do it in the street and frighten the policemen. Second, the basis of property transmission is the family, and whatever you do mustn't disrupt that lifeline. Sexuality is a matter of wild oats (when you're young) of escapades and asides. But the family and honour are your status, your business, your privilege, your career, your employment exchange and your insurance.

The working-class was infected with middle-class puritanism, via evangelical propaganda, or had to defer to it, since charity only went to the deserving poor. Many working class people were sunken middle class anyway, or formed a 'labour aristocracy' which wanted to impress the middle-class and itself with its good character, so as (1) to get the vote and (2) disapprove with a clear conscience of all that nasty, dirty, brutal unskilled labour. In any case, hard times need self-control, and in pre-contraceptive days self-control means puritan-type restraint, so even the non-puritan tries to live up to puritan-like ideals.

The left-wing challenge to puritanism comes from a variety of sources. There are those intellectuals who having read Freud, Lawrence, et al, feel fancy ought to be free. There's no incentive to retain the family system as a property-transmission belt, if anything, the desire would be to limit it to a husband-and-wife group. Remarriage, adultery, divorce pose fewer problems. Cupid flutters free as a butterfly from the chains of Mammon. There may also be psychological differences. Anti-libertarianism, anti-feminism, authoritarian and pro-status attitudes may all spring from identification with the father, who jealously guards his privileges, of having mother, and all her good things, for his property. The left winger identifies with a son who demands his fair shares of mother even though he's smaller, ie. lower class. Whence the sort of folk-myth that rightwing people act older than their age and leftwing people never quite grow up, unless they become successful revolutionaries, when they turn into the leftwing's rightwing, ie. bureaucratic tyrants. The leftwinger assumes that only brutal father is keeping mother from giving herself to all (ie. him), a fantasy which would account for the leftwing combination of idealism, feminism, and unmolested morality, while the rightwing insistence that one must respect the saintliness of motherhood means 'Hands off' and goes with a tendency to deprive women of property rights so that they can't be independent, ie. it conceals a deep fear of women's natural promiscuity.

A more middle class kind of libertarianism originates in inverted puritanism. The early puritan was if anything more respectful of sex in principle, but strict about observing his principles, than the traditional Christianity of his time. He found God through the book and through conscience; he respected learning and the inner light, and God is what they say he is. The cast iron certainties of 19th century science gave knowledge an agnostic slant, and the inner light, agnosticised, becomes psychological self-awareness. The very severity of puritanism provokes reactions, and though the standard middle-class attitude remains a (evolved, sentimentalised) puritanism, it becomes a few doughty groups who turn puritanism against nationalism-with-a-conscience and who identify, through guilt and pity, with the downtrodden, yet scorn to take advantage of their libertarian principles for merely personal, physical pleasure. Oddly, this puritan anti-puritanism produces either masochists or extremely inhibited characters, the Hellfire Club, and Sade, all came from aristocratic backgrounds.

It's true that various sectors of the establishment cling to the old traditional mixture of puritanism and obscurantism where sexual morality is concerned, and that the New Morality associates itself with left-wing intellectuals and with the old 'folk' morality (the non-puritan, lower-working-class sectors).

But the Left has its puritan tradition, derived from the upper-working-class connections with the middle-class, and we ought not to be in the least surprised to find Labour MP's crying out against all this filth and satire. A strange twist to the right-authoritarian, left-libertarian axis is given by such studies as **The Uses of Literacy**, or the stance adopted by the New Left of the '50s, when they appeared unable to think about affluence without sounding like the joy-through-self-denial brigade of the Salvation Army. Behind this lay Dr Leavis' glorification of the village community and 'handmade' literature as against the city and the mass media. The fact that a whole generation of left-wing youth took its cultural norms from a liberal reactionary is only one example of the extent to which the English leftwing elite is saturated with middle-class idealism, whether through family backgrounds or through the classroom (and make no mistake; the battle for a leftwing Britain was lost in the sixth forms of the grammar schools. Today the commercial rightwing (eg. the commercial TV lobby, the pirate radios) can pose as the torchbearers of the ordinary man's liberty, as the champions of affluence, as the workingman's buddy rather than his schoolmarm.

T FASCISMS &

David Holbrook's sermonising would make one laugh if he didn't make one weep, precisely because his weird mixture of sensitivity and moral sadism, of idealism and paranoia (ie. misdirected aggression), so thoroughly queers what might have been a promising libertarian pitch. If he's worth, and he is, the courtesy of our love-hate, it's not just because he symptomises, in conveniently extremist form, a new twist to the school marm attitude. He moves from libertarianism a la Lawrence to an unreasoning hatred of all other temperaments and styles. Yet much that he says, in criticism of the New Morality, is basically sound.

Meanwhile, let's not forget the libertarian right. Bold Sir Jasper stroking his mutton-chop whiskers as he menaces the poor-but-honest tenant's English rose of a daughter; the Victorian pater-familias knowing that brazen servant girls were pretty meat for their social master, the lover of freedom who thinks Cuba should remain the brothel of the USA.

Nipples or Nozzles?

Feminine emancipation, for one thing. As family status is replaced by jobskill status, the ratrace must try and conscript the ladies as well. Of course, the working-class woman has been out working for about two hundred years, which may be one reason why she's tougher and coarser and some of the things intellectuals like about Lauren Bacall and Angie Dickinson, and why the working-class Mum can acquire such proportions (the younger girls are working). World Wars 1 & 2 proved that the middle and upper classes could be conscripted too. The freedom of women to work is like the freedom of men to work, or die for their country, or like the freedom of children to go to school, have their heads filled with nonsense, be kept in and given lines. The achievement of our society is that it makes not working as intolerable as not learning. But emancipation will leave women no freer than it leaves man.

Woman as a sheltered, stultified sentimentalist is a familiar figure of pathos, as is the man on whom she makes her cloying demands for sustenance. Typically, perhaps, she is the product of a little experience of reality—insufficient to teach, sufficient to arouse resistance. No doubt this type will survive, and thrive, as the American 'do-godder' thrives—but more militant hitherto. The more educated and intelligent women will lose all proneness to hysteria, frigidity and tears, become more prone to obsessional disorders and to kinks. The biological will become trivial and meaningless rather than obscene; and all poetry will fly to those phantasy realms in which contact itself is blurred and half-obliterated. The image of intellectual liberal happiness will be: two beautiful people, of neither-nor sex, moving through a jungle of movie-images of their bodies, drowning together in incense and environments, aiding one another to symbolic suicides by needle, pill and other mechanical appliances. These will be worthwhile, maladjusted individuals. The pinstripe machines will fly to the Khatmandu and Hawaii holiday-camps, drench themselves in de-deodorants, wonder where life went but be too sweetly busy to pause to find out. It's not so nightmarish—rather attractive, in fact? Precisely . . .

Was I Right to Embrace Hugh Heffner without Divorcing Berthold Brecht? by Ken Tynan

The Playboy-Penthouse philosophy sells by sex but it doesn't sell sex. It sell what the magazine names imply: luxury, of which the girls are so to speak, the lushiest cusions, the mascots, the all mod cons. The girls are the bait for selling the aftershave lotions, the superchargers, the personal products, the escort agency, in brief, the bunny, in one form or another, and her accessories. What's presented as a radical crusade against puritanism is something rather different. It might seem a massive and desperate bid to offer us incentives for working harder.

But it isn't even that. All it offers is a luxury dream of which girls are part. That's why ironically, Penthouse can't afford to let OZ mention sex in its advertisements. Sex offered in any other context, and paricularly in a hippy one, ie. detached from status, shatters the implication that the sex ethos naturally belongs in, and calls for, whatever version of the philosophy your wallet will stretch to, and that your playgirl is likely to be melted by.

The link is a fragile one, because you know she knows and he knows, and she can separate your person form your playboy mask just as fast as Messrs Heffner and Guccione can pretend that the latter can become the former. They know, and OZ readers know, and only the idiots who subscribe to P & P don't know, that a passionate, reckless, sensitive and generous temp erament will get very ugly men and women so much loving so fast that the supply will vastly exceed the demand. In this open-plan world (tubes, cafes, informality) only one thing makes computer date agencies necessary, or makes loneliness a psychic scourge; and that's a state of continuous, intense and abject psychological terror. And no amount of moralising about bed will make the least difference to a human poverty which won't be solved in bed at all, but by transforming in every layer of responses from from the unseeing glance to the hidden fantasy.

Imagine, for a moment, if you can, a day without terror. A violent world, perhaps—but a resilient one . . . And contrast that with the logical conclusion of the P-P philosophy: the Playboy Club, where untouchable bunnies sell you ordinary entertainment slightly more expensively. For if you felt you could touch, you'd feel you ought to try (to prove you're a man, you're with it, to have fun, etc) and if you were faced with the prospect of trying, you'd be faced with the prospect of failing and you'd be back in the same old terrorised state from which you started. But you can't. How restful totalitarianism is.

Heffner's brilliance lay in seeing that by stressing the prohibitions (bunnies aren't allowed to . . . .)you render the daydream safe. 'I don't have to try, but she might if she could.' continued OZ 45

APPLE

Paul McCartney asked me to point
out that Apple is not in competition
with any of the underground organisations, rather it exists to help, collaborate with, and extend all existing
organizations as well as start many
new ones. The concept as outlined by
Paul is to establish an 'underground'
company above ground as big as Shell
BP or ICI but as there is no profit
motive as the Beatles profits go first
to the combined staff and then are
given away to 'the needy.'
Miles

The Yellow-on-Orange Press

7. A magic number. Turn it upside down and it becomes a fat feminine 2. What relation has 2 to 7? It's a part of the incomprehensibility of symbols. Incomprehensibility plus fact equals error:- "Nude picture campaign in Belgium." (courtesy of The Times). Caption talks about campaign. For nude pictures? No. The article chronicles Belgian police raids on art galleries. Grey press readers are expected to read headlines backwards. The breakdown and falsification of the simplest facts in commercial communications media is easy to demonstrate. Partly resulting from hide-bound traditions in error-making partly a conscious effort of controlled communications to inure subscribers to false thinking and lie-acceptance.

The Underground is supposed to be different. It is.

But is it any more effective? Effective in the role of communications? There is an easy attitude that suggests that just because the underground presses exist and have been able to survive they are successful.

The wrong yardstick is being used. Underground publications are made by people who do not belong to Fleet Street and establishment publishing groups, and they behave differently. They make a different product. But they have torn down one kind of incomprehensibility and replaced it with another.

On the news front, they kindle the same kind of hysteria as the fatuous leader-writers of the dailies. They fight the same battles, but on the other side. To meet the effete philosophies of the establishment in a head-on clash that will awaken a response (not only amongst the faithful and converted, but outside amongst the hosts of Midian) means that far more effective thinking and writing must be recruited if truth is to bloom.

Central to the business of communication is impact. It is disputable what percentage of literate people are scared off unbroken paragraphs of solid type in the New Statesman and The Times. It may not be any greater than the staunch un-readers of the Express and the Mirror, those that hate every screamer and slice of cheese cake and would rather spend their reading time with the London A-D. But it is easier to assess the great majority which is put off by misprints, overprinting and press-gram, and who will not read anything litho-ed yellow on orange.

Even supposing that such barriers are overcome, and a whole new public is prepared to dump its biases and read underground publications, there is a need for subject matter to attract participation. Uncensored news is not necessarily much more interesting if it is merely an expanded version of tabloid abbridgement. Nor is there much satisfaction for a reader finding in these clandestine pages reference to something that was too dull to make the papers.

Loyal undergrounders may be forgiven for wondering at times if editorial, besides lacking convincing and attractive writers, is not also short on straight reporters with news sense. And what is underground news sense anyway? It should be more than taking in each others' washing.

Unconvincing rediscovery of the product of great minds by birdbrains is a lamentable waste of time. Such timewasting is further compounded if these lightweights commit the extent of their findings to print. Reassessment of values by the underground is a laudible activity, but it must be carried out be those mentally equipped to do it.

The Square press sins most by ommission. No just because of censorship and commercial pressures. It actually leaves great areas of thought and action unexamined—in the mistaken belief that nobody wants to know. Just how long growing sensitivity will allow this state to continue, how long it will remain economically viable (with evening papers at 5 pence a time) is hard to say. But there are signs that a paper-hungry community is fed up with consumer advertising and consensus politics, laced with mayhem and tease-sex. If that is all that life is about, more and more will turn to and seek for something better. At the moment they won't find it.

Another hold up is ubiquitous. The hedonistic fun thing. The suggestion from the underground that a wise man lives on a diet of milk, honey and lotus. Even if this were true it would evoke suspicious hostility from the outside world. The conception that you work at what you like and like what you work at needs keener explanation- otherwise in puritan Britain and probably elsewhere the argument will find few takers.

Whacky pictures are alright, but not exclusively so. The earth is crawling with good artists, illustrators and photographers, so why get stuck in a rut? Steadman and the rest of them don't make a summer, and most free presses want to publish the year round. In Nazi terms, repetition may achieve its ends, but it never was satisfactory unless it could be imposed blanket-style.

Generation-gap troubles too. Outside a few sacred old men and flash middle-agers, underground press workers and contributors are in the same age bracket (and it must get older). Even if in fact it is, the underground shouldn't be a youth club, nor should it be allowed to senesce into a society for oldsters to camp about in bermuda shorts and school-caps. Currently, free publications are chained to youth. That sort of bondage can be dull.

Perhaps the youth flavour explains why optimism is in the saddle. A putative long-life stretching won't help to make its inheritors interested in forcing the pace of change. It may be little use pointing out that everyone gets older–fast but the dirty and leisurely course of human history suggests that gradualism has consistently choked off the millenium. Rosebud gathering ends in a stench of corruption.

This is not to demand that the underground should show itself more committed. It's just that happiness, the better life, and the rest of it are not going to come about by chance—nor will they come any nearer through the good intentions of the Establishment Go-Slow. Those who have opted out of the non-life have a right to expect a little more action. They could (should?) find it in the underground press.

(new readers, begin here)

Sheldon Williams

ANTI-U

Alan Krebs

The Antiuniversity of London is a response to perceived madness. It is not the only response possible, it's far from a perfect response, but its existence, in the concrete, is intended to be an explicit statement of what we think the educational system of the West has come to be.

Meaningful education comes to an end at the age of five. At about that time learning to differentiate hot from cold, good animals from bad, the meaning of frowns, inflections, smiles, the techniques to control (or at least limit) the actions of the Titans who tower over a kid come to be differentiated from 'real learning'. 'Real learning' takes place in a special building at appointed hours at the hands of paid officials. It is first and foremost an initiation into the properties of methodical submission. We learn how to be students, how to be passive, how always to work within a situation with predefined limits without ever questioning those limits.

Knowledge comes from School through the instrumentality of the Teacher. It is a sacred thing, divided into certain sacrosanct areas and approached in stylized form with a host of attendant ritual acts: silence, decorum, respect, neatness, cleanliness, order. If blood must flow (and flow it must) it must be directed laterally: 'Whose performance today was best?' 'Whose lesson was the neatest?' Who learned to spell the most words today?'

And let us not think for a moment that this programmed rape is without its biographical significance. Which of us will pass through the filter? Who will be streamed in which direction at the 11-plus? Who will perform the best on O-levels? Who will perform best on the A-levels? Which will go to Oxford? Which will go to Cambridge? Which will go to City University? Which will go to Slag Heap Tech? Which will go no place at all?

For Western industrial man the educational system is first and foremost THE mobility escalator in his society. Barring the Pools and a fortuitous homosexual relationship with Lord X it is the only technique available to the majority of white westerners to improve their lot in comparison with their fathers. The structured insanity of the industrial nine-to-five as millhand or clerk or even the motor trade or the life-time sale of yard goods provides initiation first to the parents—then later to the child; whether the fears and nightmares, the futility and horror is ever recognized, whether the transmission system is ever noted, whether the emotional 'guidance' provided is ever remarked—its articulation is irrelevant. The horror exists.

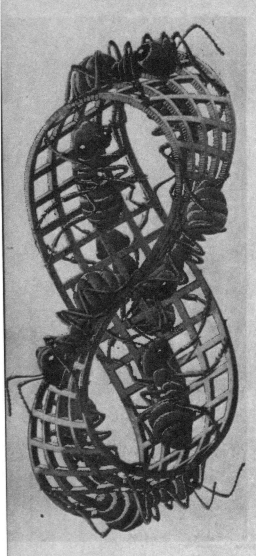

Who can blame them if two-thirds through the Twentieth Century they took their social orders to be permanent fixtures of mankind? If they agreed that for the sake of the telly and the HP, the week's supply of paraffin and the Queen they tried to do the best they could for their children. And who would blame them if their institutions were geared to produce more clerks and engineers, teachers and Post Office workers—docile submissive, respectful, unquestioning?

The educational system exists primarily to produce the skilled manpower that those who run the social order require. The managers need those who neither rebel nor daydream, innovate excessively or quarrel. Just good, respectable, methodical, home owning workers.

By the time the gates of heaven are opened, the grant obtained, university admission secured, the damage has already been done. That only 5% of the age-eligible population of the United Kingdom can obtain entry to the 'facilities' of higher education is a saving grace. It is not that only 5% can obtain entry; rather that only 5% are certifiably destroyed. It is those who have managed to hop through so many hoops, to pass through so many of the filters, to have so bridled and constrained not only their minds but their bodies as well that the best of them will spend a good proportion of their ensuing years unlearning the destructive effects of their earlier education.

'Nonsense,' respond detractors, 'why, many of us will become teachers. We will become educators and given complete freedom to pursue researches wherever our curiosity might lead us. Instead of grinding away at a dull and terrible job in the Underground we'll have our minds free to explore ideas—to consider the relevance of Yeats to Joyce, to examine the philosophy of Hume, to explore the contribution of Weber.' Surely.

'Nonsense,' respond others, 'think of science (i.e. apart from chemical—bacterial warfare hydrogen bombs, rockets, flame-throwers, etc.) think of outerspace, the configuration of matter, the leaps and bounds of the new physics, the development of new contrivances, of transplants.'

Surely. Particularly in a social order in which all innovation is scrutinized for its destructive potential.

From the perspective of damage already inflicted, then, the construction of an anti-university is an obscenity. More than anything else it is a drawing together of cripples who, at least, have an inkling of their infirmities. The majority who attend will always already have been wounded—their injuries will always be carried over into the new organization. Thus, at the Antiuniversity of London, the dominant question (with those who have already had their brains constructively orientated by the establishment, will be how to destroy the whole previously existing structure of learning, the sacrosanct student-teacher relationship, the injunction to passive silence, the awe of great figures, the humility of the Humble when facing the source of Light.

As for the 'unfortunate' 95% who never merited the favour of the establishment, not surprisingly there are few. Why, after all, should people take time out from making money, drinking, screwing or sleeping to sit down in classrooms and listen to teachers intone. Even if teachers intone ideas never intoned in Western classrooms before, there is—in the very process of intoning—something of the smell of impotence and death. If these brethren were with us, the obstacles faced by the place would be even greater: how do you create relevance, in the Twentieth Century, with words? Unless the words can be translated into some meaningful act, unless they derive from some felt and visible material circumstance, then what good are they at all? This is a question the Antiuniversity has yet to be even in a position to answer.

ANTI-U2

Bill Mason

It has been necessary to give up the premises at Rivington St. because of lack of funds, and until we have more money, courses and seminars are being held in member's homes and other places. Information about all meetings can be had by writing to 1 Sherwood St. N1., or by telephoning Bill Mason at 01-289 0998

The registration fee is now £5 a year, starting in September, and will admit members to all courses. But unless cards are shown, a visitor's fee of 5/- will be charged.

Information of all public lectures sponsored by the Anti-University will be first sent to members, who will be able to attend at half price. We hope to arrange that membership cards may be used to obtain the usual student discounts. Any members who have already paid for the summer session will be sent a years membership.

A room will be rented in a pub for a general meeting and a get together on the second Friday in September, when future courses will be discussed. The time and place will be known by the last week in August. Ring Bill Mason after that for details.

Courses now meeting are:

1 Action Research Group on Racialism / 2 Roy Battersby, Leon Redler, Roger Gottlieb - Time & Timelessness / 3 Bob Cobbing & Anna Lockwood - Composing with sound / 4 David Cooper Seminar / 5 Roberta Elzey Berke - On Finnegan's Wake / 6 Guerilla Poetry Workshop / 7 Jim Haynes - Dialogues about Relevance and Irrelevance / 8 Jerome Liss — Workshop Sensitivity training / 9 Alex Lowsiewkee — Chinese Language & Philosophy / 10 Julian Mitchell — Literature & Psychology / 11 David Mycroft - Linn Think / 12 Peter Payne — Self Defence & Body Awareness / 13 Ian Sutherland — Joy/14 Morton Schatzman — Analysis of the Family/15 Tony Smythe — Civil Liberties in Britain.

This will be extended in September to include the following courses and seminars: 1 Nool Cobb — Spiritual Amnesia & Physiology of Self Estrangement / 2 Alan Krebbs — Life in a Television Set / 3 John Latham - Anti No / 4 Paul Lawson - Demystifying Media / 5 Gustav Metzger - Theory of Auto Destructive Art / 6 Jesse Watkins Group / 7 Mazin Zeki — Alternative Press.

Instead of a formal catalogue, regular news bulletins will be sent out and members are invited to use them for comment and communications.

The Institute of Phenomenological Studies

During the summer of last year, The Institute of Phenomenological Studies organised the Dialetics of Liberation Congress. This was concerned with the Demystification of Human Violence in all forms, the Social System from which it emanates, and the exploration of new forms of action.

The proceedings were recorded, and Inter Sound of 20 Fitzroy Sq., London, W.1, are releasing them as a series of 23 long play records and are now accepting orders.

Records are available individually or in sets. For example the Anti-Psychiatry set: 1 Gregory Bateson Conscious Purpose vs Nature; 2 Bateson concluded/Ross Beck concluded; 3 David Cooper Beyond Words; 4 Ronald Laing The Obvious; 5 Ross Beck Politics and Psychotherapy of Mini and Micro Groups. The Anti-Psychiatry set costs £6 or $13.99.

Other speakers include Stokely Carmichael, Herbert Marcuse, Jules Henry, Alan Ginsberg, Julian Beck, Paul Goodman, Paul Sweezy, Simon Vinkenkoog.

Records are available individually of all speakers at £1.5.11 or $2.99.
Enquiries to Inter Sound, 20 Fitzroy Sq., London, W.1.

3rd World

Norodom Sihanouk rules Cambodia with the verve and guile of a latterday Lorenzo the Magnificent. Something of a South East Asian Superstar (he makes movies, composes songs, hosts Jackie Kennedy), he has maintained the integrity of his threatened kingdom by counterbalancing the Americans with the Chinese. In doing so he has been forced to articulate many of the 3rd World's hopes and fears.

In the general world situation today and in particular — in the present situation in Asia, Cambodia has no desire to adhere to regional organizations the real aims of which are seldom clearly defined. At this time, our preference goes to bilateral relations outside a rigid framework, which would deprive us of the freedom of manœuvre we require to ensure our survival, and to safeguard our non-aligned status. We attach supreme importance to retaining our freedom to have the sort of relations we want with the countries we want to have relations with in conformity with the principle of reciprocity, with due regard to the international conjuncture and to where our national interests lie.

I need hardly add that it is our ardent desire to see the establishment of an authentic co-operation between all Asian countries, irrespective of the sort of régime they may be subject to, or to the political options they may have taken out : co-operation on the lines envisaged at Bandung in 1955. But it is evident that solidarity in this beneficial form demands a strict application of the principles of peaceful co-existence, together with the liquidation of American neo-colonialism, particularly in its most brutal aspect as currently displayed in the attack on Vietnam.

There is only one way of bringing the war in Vietnam to an end. The problem is a very simple one. Are the United States prepared to respect Vietnam's national independence, and to recognize the right of the Vietnamese people to settle their own affairs free of military intervention, and foreign interference? If the answer is a positive one, let them withdraw their armed forces at present engaged in an invasion of South Vietnam, and the war will come to an end at once.

Cambodia under the «Sangkum» régime continues to develop as a nation by relying on its own resources or— as we are in the habit of expressing it — by « self-aid ». It is our belief that this is the sole policy, in final analysis, calculated to preserve in effective fashion our national independence, and to place our economy on a sound basis. Moreover, the progress accomplished during recent years provides ample proof of the truth of this contention.

We are of the opinion that no foreign aid, whatever form it may assume, is furnished without ulterior motive, but that it serves first and foremost — and this is natural enough — to promote the interests of the donor. We are well aware, to be sure, of the difficulties with which all developing countries are faced, but it seems to us that these would

be greatly attenuated were ou « third world » to find some wa of uniting to end an absur situation or — in other words – to put a stop to further exploita tion.

We are demanding that th great powers finally adm the fact that every countr in the world, whether it be larg or small, rich or poor, has a equal right to insist on comple respect being shown its nation independence and territorial inte grity. In short we are asking t be accorded the indentical righ which the great powers insis on being invested with them selves. So far as our traditionall expansionist neighbours ar concerned, we trust that the future rulers will have the wis dom to adopt another approac in their dealings with Cambod and — more especially · tha they will renounce their desig on Khmer territory.

If these neighbours flout o sovereignty, and show no respe for our territorial integrity, the do so in the knowledge tha our people will rise in defenc of their sacred rights, alone need be, or with aid supplie them by friendly countries, as the case with the Vietnames people today in the face of th American invaders.

NORODOM SIHANOUK

30

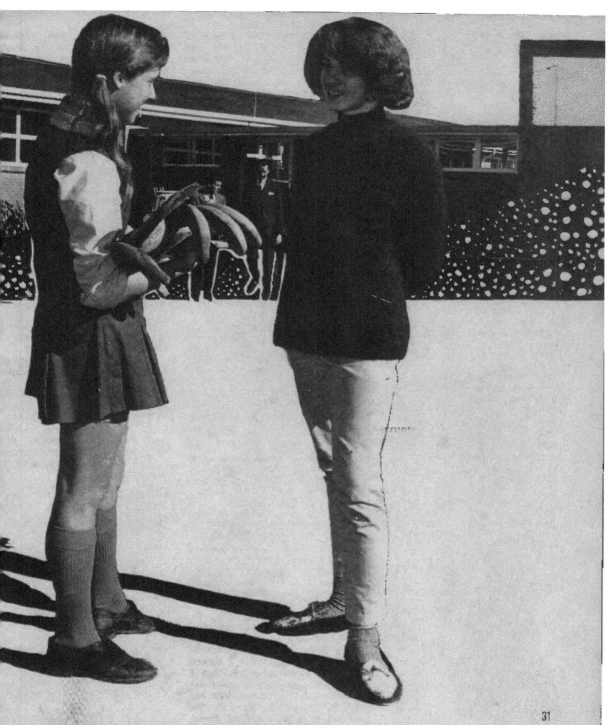

THE HAIR OF FABIAN DOUGLAS
by Neil Douglas

The Great Altback 2

Last year, 15 year old Fabian Douglas was expelled from Hurstbridge High School, Melbourne, because the headmaster ruled that his shoulder length hair was too long. Now he is appealing to the United Nations Human Rights Commission.

The freedom to go to school long haired is not an issue of world shattering importance, but the conflict between Fabian and his headmaster is not about hair. It is a conflict of consciousnesses. *In his extraordinary and eccentric autobiographical story, Neil Douglas, Fabian's father, establishes—among other things—that the first hippie was undoubtedly a Victorian.*

A Very Simple Story—

1. *WHY BACK YOUR BOY FABIAN IN HIS PLEA TO U.N. HUMAN RIGHTS COMMISSION FOR HIS LONG HAIR?*

I am not, and he isn't!

WHY DO YOU BACK YOUR BOY IN DISOBEYING SCHOOL RULES AND THE HEADMASTER?

I am not, and he didn't!

I cannot get this simple story correctly published as a whole in Australia. and so write 12,000 miles to LONDON OZ, who alone have offered the space to show what we can't get, and what warrants an appeal all the way to U.N., is that we want to be told the facts either way, by experts, and not by the sort of Authority which apparently fears even their own experts, as I will show. *Definition of self expression for original types at schools SHOULD be made by the properly qualified experts, instead of by untrained and authoritarian officials!* This little question affects all the biggest issues of our lives and in schools, I believe we ARE damaging our creative kids.

2. **WHY SHOULD MY 15 YEAR OLD BOY FEEL SO STRONGLY THERE ARE ALTERNATIVES TO THE RATRACE? WHY DOES HE SO URGENTLY WANT THE EXPRESSION OF THIS AT SCHOOLS?**

So would you, if, like Fabian, you grew up in a more effective and beautiful life than the ratrace!

BEGIN YOUR NEW LIFE HERE . .

One day, when I was a boy myself, two businessmen stood over me. It was an arranged interview for my own good. They told me my father was right, —I had to earn money for my living, and so had to Be Successful in Business. Businessmen were Practical—all Governments and Schools centred around Business. I must be practical too, and be efficient, and stop fooling in the garden all my time, and get a job, and conform to society, before I could be accepted in Society. And I knew it was the Final Ultimatum . . . .

When I was asked for a reply, I said, 'But but ' (then I had an absolute inspiration and I said,)

32 - but I HAVE RETIRED.'

. . Remember this was 40 years ago! I followed up the astounded silence coming from what I didn't know in those lonely days was an intense psychedelic advantage! - by expertly talking very fast about my plan for turning our four acres of land, 20 miles from the City, into an -

OASIS IN THE RATRACE FIT FOR KIDS, A ROBINSON CRUSOE KIND OF EDEN,

- I said - with a world wide collection of rare vegetables and fruits for all seasons, and wonderful herbs for connoisseur approaches to home grown food and home brewing and cheeses made from cow or goat! There would be chooks, and bees, and a kiln for pottery, and some natural and beautiful girl without artificial gunturrets and commercial warpaint, would come and weave and spin for clothes and make handcrafts! We would be self supporting, yet with enough money   all our friends would be people instead of rats on the treadmill!

3. ALSO I WOULD NOT HAVE MY CHILDREN FORCED OUT OF PARADISE INTO THE TREADMILL!
I said fiercely—into the sardine commuter trains for forty years, into the time payment penance, into the insulting fortnight of free time once a year for the rest of their lives, into guilty silences in order to get on, —my kids would also be people and their wives wouldn't have to go out to work! Be People, I said— not industrial automatons who can walk past others on the footpath screaming for help, as happens in all industrial societies and lately even here in Sunny Australia, the Land of Mateship! We won't soil our suit even to help someone in terrible distress these days!

OH I wouldn't wear this uniform and feel like a chook in a battery in return for wage-spiral money buying built in obsolescence– striking even before the payments are done!

OH IT WAS A SAVAGE REPUDIATION and I burst into tears for myself and my future children and all kids I knew stifled and twisted and silenced to fit into set patterns.

4. Invoking my future children against their Business Heavy weights amused my parents, except that my father said, half convinced, that my poor future girl would probably rather I was in the ratrace!

— 'I would rather you were in the ratrace,' said every lovely girl I met for the next twenty years, while I achieved in fact and reality the most awful frustration, but also a garden which was

THE MOST PERFECT PARADISE ON EARTH I HAVE EVER SEEN, FULL OF VERY CULTURED FLOWERS!

In among the Artychokes sprung up Barry Humphries, John Perceval's ceramic angels among the Passionfruit. Behind the Perfect Posy for the Prettiest Girls always appeared Max Harris, and behind the perfect Poesy smiling Barry Reid, Sidney Nolan nibbled the nuts, and the Early Boyd promoted in paint the New Diet of Worms, and Sunday came any day of the week . . . . oh what a garden from which to watch, heh, heh! guess what I watched!

5. I WATCHED THE BIG PRACTICAL BUSINESS WORLD COLLAPSE!

Businessmen suicided (very practically) on every hand, —a long depression, terrible to see last so long, and then wars precipitated by business, then we had a Bank Run, and then the sinister New Guard, (local fascist group– e and even the Military in the Coalfields. But even worse than the Price-wage Spirals was that–

EVERYONE HAD COUPONS FOR FOOD A CLOTHES INSTEAD OF FOR CHILDREN LOVE

GET THIS—
THE FOOD THAT GREW ON MY VINES WAS FOR FREE!

Fiercely I looked out at the broken and discredited Business World from the Gardeners' happy grind where the only SPIRALS were around the hives, and the only QUEUES, the lines of carrots or fruits along the boughs and into my hands themselves did reach the nectar, me and curious peach . . . .

6. INEVITABLY THEN, TO SUCH A SUCCESSFUL ALTERNATIVE WOULD COME A MAN LIKE FABIAN!

and so it was that one day a girl who had been half starved in the big depression both for beauty and for food burst into tears when she saw the huge rambling Garden, and Fabian at length became Fabian of a green thought in a green shade and Paradise was soon neither rural nor solitude along with Linden and Rowen his brothers named for our trees, and Fabian mess grower of beans (as well as brains over brawn. to put the old legend crudely!

7. NOW THE NICEST PEOPLE MUST ASK THE NASTIEST QUESTION:–

WHAT sort of a HOUSE would such 'NON-CONSUMER GOODS' children GROW UP in than?

So see Fabian with birds nests by his attic bed in 'a home beautifully expressed' as someone called it at once, a historic pioneers cottage like Dylan's poem, Fern Hill, in the Bush! It was made with no nails, of stingybark, and blackwood, wattled into natural timber effect

'a wooden shingle roofed attic, where tame
...tails stole Fabian's bedside apples at night
...window views showed long aisles of fun-
...d for) expensive and exclusive flowers
...hing in bowers away into the wildgarden
...hard and the Bush, and all the proper price
...kers were also missing from the tree high
...untains of fruit!

...d our furnishings?—all were of gentle hand-
...le style, wood basketry, pottery, handwovens,
...d wrought metals made by friends in exchange
...barter.

Was it any wonder that Fabian came to
...one day and said, 'NEIL, I WANT MY HAIR
...NG! I DON'T WANT SHORT HAIR LIKE
...E CHEEKY TAXIMAN. I WANT TO LIVE
...AL' NOT WORK! I WANT MY HAIR
...NG LIKE MATCHUM SKIPPER MY JEWEL
...KING MAN. I WANT RINGS IN MY EARS
...D AND HE IS ALWAYS LAUGHING. I
...L WORK REAL, LIKE IN THE GARDEN
...D FIND NATURE ALL MY LIFE.

...WAS NOT YET FIVE YEARS OLD!

At five he went off to school with his
...g hair and was so very confident although
...re were no other long haired boys in sight
...he days.

...AM A SISSY SO IS SAMPSON he told
...my suburban kids, but as always was accep-
...because of his exciting and expert ways with
...re- pets, excursions, snakes, butterflies,
...pions, bush orchids, – the love life of kangar-
...–and Kissing Gouramis!

...W! GOT BULLIED OVER FABIAN!
...U'RE DOING IT TO HIM! said all the
...ibles! They couldn't see a born aesthetic
...Australia, a Man's Country, and like Huxley
...'d have to take mescalin or some other
...e even alcohol to see the world with a
...cock edge to it like Fabian does every
...ute of every peacock day, naturally, and
...ght he said I will wear my hair right down
...back like a Peacock!

...THE VILIFICATION, I said many people
...Id soon be like Fabian and give up trying
...win Lotteries or Be the Boss and try to
...ture their lost innocence, the warm earth
...ask the most powerful of all political
...stions: –

...we live to work or do we work to live?'–
...O MEAN IT.

...IT WAS A LONG SPEECH I MUST SADLY
...Y IT LASTED SOME YEARS while I wore
...wer in my buttonhole all my life, but
...denly, Hullo! as I knew it would because
...h grows spontaneously, up sprang every-
...re the vast discrediting of the ratrace by
...he people who walk with long hair and
...feet like good gardeners like to, except
...many were so damned innocent they

harmed the cause so much. I nearly stopped
wearing my flower after forty years, but
they did and do ask that one real question
AND MEAN IT.

10. AND IS FABIAN AFFECTED BY THE
TAUNTING, YOU ASK?

BAD GOD, MAN! FABIAN'S ONLY JUST
BEGINNING TO ATTACK THE RATRACE
RELIGION OF HUMAN UNINVOLVEMENT!

A school suburban type ringleader, hoping
for a laugh on the playground, picked Fabian
one day! A ring gathered, and waited for
Fabian's reply. Fabian walked up to him and
looked the suburban bloke over very quizz-
ically very closely, like he does a specimen,
and then said brightly at his hair 'Ah! I've
got it—a lavatory brush!—I don't fight
lavatory brushes!'

The bloke walked away from his mates to
leave the laughter and everyone stayed with
Fabian.

11. AH! THE FIRST 'STUDENT RIOT'
I SAW was when Allanah Coleman my fellow
Art Student, later of London, innocently wore
the first slacks seen in Australia, the land of
MEN! She stopped the whole city and as
always they said, 'YOU caused the Riot!'—
and now they have slacks in every family, and
still they scream the same way now at Longhairs—'YOU cause the trouble!'

12. MEANWHILE FABIANS 10 SUCCES-
SIVE HAPPY HEADMASTERS, INNOCENT
AND UNAWARE SET THE CANNON FOR
FABIANS SUBMISSION TO U.N. BY PER-
MITTING INDIVIDUAL EXPRESSION AT
SCHOOLS! AND LIKING HIM!

Yes, in three schools, these heads made use
of Fabian's abilities to demonstrate various
wonders for classes, and they actually appreciated interesting specialised types of boys at
school, and even lifted compulsory sport for
some brainy types, and had them in the library
or in congenial work which saved them the
hated 'torture' such as Religious Instruction. . .
(hows that for any scientific mind like
Fabian's?) and they all allowed waist length
hair at school for Fabian!

THERE WAS NO INCITEMENT TO IN-
DISCIPLINE, BUT THE REVERSE, NO
PROBLEM OF DISCIPLINE THESE 10
HEADMASTERS COULD NOT HANDLE
WITH THE GREATEST OF EASE, NOR ANY
PROBLEM OF TELLING GENUINE FROM
PROVOCATIVE SELF EXPRESSION BY
SIMPLY STUDYING THE CHILD AND ITS
BACKGROUND.

They all did this, and came to see us often
socially, and shared of our life and friends.
They sent classes up to see the native garden

etc., the paintings, Fabian's collection, and
specially on Public Occasions, when our home
was used for Open Days for Charities like
International Social Service or the Arts
Council, and, as at school, Fabian was always
in demand with his dramatic talks, and his
charm, and his charming snakes etc!

SO HE WAS A SUCCESS AT HOME AND
AT SCHOOL AND SO WERE HIS PARENTS.

13. THE ELEVENTH HEADMASTER
SAID, 'YOU WILL NEVER GET A JOB IF
YOU LOOK LIKE YOUR PARENTS OR
YOUR PARENTS FRIENDS. LONGHAIRS
ARE DISREPUTABLE. YOU WILL CUT
YOUR HAIR. I HAVE TO THINK OF THE
GOOD NAME OF THE SCHOOL. I CAN'T
MAKE THE RULES OF THE SCHOOL FOR
ONE BOY! A STANDARD HAS TO BE SET
BY THE MANNERS OF GOOD SOCIETY
AND ADHERED TO. I WILL MAKE THIS
BOY CONFORM FOR HIS OWN GOOD!
I AM DOING HIM A FAVOR!'

He repeated this to schoolteacher friends who
objected strenuously to him and to me and all
pointed out the 10 Headmasters hadn't needed
a rule for one boy!

14. Fabian was faced with a terrible choice.
He had long looked forward to secondary
school to do sciences on the way to
entymology and biology, but if he cut his
hair it was admitting our indecency!

Before he started in the new year, 1967, he
had to agree to 'behind the ears, and above
the collar,' as the ticket to his further Education!
The Headmaster, represented this to him as
an honourable compromise on his part. Fabian
said, 'I wish it were possible for me to force a
similar 'honorable compromise' on his part
that he would feel as upset and dishonoured
about as I do.'

I left the matter to Fabian.

BUT FOR SIX MONTHS THE HEADMASTER
TRIED TO GET FABIAN TO CONFORM
INWARDLY TOO!

I said 'Take it all very politely and do not
become rude. He has never been out of the
suburbs in any real enough way and really believes he has to indoctrinate you towards the
mass produced pattern for both you and he
to 'get on'.

One morning when Fabian was late, I found
him in tears with his brother (inden helping
him to do the hair in a very clever way so
that it was longer than it looked, and pressure
of time made the protracted process a domestic
crisis! This became a recurrent crisis and a
point of honour!

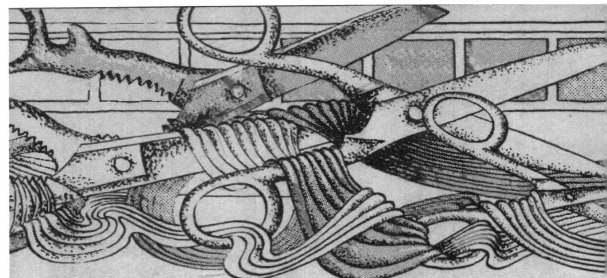

THEN FABIAN HAD A POSSIBLE JOB OFFERED HIM ON THE TELEVISION AS A LONG HAIRED NATURE DEMON STRATOR FOR A 'YOUNG SESSION' IN THE WILDS OF THE BUSH AT THE SAME TIME THE HEAD WAS SAYING HE WOULD NEVER GET A JOB!

THE HEADMASTER RUBBISHED THIS OPPORTUNITY SO HE BEGAN TO IN- TENSELY HATE AND DESPISE THE HEADMASTER HE HAD HITHERTO AD- MITTED WAS A GOOD TEACHER WHOM HE LIKED APART FROM HIS PHOBIA, and grew deeply resentful, not of school, but of situations possible at school, 'so private from the public' he said.

His tension was increased by another mark of public esteem. The Eltham Arts Council advertised a nature walk for the building fund during the Eltham Festival, 'to be led by Fabian,' which they could not do if he was a threat to the school with his well known ideas. To this walk came 72 children and adults of the district. It was a wonderful day but—Monday was school again!

Imagine my worry when of all people he began to lose his confidence, and lost his powers of concentration on his beloved interests, and work connected with them, like watering his pets, lost volition generally and became most uncharacteristically tearful and aggressive personally, and forgot home jobs vital with both parents often away. Worst of all he began to stutter badly and to talk—Fabian, mind you!—with his head down, which I had been amazed to see other kids do to the Head at School.

'I want to wear my hair to my shoulders, why can't the Head be like all the other teachers and get on with the lessons and forget the hair. There are terrible boys at school whom he never worries as much as he does me. It's because he is bald. I have tried both ways and I get on better with kids with long hair and grown ups too, and also with myself and what I want to be.'

He burst into tears and asked me to see the psychology and Guidance Branch of the Ed- ucation Department, whose officers he knew personally.

Meanwhile the hair needed another trim— it couldn't have come at a worse time psychologically:

'DON'T COME BACK TO SCHOOL UNTIL IT IS CUT.'

FABIAN WAS IN SUCH A STATE, THAT I MADE OUT A LIST OF TWENTY ONE DIFF ERENT CATAGORIES OF ACTUAL EDUCA- TIONAL VIOLENCE—i TO FABIAN'S
34 SCHOOL ATTITUDES, ii TO HIS TEACH-

ABILITY, and iii TO HIS PERSONALITY.

15. I TOOK FABIAN AND WENT TO SEE THE HEAD, AND APPLIED FOR AN INTER- VIEW WITH THE EDUCATIONAL PSYCHOL- OGY BRANCH, AS HE HAD REQUESTED.

AS A PRECAUTION I HAD PREVIOUSLY TESTED OUR ARGUMENTS WITH EDUCATIONAL PSYCHOLOGY FRIENDS WHO SAID WE WERE RIGHT TO WANT THE SAME TREATMENT AS THE PREVIOUS TEN HEADMASTERS BELIEVED IN.

I used their words to the head 'I feel Fabian is being ground between the millstones of two totally different approaches to life,' and recited a list of alleged damages I wanted expert assurance about, such as the stuttering be- coming permanent under more of the same inductrination and intimidation and division that had brought the trouble, and that there- fore a conscientious parent, without this expert assurance, could not comply with the order, as yet. We were not disobeying, but asking for expert supervision, I cited the ten previous Headmasters as a practical demon- stration, after all, that it was not a case of making the rules of the school for one boy, and the benefits to both school and group and individual by this type of authority. I mentioned also the job on television, and said also that the Headmaster was involving my own integrity and decency as a direct challenge to me also, as well as the boy he was supposed to be educating.

To each part of my speech he replied, OBEY MY LAWFUL ORDER OR I WILL SUSPEND THE BOY. HE ACTUALL THEN SAID HIS PSYCHOLOGY AND GUIDANCE BRANCH WERE IRREVELANT TO THE CASE, WHICH WAS OBEDIENCE TO HIM ALONE WITHOUT QUESTION!

'But you are not a trained Diagnostician and do not know if the stuttering could become permanent these things are very complex. The boy has a high regard for you, warring with his own personality and home exper- ences, to the opposite of what you make this whole school seem.' I said, 'His lessons are suffering and could suffer more, therefore I demand expert supervision of our obedience. If I am so wrong surely I myself need expert advice from the men my tax money pays to advise me. What has your true authority to fear from your own Experts? What may be shown to be wrong opinion in a wrong area on a wrong premise will not help your true authority nor will controversy about your authority as a Psychologist'.

UNMOVED HE SUSPENDED FABIAN IN MY PRESENCE.

I then drew his attention to the important

point that nobody knew of this interview in his office, the hair was not even noticeabl past ears or collar, Fabian had NOT SAID H WOULD NOT CUT HIS HAIR, BUT ASKE TO SEE THE EXPERTS, this was not a chal lenge to him personally, could he then sus pend his judgement instead of the boy while we rang them from his office? Say for five minutes? He was unmoved even by this appeal?

16. SO WE WERE PUT ON CORRE- SPONDENCE COURSE—SOLITARY CON- FINEMENT LESSONS FOR THIS GROWI BOY NEEDING TO RUB SHOULDERS, AND TO INFLUENCE AND BE INFLUEN BY HIS GROUP HITHERTO SO SUCCESS- FULLY FOR ALL

IT IS IMPORTANT TO NOTE THAT THE IMPROVEMENT IN HIS PERSONALITY WAS FROM THIS MOMENT FAIRLY RAPID.—

The stuttering vanished and he held his head properly again under home criticism, and to all other worrying symptoms except for a slight trace of mumbling instead of speaking at times,—but this is going. I realise now a boy of fifteen cannot possibly cope with six months pressure from an adult he likes a is in two minds about.

He passed his two failure subjects, French an maths, on correspondence, and did better a round.

THIS WAS BECAUSE DELINQUENT BOY TOOK UP THE TEACHER'S TIME IN CON STANT SCENES, HE SAID, AND POINTE OUT THEY WERE STILL AT SCHOOL, WHERE HE WANTED TO BE BUT THEY DIDN'T!

17. 1. WERE WE GOING TO ACCEPT THE HEADS' PUBLIC LABEL—DISREP- UTABLE?

2. WAS I GOING TO LET THE UN- TRAINED DIAGNOSTICIAN JUDGE FOR THE TRAINED EXPERT WHETHER WE HAD A CASE OR NOT, AND ACCEPT TH PUBLIC DISGRACE OF SUSPENSION BE- CAUSE WE WANTED TO BE PUT RIGHT BY EXPERTS?

Hoping it would help, I withheld all publicit until the OFFICIAL ENQUIRY INTO THE SUSPENSION.

This 'established' our disobedience, again without checking their own Experts to find if damage would be done to the boy by obeying, and more of the same treatment.

Fabian felt he was fighting for many other individuals denied legitimate self expression because 'different' types to the suburban pattern.

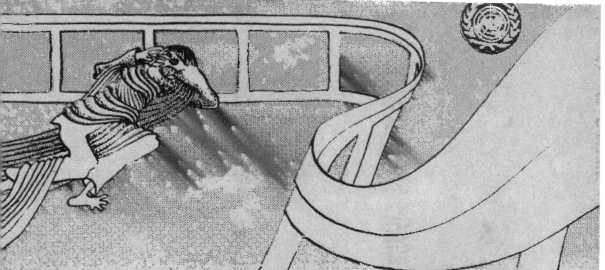

If we should submit we prove what they think of us for them, that we are disreputable.' Fabian said, 'Keep fighting Neil, for many boys, is school a sheep shed?'

18. I THEN BROUGHT A CASE IN THE SUPREME COURT OF VICTORIA, AND THE HEADMASTER, MR. McINERNEY.

I WENT TO THE COUNCIL FOR CIVIL LIBERTIES.

I APPEALED IN THE PAPERS TO THE LAW-MAKERS INSTEAD OF THE LAW KEEPERS.

I WROTE TO THE MINISTER FOR EDU-CATION.

All these approaches were allowed to fail, for one magnificent reason or another, to do the simple job of GETTING EXPERT OPINION HEARD AND   EXPERT JUDGEMENT MADE ON THE DEPARTMENTS EVASION OF THEIR EXPERTS!

THEN I WROTE AN OPEN LETTER TO THE MINISTER FOR EDUCATION, SUBMITTED IT TO PARLIAMENT, THE PREMIER AND LEADER OF THE OPPOSITION, THE NEWS-PAPERS, THE EDUCATION FACULTIES OF UNIVERSITIES, HEADMASTERS ASSOCIATION, AND SO ON.

FINALLY A REALLY TREMENDOUS ROW BEGAN IN TRAINS, TRAMS, DEPART-MENTS, AND FURIOUS EXCHANGES IN NEWSPAPER COLUMNS, BETWEEN IN ONE CASE for example THE PROFESSOR OF EDUCATION AND THE PRESIDENT OF HIGH SCHOOLS PRINCIPALS AS-SOCIATION! NO PUNCHES WERE PULLED! ALL KINDS OF NOTABLES FLEW AT EACH OTHER! TWELVE OF FABIAN'S TEACHERS INCLUDING TWO SENIOR MASTERS BROKE PUBLIC SERVICE PROTOCOL AND WROTE TO THE PAPERS SUPPORTING FABIAN!

ALAS BY THIS TIME, HEADLINES, CORRESPONDENCE AND FIGHTS WERE TAKING PLACE DAILY BETWEEN IM-PORTANT PEOPLE WHO DID NOT KNOW THAT OUR TRUE SIN WAS NOT FLAT FLOUTING OF AUTHORITY BUT AN APPEAL FOR EXPERTS, AND THE WHOLE THING GOT OUT OF HAND!

I REPEATEDLY RANG CHIEFS OF STAFF AND SPOKE TO REPORTERS AND WROTE LETTERS BUT COULD NOT GET THIS SIMPLE FACT PUT RIGHT.

I THREATENED AN APPEAL TO U.N. WHEN EIGHT WEEKS WENT BY AND THE MINISTER HAD NOT ANSWERED MY OPEN LETTERS APPEAL TO BE ALLOWED TO SEE THE EXPERTS.

AT THIS NEW SENSATION WHICH WAS WORLD WIDE, HE THEN SENT ME A LETTER SAYING OBEY THE AUTHORITY OF THE HEADMASTER!   GO AND SEE THE NEW HEADMASTER THIS YEAR.

WHEN I DID THIS, TAKING FABIAN WITH ME, I FOUND THE NEW HEADMASTER WANTED ME TO SIGN A DOCUMENT THAT I WOULD OBEY THE AUTHORITY OF THE HEADMASTER!

—AND WITHOUT GIVING ME ANY GUARANTEE THAT THE PRESSURE WOULD BE TAKEN OFF FABIAN OR EXPERTS CONSULTED!

To the newspapers he said:

'I cannot make the rules of the school for one boy!—His father's attitude is keeping him out of school!'

To me he said, 'I have no knowledge of ten other Headmasters!'

Meanwhile damage was still being done, and cruelly, to a naturally popular and gregarious boy, with both staff and school, who is on Correspondence in a home with both parents away at work, in an atmosphere of de facto solitary confinement for a crime the experts may well find was only in the imagination of his accusers.

'FATHER MUST TOE THE LINE,' said 'The Melbourne Age' newspaper. 'The Sydney Morning Herald' said, 'IT IS BECOMING TIRESOME TO HAVE HIS SON REPRE-SENTED AS A TRAGIC VICTIM OF IN-TOLERANCE WHEN SO MANY REAL ISSUES OF CONSCIENCE ABOUND'.

AT THE SAME TIME 'THE AGE' ran a major double weekend article by Robyn Boyd on all the major ills of toeing the conformant line in Australia!

AT THIS SAME TIME 'THE HERALD' com-plimented the Commissioner of Police (who almost caused a riot in the Police Force in the Mellish case, of the mad gunman holding his wife hostage) 'for taking the advice of Psychologists against all comers!'

I wrote of course but they did not correct the poor public image their determined inconsistency had given our true application being: 'for the advice of Psychologists against all comers!'.

(How do they reconcile this behaviour with their membership of the Journalists Asso-ciation?) And I would ask why did they change their original policy of very sympathetic approval? And WHO bashed in their sym-pathetic staff? 'AN ORDER HAS COME DOWN, they said!

19.   WHAT NOW?—IS IT REALLY IM-PORTANT? WELL, I CAN'T SEE THE DEPARTMENT EXPERTS TO FIND OUT! BUT THEY CANNOT SPEAK PUBLICLY UNTIL THE HEADMASTER ASKS! BUT WE WANT TO BE TOLD BY EXPERTS PUBLICLY IF SCHOOL REALLY DOES AFFECT OUR PUBLIC-LIFE, and fate as a Nation? IF SO ... Official's Policy must be revised urgently towards their own Experts advice about true discipline for specialist extra-type kids possibly being buggered up by Blimps! And so in Human Rights Year, am I going to be told YES or NO by the proper Experts or all comers?

This is a very simple story.

THIS IS A VERY SIMPLE STORY

THIS IS A VERY SIMPLE STORY.
—or is it?

Neil Douglas
Research Post Office 3095
Melbourne
Australia

CREDITS

BBC, Black Dwarf,
Black Panthers

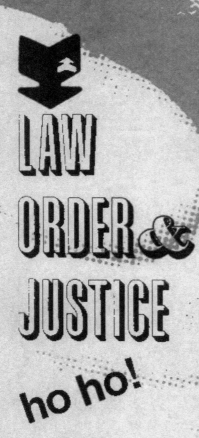

LAW
ORDER &
JUSTICE
ho ho!

a documentary

Commentator: And that is a disturbing question. We have seen four cases where the courts have upheld charges of wrongful or malicious prosecution against coloured people. Are these the exception? For every coloured man with the means — and the will — to fight his case how many others find it easier and quicker just to plead guilty — and get it over with? And more significantly — are these cases symptomatic of radical prejudice among our police? Sue McConachy talked to an ex-police constable from the Metropolitan area, who resigned from the force last year.

Ex-Policeman: Well I think in the police force you find a complex of prejudiced minorities. For example you might find that a certain number of police officers would be prejudiced against taxi drivers, bus drivers or against Jewish people. But I think the coloured prejudice is virtually absolute. In other words it extends probably 99%.

Sue: What efforts were made by senior officers to counteract it?

Ex-Policeman: None at all that were apparent. Either they were unaware that it exists or they just chose to ignore it.

Sue: How much is this police attitude a reflection of the general public?

Barrister 2: I would always argue that the whole society is a racist society and it is almost totally impossible to ask a policeman to be non-racist in a racist society. That's just a basic contradiction. But because of the immediate inconveniences of the police framing of black people, one must demand this.

Sue: Do you think that the administration of the law affects the way the police operate?

Barrister: The magistrates rubber stamp the police evidence. I had a case quite recently where I had two policemen giving evidence and I had some quite respectable middle-class white witnesses giving evidence quite contradictory to the police evidence. And at the end of the case the magistrate simply convicted, saying "I accept the police evidence". And you get this rubber stamping throughout. And of course some of the worst offenders of rubber stamping are Stipendary Magistrates.

Sue: What's the answer to all this?

Barrister: One of the answers is I think, that we've got to start being honest about this. I think that, for instance, most black people know what policemen do to black people, but other sections of the community don't. Most working class people have some idea of the police. I mean, there used to be an old saying that if you saw a policeman, you'd cross over to the over side of the road and get out of the way. I think that, even more important, is that most members of the Bar who practice in the Criminal Courts know what goes on, but they keep silent. And I think that one has to blow the lid on this because I think there is always a danger here that you put the interests of maintaining law and order before the interests of justice.

Barrister: I know what is being done now is not going to solve anything. And one must be very direct here and say that the police must stop it or the black communities will have to stop them from doing it...... it's simply this. And in the United States one sees this is exactly how it turned out to be. So they have a lesson to learn from the United States.

...right of police persecution, not difficult to understand. It is important that police...

What To Be When Cops Lay Their Hands On Black Man at The Speakers Corner.

...
...dump them in a Black Maria, and...

...undreds of black man stood there watching...

...the reason the cops got...

...ay their hands on black man in that park again, we will all know exactly what to do...

...brothers hear of it in both case... the cops are ...the box, ...take him away ...be done ...:

...down and ...oment the news of ...Any Black man who ...and must be...

...oncentration of ...ront of the fence, ...leads to the box ...olding the arrested ...other.

...pushing must start at ... the ...y in front must grab hold ...ain pushing and pulling ...down. this will make all ...side of the fence and ...it.

...hers must leap over the ...and run towards the box ...to rescue the arrested brother being ...held there. This will make the police, at least some of them, leave the line and chase after the 5 brothers.

6. In the struggle and confusion a third lot of five brothers will...

9. If any white man who appears to be a bystander suddenly joins in the fight and defends the cops, you must know at once he is neither a plain-clothes cop or a viscious fascist

10. It must be seen that at the end of the rescue operation no single cop must be standing on his feet, able to recognise or identify anyone.

11. Everbody must disappear immediately after the rescue job is done and be miles away before police re-enforcements arrive on the scene.

12. If by some miracle, the rescue attempt is a failure and the cops manage to get the arrested brother to the police station it is the duty of all the brothers present to march straight down without delay and as one united body to the police station and see that the brother is bailed out and released as soon as possible. Then we must all go home not with our heads bowed down because we have failed, but to find out why and where our plans went wrong and with this improved knowledge and experience, be better equipped to strike back next time.

...ken him there ...waiting for the ...ck maria t... We shall consider the ...o cases...

...the arrested black man is taken to ...police waiting box.

...his method must be employed if the cops ...rested black man near the platform of a ...ack speaker or near a big black crowd. The ...oment the cops lay their hands on a black ...other, it is the duty of the black brother ...arest to the spot to call the attention of the ...her brothers to what is happening at once ...d the news must spread like wild fire in ...e park.

...e black crowd must surge forward like ...e big black steam-roller to catch up with ...e cops and the black brother being marched ...ay towards the police box.

...who earns his living by voluntarily ...aking himself an instrument and a ...nom ous custodian of a fascist whitey ...stem that has oppressed out people for

WITH THE EMPHASIS ON ENJOYMENT

London OZ is published
approximately monthly by
OZ Publications Ink Ltd,
38a Palace Gardens Terrace,
London W8. Phone: 01-
229 4623 . . . 01-603 4205.

Editor: Richard Neville
Deputy Editor: Paul Lawson
Design: Jon Goodchild

Typesetting: Janet Farrow
Big O Press Ltd, 49 Kensington
High Street, London W8.
Phone: 01-937 2614.

Advertising: John Leaver
3 Gunter Hall Studios,
Gunter Grove, SW10 Phone:
01-352 7258

Photography: Keith Morris

Pushers: Felix Dennis and
Louise Ferrier

Distribution: (Britain) Moore-
Harness Ltd, 11 Lever Street,
London EC1. Phone: CLE 4882
New York DGB Distribution
Inc, 41 Union Square, New York
10003
Holland Thomas Rap,
Regulierdwarstraat 91,
Amsterdam, Telefoon: 020-22706
Denmark George Streeton,
The Underground,
Larsbjørnstraede 13,
Copenhagen K.

THE ELECTRIC CIRCUS

We now live in a global village - a simultaneous happening.

Art is anything you can get away with.

There is absolutely no inevitability as long as there is a willingness to contemplate what is happening.

The Electric Circus is a new section of OZ concerned with environment.
Which to you, *media freak* means, television, movies, sound radio,
etc. Because that's where you live now.
All the rest is geographical accident.
You will find informational input into the Electric Circus is pretty much
raw data.
(Check out the Godard press conference on Page 42.)
That's because the conventional perceptual processes are now only
so much civil defence against massive media fallout.
So don't don't get bugged by spelling mistakes.
You probably weren't meant to look at the words anyway.

So, continue. Infiltrate the new electric infrastructure.

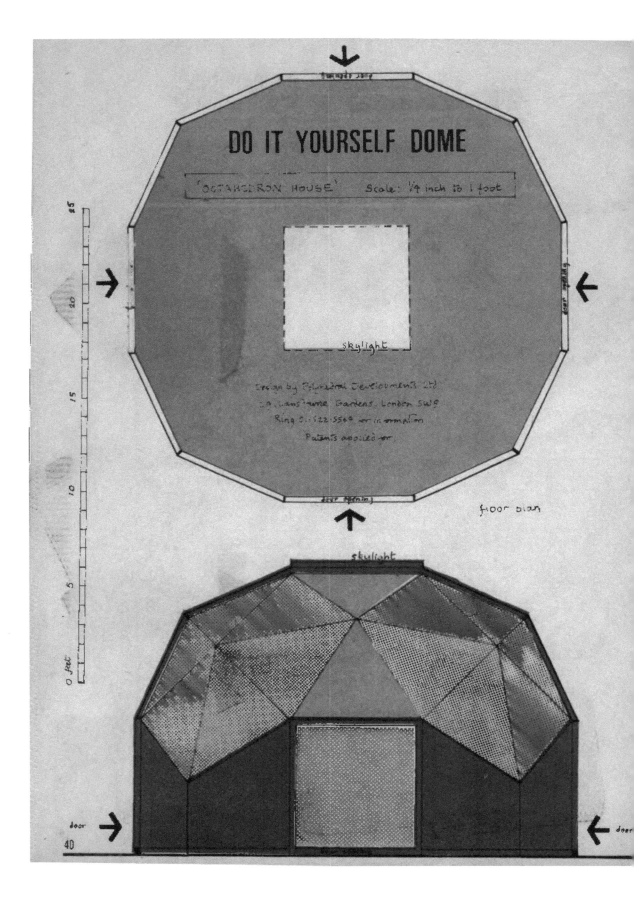

DO IT YOURSELF DOME

'OCTAHEDRON HOUSE'   Scale: 1/4 inch to 1 foot

skylight

Design by Polyhedral Developments Ltd
4 Ransome Gardens, London SW9
Ring 01-622-5564 or information
Patents applied for

floor plan

skylight

door

door

40

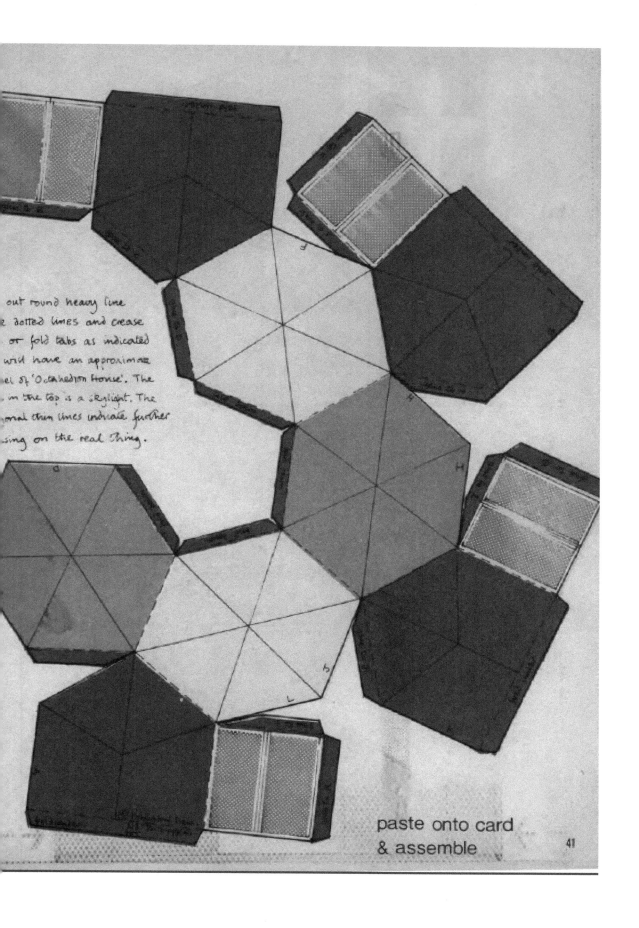

out round heavy line
dotted lines and crease
or fold tabs as indicated
will have an approximate
el of 'Octahedron House'. The
in the top is a skylight. The
onal thin lines indicate further
ing on the real thing.

paste onto card
& assemble

41

2 or 3 tapes of a Press Conference

You seem to be saying that you want to make yourself invisible.

Yes, I think this is especially since what happens in France, about three or four months ago it was happening, especially with the students, still considering myself a student in the audio-visual form, it shows me that a lot of people, who were younger than I was, were discovering a lot of things that I had maybe not yet discovered. Things that I was discovering at the same time but that I had been working on for twenty years and they discovered it very easily, and I mean, the good in their movements was not coming from us, it was coming from them. So, we were speaking of culture, art and a lot of things, and they, they found things apart from us. So we have to learn from them instead of pretending to teach them. That is why we cannot speak of being a person as an artist or making a piece of art. This has to be completely destroyed. We must be very, I think so, very simple. This is why this movie is called just One Plus One, because this is the beginning and already two plus two is too complicated.

Why is it called One Plus One? Because there are just several people or groups or tribes or societies. There is the musical society, The Rolling Stones; there is the black society, or if not a language society, there is a music language, black language, the European or democratic language, there is the Fascist language which is always the same. It was called Hitler twenty years ago and today it's De Gaulle in France, or Wilson here, I mean, people like that. Of course, Wilson is not exactly like Hitler, but something which astonished me very much is when there are speeches, political speeches by leaders of today, they are saying exactly the same thing that Hitler or Goebels was saying.

Exactly the same   If we say Wilson had said that, nobody will find those things funny. They will say, "OK, yes, Wilson could have said that very easily."

Etes-vous soigne d'être prophetique completement de ce film?

No, not at all. I don't think there is anything prophetic. Prophet, it means religion and I think religion is a masked form of Fascism too.

There's something quite vocational about the way you make films because you do try and relate. I mean, when one sees them it seems something has been said about the society we live in. I mean, after all almost all your films. And you also often talk about propaganda and use quotations from several works of propaganda in your films. How much do you think that films themselves can be propaganda?

Well it depends what you call propaganda, I mean there is good propaganda and bad propaganda. I mean, quotations, well every word you say is a quotation from the dictionary. So if someone has said something better than I could say it then I don't see why I shouldn't use it. It is not quotation, it is just part of more general speech into which I put, I am bringing, my own stone.

Do you think the language of film is a language like any other than?

Yes exactly. Just it is to express himself into films and it makes an express into literature or music, but it's a part of a general language. It's like science, you can express through mathematics or physics or chemistry.

The language of science is more objective?

Well when I say language it's not only the tone but the meaning too. I mean, the thought.

Sometimes you express yourself through violin, sometimes through a piano and still is music. And there is Mozart and there The Rolling Stones. It's music. I think there is more difference for example between Mozart and The Rolling Stones than between a modern movie and a modern book.

Yes certainly. What I am still puzzled by what you first said a about . . .

Well forget about what I first said.

em . . . film-making now being a process of learning for you, you're having to learn from the students.

But to learn is to learn from them. I think we, as moviemakers, in order to change movies, the only possibility to make good and new movies, it's to make movies with people who never made any, who are not the movies. Because if you work with people who are in the movies, sooner or later you are doing again the same kind of movies. You have to go to people who don't do movies. Just to learn how they . . .

Jean Luc, can I just interrupt, because this very interesting for us because you know your three producers, we haven't had a lot of experience, but if you say you would like to make movies with people who haven't made movies before and you come up against the difficulty of lack of experience in the technical sense.

Well forget about the technique. We have to make simple things there are no difficulties. You bring the difficulties, I mean, not you personally, I mean the technicians. Because they are used to work in such a complicated way like privileged people.

Always saying we need this and we need that. When of course there are some young people like Dovshenko. When he was twenty or eighteen, he was a worker, and he was passing a street and he saw a house and some people working inside and he looked in the window and he said, 'Oh I am very

interested and I would like to do what you are doing' and that's how he began movie-making, Dogvshenko. But today, if somebody goes to Algumol?I Algumsted and looks in the window and says 'I want to make a movie' they would throw him out and say first you have to do this and that and go and get certificates and things, and after that they would say you are not able to because we need such you know. And so they build themselves a castle and after they say to the peasants who want to come into the castle, 'No, to come into the castle you have to be a king or something like that.'
But isn't it true also that with equipment that isn't suitable for many people to use that one man cannot pick up a camera and do everything?
This is the trouble because today you make one movie with a hundred men, instead of a hundred movies with a hundred men. There are very few movies. Each year there is about three thousand movies which is very few. For how many people in the world? It is always the same who are going from one theatre to another one. The people in Manchester shouldn't see the same movie as the people in London. Why . . .
But would you say that this is a problem of the society or a technical problem that? . . .
Oh no, this is a much more general problem. And we haven't developed the individual camera that can do it?
Oh it's deeper than that. It's more technical. It's going to people in the country or students or workers and trying to learn how they speak first, what is their language. It's not saying as in the left, we must do movies for the workers. No we must do movies from the workers. The movie has to come from the workers. The movie is not to be brought to the workers, the movie should be built by the workers; if they don't want to built it, at least we should learn from them how do they want a movie to be. But we are

so far away from that the theatre it is the same, there is no need to go to a play – like very often, every strike there is, the theatre goes into factories and plays some Brecht and things but the trouble is its only on strike, ot should be every week. That means the theatre is brought by the king of the theatre to the workers. The contrary should happen, but even the workers don't know that, They are very glad, because if they are feeling miserable, they are glad that when there are strikes at least people are coming to see them. They don't even think they could have their own form of theatre, they just think that theatre and culture or movies are a privilege. We start with teaching in a university and then you get a degree. You have a degree in Hollywood for the movies. Thats what I mean when I say that you shouldn't go to the people in movies. You have to go to people who are not in movies. You just have to go to people because we are in a castle. And this is very hard to leave, this castle, because its very nice in the castle.
Is this why you wanted a man who is actually a black power militant?
I prefer it but I was a bit afraid to because its more honest for me to take actors because if black power people say 'you were not right saying that,' because I'm not so good. Well then I can say, well maybe I'm right, maybe I'm wrong but at least people know it is actors and will not take it as if it is a real person. For example, we though Cassius Clay could play the thing, but if he were on the screen he would not be able to express what I want him to express. Maybe he doesn't like Leroy Jones or maybe he doesn't agree with him so it's not possible.

You said something to me once which I have remembered and if you would like to say a little more. If the technicians have

been used as tools is it possible to break through this, or do you think it is a human problem?
It's possible but in evidence it is very difficult because we have to do everything twice or three times. There are knives and forks and its just like asking a fork to work as a knife And the fork, says I'm only a fork. He's not but so many people tell him he is a fork so he believes it.
You talk of language, not in terms of linguistics, but as being a whole ethos of the person. After being in England how would you describe the language of the British?
I've only been here a very few days. I would not pretend to know.
Yes but you said it was an attempt at making a British film.
In what sense?
Then comes a cut in the tape and no sense can be made.

spontanteity . . . . (cut)
Why did you come to England to make a film?
It was interesting to go to a new place and find how it is and I came because I was asked to come, and then I thought it would be nice to go to the most conservative country in the movie making world to see how it is.
Have you spent a lot of time in England at all before?
No
And you don't have any special feelings about England?
No I was just glad to begin this picture with the Rolling Stones.

Do you consider English moviemaking more conservative than American?
Even more. I don't know how it is possible but it is.
Would you like to say something about the difference between French moviemaking and British?

There is the same difference between France and Britain. In movie making they are conservative all over the world but here its even more complicated because not only of the conservativeness of the movie making but also the conservativeness of the union and of your way of life even if you are out of the usual life. In France there are two or three types of conservativeness. Here there are five or six, anyway that is what I feel. Especially here you live on formulas. In movie making at least. You have been taught to make movies by American people. They gave you a formula and you have kept to it. You never change.

Isn't that because most English films are financed by American companies?

Yes of course, and it has increased. Because after all when Hitchcock went to America he was British. Most of the best actors are British. Burton, Cary Grant, Charlie Chaplin. They are British. But they are keeping to the formula. When you tell them about another formula, they are not interested. That is what Tony told me. He said, 'Jean-Luc, you asked me to shoot when the sun is coming in and out of the clouds. It is very difficult for me to look into the camera and at the clouds at the same time.' And I say, 'Well you should train to do that when you are not shooting.' He never thought he could learn to do that. He was taught to shoot with the sun in or with the sun out and not with a combination of the two. He thought I was joking but I wasn't. He could have been training himself all that time. But he didn't and it's the same all over the world, from the technicians' point of view. What the cameraman should do when he has nothing else to do is hire a Samuelson for an hour a day and take it out and start training himself. Sports people do. But in movie making the one who really works is the guy who is making tea and biscuits for the others.

He's really the only one who works eight hours a day. Everyone else worked only two or three hours a day and they were being paid for eight (Paul: he changes his tenses here so that it sounds as if he is referring to his actual crew and his experience with them, Pauline).

May I say that I think it is a lack of courage (female voice (French) I think she must be assistant prod. or something).

(interrupting) . . no, it's a lack of education only. Not courage, because they were very nice people. They were really willing to do well. It's only a lack of education.

A lack of courage on the producer's side, because at one point when M. Godard had got sufficient film but he was not shooting every day the unit had become very dissatisfied and M. Godard said to me, 'Ask them to borrow or buy cameras and go and make a movie for themselves.' And I did not ask them and I think I should have asked them.

(Male voice) No, that's not true. It was put to them and offered them but I think that once people are doing . . . (trails off at interruption)

(female voice again) Because they say 'We want to make a movie, we want to be shooting every day . . . (male voice now) Jean Luc, although you haven't finished the film as yet have you been disillusioned with your experience in England of making a film? Maybe two or three years ago I would have been but not today, no, I'm very glad.

Would you come back to make a film again? Oh yes, anywhere. But I think the director is now . . . well . . . the only thing I discovered from what happened in France from my personal experience as a movie director is that I was very proud of directing the . . what we call in France, mis-en-scene. Well, directing was . . . I don't know how you say it, we say . . patron, well directing was being the boss. And so I was again the boss in the . . It doesn't mean that someone has not to do the movie at the right time but not always the same person. Because why should twenty people obey the fantasy of another? The artist can't be the boss, this is no more.

Do you think the American movie as it is serves any purpose at all?

The purpose of the bankers and the purpose of what we have to call, even if it sounds too much, cultural imperialism, because it is. Black people who want to make a movie can't do it. If Stokely Carmichael wants to make a movie about Malcolm X, he can't do it. And even if he finds the money, if Mao gives him the money, or Kosygin, but I don't think he would, then no theatres will show it.

It's a very deep problem. It's not just a matter of film making. It's a whole social structure.

So it's very difficult to change it in film alone.

No of course, but since we are the beginning we have to be. And since people like Guevara, well-known people or completely unknown people are doing the same, are giving their life, at least we may give our time. Because we don't risk our lives doing that.

Most film-makers have a preconceived audience, which they visualise are going to see their films. Do you have any preconceived idea about who is going to see your films?

No I never think about it.

Does that relate in any way to why you wanted the Rolling Stones? Was it just them as musicians?

No, it was also because of the way in which they represent something, a certain kind of society, to which I am . . .

So in terms of this film, if one can visualise ahead, you hope that young people are going to see it?

I don't know. I don't care . . about young or old just . . .

Do you care about your audiences?

Sometimes, yes. The work of art is always related to money. So that's why you ask 'Do you care?'. It means do you care for a lot of people. No, I don't think a lot of people should ultimately see everything. Why? (should they) when there are books on mathematics known only by three or four people who know about mathematics and they are not ashamed if everybody doesn't understand. There are some movies like that.

There are some movies where it is very important if they are seen by quite a lot of people. Like some books and some music. There are no rules. The trouble is there is that that they try to make rules. If you go to the bottom to find what is beyond the rules you find money.

But you seem very often to draw back to education. Education you think is one of the main failings of society in general?

Yes because you find money behind education too.

So it's the whole basis of it.

Yes. Every goes together.

What is the more important aspect of film-making? Communication or propaganda? Well I think it can't be put like that. It is automatic communication. To me there is no difference in film. It exists but there should be no difference between film and television. There is a difference because they are badly done but to me there is none. One is brought by a electronic device and the other by a photograph, a chemical device.

The fact that it is a confined screen . . .

It's only because they don't want it to be a huge one because people would like it too much. If there is something very bad for the government, if you had all the wall of your dining room it would . . They could build it very easily but they just don't want it. They keep it very tiny.

And sometimes, if it is a very straight (?) thing to have just a tiny thing is very good too. I mean radio is still going and there is no image. Music isn't bad.

But you say the workers don't actually see your films.

Well, a hundred years ago Marx was sent away from France to England or to Belgium. After all what he wrote with Engels helped a little bit with what happened later on. And he didn't fight. He wasn't a very strong man physically. But it helped. Literature and language and art and science can't be neutral. For example, Guevara was very glad that Debray (?) was to him and he tried to tell him to go away from Bolivia and tell the world. Publicity would help us he said.

You can see in Greece today that the colonels are against anybody who writes, makes films paints . . (cut).

For example what happened about the dockers and the black people here and Enoch Powell. If he were Prime Minister, it wouldn't be exactly the same. And it depends how you do it. If Peter Brook had staged Murat Sade each morning in front of Buckingham Palace in front of the people, the police would have thrown him in jail right away.

What is your primary dissatisfaction with the film industry?

Working too much as an industry on formulas, which could be good sometimes but not always. It's not a matter of people, because all the people I had were very nice and but they are badly educated, that's all. And so you think that people in film industry are badly educated?

Oh yes. Totally.

Do you think it is more important to be instructive in films or to be just entertaining? Instruction, but I don't see why instruction shouldn't be brought through entertaining. And is that the element you are looking for in your films?

Yes, I think actors very often should be used not only in plays and movies but in universities just to play the teaching sometimes, the lines of philosophy.

With the feelings for society that you have would your purpose be better solved by doing something like a television programme? This would yes, but not to me but to a lot of people. That's the way television should be. One hour of television should belong to the Labour Party and the next hour Rootes or to Manchester United. And everyone could express themselves.

. . cut

44

efferson Airplane

live in a society which consists of highs...
ims Murray Roman (Tetragrammaton
). And it's true. Music is a high—what's
e they can't bust you for it. So, why
sn't somebody release

live in a society which consists of
hs . . . .' claims Murray Roman (Tetra-
mmation 101). And it's true. Music is a
h—what's more they can't bust you for it-
like they already have L.P.s called Songs
Swingers and Music for Lovers why
esn't somebody release Music to get High
The CBS Rock Machine album comes
tty near it with tracks from people like
nard Cohen, Moby Grape and Blood,
eat & Tears. It would be nice if everyone
ld cut a record like that with their own
lve favourite tracks on it. The only drag
hat everybodys selection's got tobe different
eveyone else's. My own
um as of now would contain tracks from
s that you maybe won't have heard yet.

'Castles in the Sand'—Jimi Hendrix
om 'Axis Bold as Love' on Track) You
uld already know.

'Dynamite'—Sly and the Family Stone
om 'Life' on the Epic label) You can
y get this album on import at the moment
m somewhere like One-Stop, Town Records
Musicland. If it's released in this country
be on the Direction label. Sly and the
mily Stone are probably coming here in
stember. They're an incredible group who
ve all the time but you can't put them
o the ordinary soul bag.

'On the Road again'—Canned Heat
um 'Boogie with Canned Heat' on Liberty)

It's good that Liberty released this as a single.

If they hadn't the L.P. would have been
almost worth buying for this track alone. As
it is the other tracks are nearly as good.

4.   'Politician'—Cream
(from 'Wheels of Fire' on Polydor). Cream
are always best when they work within a
standard blues framework. This track, com
posed by Jack Bruce and Pete Brown,
features a typical wailing vocal and evil bass
line by Jack Bruce and of course Clapton
(or as the Americans spell it—God).

5.   'Feelin' Good'—the James Cotton Blues
Band (from the James Cotton Blues Band'
available on import on the Verve label).
The album from which this track comes
features a good selection of R&B numbers
(listen to the classic 'Don't Start Me Talking')
but it's a pity they included 'Knock On Wood'

6.   'Old Songs New Songs'—Family
(from Music in a Dolls House on Pye). The
Family are almost as good on record as they are
are live and that's a compliment. The outstanding feature of an outstanding group is
the voice of Roger Chapman, the lead singer
who sound incredibly like Buffy Sainte-Marie.

7.   'Rondo'—The Nice
(from 'the thoughts of Emerlist Davjack' on
Immediate) I prefer the Nice's treatments
of other peoples' material to their own
numbers. It's a fantastic experience simply
to watch them perform this number.

8.   'I Started Walking'—John Mayall
(from 'Bare Wires' on Decca). This is John

Mayall's best L.P. since 'John Mayall's
Blues Breakers with Eric Clapton' mainly
because of the brass selection of the group.
This particular track features an angry
guitar solo by Mick Taylor.

9.   'Wine'—The Electric Flag
(from 'A Long Time Comin'' on CBS). The
nice thing about the Electric Flag is the variety
of the numbers they do. This particular
track is pure rock-and-roll. On the sleeve
Michael Bloomfield says he thinks of the
group's music as 'the music you hear in the
air, on the air, and in the streets; blues, soul,
country, rock, religious music, traffic, crowds,
street sounds and field sounds, the sound of
people and silence,' which must be roughly
where it is

10.   'America'—Simon & Garfunkel
(from 'Bookends' on CBS). Every track on the
the L.P. is superb but 'America' is the best.

11.   'One More Heartache'—the Paul
Butterfield Blues Band
(from 'The Ressurection of Pigboy Crabshaw
on Elektra). This number features Paul
Butterfield's excellent harp playing. The
group's big brass section grooves all the way
through the album.

12.   'Murder in My Heart for the Judge'
—Moby Grape
(from 'Wow' on CBS). Moby Grape are
another group who don't specialise too much
The album even contains a number 'Just
Like Gene Autry; A Foxtrot' which is such
an authentic 1920's sound that you have to
play it at 78 rpm.

John Leaver

do yourself a favour
go to a record shop
listen to this album.

if you dig it
that's nice

if you don't
others will.

CZECHS
TOLD

[he] Writer of this article is a Czech, very prominent in the movement towards [dem]ratisation. Outspoken, and plainly so, for [the] time, he no longer feels free to write [un]der his own name. Hence the pseudonym. [We] respect his fears that the least indication [of] who he is may endanger him and his [fam]ily.

[The] present situation of Czechoslovakia [se]ems to be obvious beyond any doubt. It is [prov]en by the presence of the occupational [un]its and by the acception of the Moscow [di]ctate which has been more than once [co]mpared to the Munich dictate. While the [oc]cupation of the foreign armies still lasts, [th]e basic democratic freedoms are again [re]strained. What will be the attitude of the [C]zech and Slovak nation to this reality? What [ar]e the prospects for the nearest future? Will [pe]ople defy this situation or will they [su]bmit? Will there be more shooting in the [str]eets of Prague or will fantastic [ac]cusations and selfaccusations be again [he]ard in the courtyards?

[Th]ough the present state of affairs makes us [dr]aw rather pessimistic conclusions, let us [tr]y to see things in broader perspectives. [Th]en it appears that the present [C]zechoslovak situation reveals a lot of very [po]sitive factors which certainly will come [in]to effect in the nearest future. [Un]doubtfully the most positive moment is [th]at a political and economical program has [be]en worked out after tens of years which is [ac]ceptable even for the young generation [al]so in the pro-Soviet regimes, traditionally [ke]eps apart from the political life. This [pr]ogram of the democratic socialism has not [fai]led its fulfilling has been interrupted by

force at the very start from the outside before its inner conflicts could have be fully revealed. Thus it remains still very attractive both for the Czech public as well as for the public in the Eastern countries, if not for the whole progressive public in Europe.

The second important factor is the inner renaissance of the Communist party which turned from the bureaucratic and politically almost ineffective organization into an active political force which succeeded in uniting the whole nation gaining it for its program. The Soviet intervention — quite in contrary to what the Soviet leaders intended — completely undermined the conservative wing of the party and strengthened the progressive wing and the centre.

The return to the methods of the past would be possible only in case of a severe attack against the Communist part itself and if the life of the country got under the control of the Soviet secret police again.

Another important moment can be seen in the fact that during the half year's duration of the so called Prague spring the progressive intellectuals managed to reveal completely and discredit the mechanism of the neostalinist government not only in the eyes of a handful of intellectuals but of the whole Czech and Slovak public. The severed contacts between the progressive intellectuals and the working class were

restored again. Even neostalinism needs at least a handful of loyal people believing in the cause; and these will be very hard to find in Czechoslovakia. It will be difficult to find them even among the quislings for they will be scared by the present development All these factors and moments — not mentioning the change in the traditionally pro-Russian feelings of the Czech nation might mean that the renewal of a neostalinist system in Czechoslovakia will be difficult even under the auspices of the Soviet troops, even if the Soviets will succeed to gradually remove the present party leadership, what they will certainly try to do.

Nevertheless the prospects of the Czech and Slovak nation will not be very rosy. After any great national upheaval there follows fatigue if not a hangover. Both Czechs and Slovaks have discovered that though supported by the whole world public, in their struggle, their fate lies completely in the hands of one of the superpowers. They have learned that their freedom is quite fictitious and that the dream of the Czech example to the world has been really just a dream. They have understood that they may differ only in minor details and in certain limits.

The fatigue will grow undoubtfully due to a serious economic situation. The bitterness which can be expected as an overwhelming reaction of the majority of people might prevent mass collaboration but will also make people to turn their backs on further struggle. They might find useless any effort in the country where tanks are watching whether the limitations of freedom are not overstepped.

The question which many people ask now-whether the Czechs and the Slovaks will accept the hard terms—may be answered that they have hardly any other alternative left. Both the Czechs and Slovaks have experienced a hundreds-years' existence how to gain some free space inside non-free conditions imposed on them from the outside. They will seek this again. It is possible that the Russians at the same time when they will feel that the border of their zone allotted to them at the Jalta conference is secured will allow Czechoslovakia to enjoy some extent of freedom. It also is not in their interests to keep up a regime which would cost them millions of rubles a day. So the Czechs hands in hands with their Slovak brothers might try to continue in their reformist program aware of all the limitations due to the fact that they are no longer masters in their own country.

And because there is no life without hope, those who cannot live just for the needs of the present day will rely upon the political development inside the socialist camp of which Czechoslovakia is a member. They know that the evolution which started in Czechoslovakia and also the way in which it was suppressed cannot remain without some response. They know that the Czechoslovak spring must bear its fruit although it is difficult to predict when this might happen.

RICHARD DEUTSCHER.

CHICAGO

EUGENE SCHONFELD

Some Yippies would welcome a bloody confrontation in Chicago this summer. They believe that, while a few people might be hurt or killed, in the long run it would do good for people in this country and over the world. Let me emphasize that most Yippies do not want violence. But those who expect and welcome violence may use their skills of orators to urge crowds in Chicago to provoke the authorities. They can easily be provoked. All the latent and overt prejudices against minority groups (including hippies) lay very close to the surface in that capital of America's torment.

Last October, I participated in the Friday demonstration at the Oakland Induction Center. At the end of the day, when automobiles were being pushed into the middle of the streets and their tires deflated, while street benches and trees were strewn about as barriers; barricades, I felt a sense of excitement at being involved in the most direct protest of any that I had witnessed.

At the same time I recognized that simply because this kind of protest was effective, it could be followed by more violent protests, and that with increasing violence by the opposition, I have learned have been realized.

There is no doubt that black people have suffered more persecution in this country than any other minority group. Claims have been made recently that there is a plot to exterminate the black man in the United States. I don't believe there is such a plot but I do feel there is a possibility of this occurring—a kind of self-fulfilling prophecy. The assassination of Martin Luther King has led to a vacuum in black leadership, recently being filled by black militants, some of whom espouse violence as a means to obtaining their ends.

The Yippies who planned the lout-in at Macy's in New York City on June 6th had no specific complaint about Macy's but chose the store because it is probably the best known department store in the United States. The Yippie leaders think this kind of chaotic action

may lead to some changes. But we need only look at Nazi Germany to notice many striking parallels.

When Germany was subjected by the world-wide depression, when money there became virtually worthless, I recall seeing old motion picture films of people carrying money in wheelbarrows to buy groceries. During the same years in the United States we had an opposite problem—the scarcity of money. However, it was far worse for a money-oriented society like Germany to find its currency worth nothing, than to have it worth a great deal and unavailable.

Because of the "safeguards" of our money, banks would not fail in the event of a depression as they did in the 1930's, at least not right away. What would happen is that the currency would just become pieces of paper.

A relatively small and powerless portion of our population consider themselves workers and identify with a "working class." Our union concern themselves not with political issues, but only with questions of increased pay and benefits for their members. Union members, for the most part, are among the "most conservative groups in the United States and truly feel they have a stake in the status-quo.

In a vacuum created by anarchy, violence and economic catastrophe, "status-quo" people look to a strong man or a leader to help them. German conservatives thought they could use Hitler and later take his power from him. They were among his first victims. Some of the Yippies feel that creating anarchy and chaos will indeed lead to a rightist reaction but then a turn to the left. German communists believed the same until they were eliminated.

Violence leads to more violence. If the Chicago Tin-in or Lie-in violence it could be of more harm to the cause of peace and black progress in this country than if it were directly supportive of the rightist right.

The Free University of Berkeley this summer is offering a course in the use of small arms. It is said

that this will be a highly popular course. I see no difference between middle-aged housewives in Detroit training with guns or black training with guns or long-haired so-called hippies training with guns at the Free University.

Fascism is fascism and it doesn't matter whether it is a black fascist, a blue-haired fascist, or a long-haired fascist.

There are ways of achieving social change without destroying the entire society. Some members of the underground and overground press believe that the present events in history will occur whatever is said, that they move with inevitable force. But I cannot remain silent, I will not contribute in a situation which potentially could lead to another Nazi Germany, or a situation which might result in thousands or millions of deaths.

I think the Yippies had an important role in forcing President Johnson to decide to step down at the end of his current presidential term. But all Yippies are not Hippies. One should distinguish the essentially non-violent and pacifistic hippie from militant New Left groups.

I think it is time for everyone to seriously decide whether the situation in this country is so odious and so unamenable to change to warrant riots, rebellions, the possibility of thousands killed or imprisoned and the eventual takeover by the right.

We have only to look to the example of Russia to know that intellectual tyranny can continue 50 years after the end of a revolution. We must ask whether the economic and social inequities in the United States are so severe that they warrant the risk of a destruction of a society and a race of people.

I say things are not yet that bad. I say the non-violent course followed by Gandhi and Martin Luther King is an ideal toward which we must strive. The alternative may be an unprecedented period of barbarism.

I'm not going to Chicago this August.

OZ 15

London OZ is published
approximately monthly by
OZ Publications Ink Ltd.
38a Palace Gdns Terrace W8.
Phone 01-229 4623 . . .
01-603 4205

Editor: Richard Neville

Deputy Editor: Paul Lawson

Design: Jon Goodchild

Writers: Andrew Fisher, Ray
Durgnat, Germaine, Tom Nairn,
David Widgery, Angelo
Quattrocchi

Artists: Martin Sharp, Rick
Cuff, Michael English,
Larry Smart, Vytas
Serelis, John Horford,

Photography: Keith Morris

Typesetting: Jacky Ephgrave,
courtesy Thom Keyes

Pushers: Louise Ferrier,
Felix Dennis, Anou

Distribution: Britain (overground)
Moore-Harness Ltd. 11 Lever
Street, London EC1.
Phone C1.E 4882.
(underground) ECAL,
22 Betterton Street, London
WC2. Phone TEM 8606.
New York DGB Distribution Inc.
41 Union Square, New
York 10003.
Holland Thomas Rap,
Regulersdwarstraat 91,
Amsterdam, Tel: 020-227065.
Denmark George Streeton.
The Underground, Larsbjørn
straede 13, Copenhagen K.

Dear Sir,

Thank heavens for the sense of
Eugene Schonfeld in his article
on 'Chicago'. A lot of young
militants strike me as plain
'rockers' and 'yobs' excusing
themselves with a nihilist philosophy. If only they would realise
the validity of Schonfelds statement: 'Fascism is fascism and it
doesn't matter whether it's a

black fascist, a blue-haired fascist
or a long-haired fascist.' I pray
that readers will stick to a
beautiful alternative of OZ rather
than the Tyranny of 'Black
Dwarf'.

John Dougill
Lockner Farm,
Chilworth,
Guildford.

Dear Sir,

Apropos of 'Happy's' comment
in OZ 14, Ray Durgnat may be
relaying his hang-ups to other
people, but they sound to me
like the kind of hang-ups that
more than 50% of the population
have. Ray scores in being able
to articulate them, which is a
hell of a lot more than can be
said for some of your contributors. If some reader (or perhaps
the editor) could provide a
commentary on Herman Kahn's
piece in No 14, or even give me
the general drift of it, maybe
I'll learn something. Or is it that
the underground sees obscurity
and rambling as virtues, even
when trying to explain its own
hang ups.

(If you think that's worth printing, and I don't please leave out
my address.)
Sincerely,

Brian Morley

Dear Sir,

I have just read OZ No 14 and I
feel I should communicate with
you and your magazine about
your position. First, for a
'supposedly' revolutionary mag
you seem to support avidly mass
commercial culture. Pop, whether
whether it be Hump or the
Doors it is still commercially
orientated, retrograde, reactionary, primitive (using primitive
chord changes and harmonies),
traditionless and superficial.
What really pains me is all the
'big hips' who shout how progressive it is without even hearing Stockhausen, Boulez or Cage.

Secondly, your letter column
seems to be filled with discon-
certed spiritualists such as Jamie
who forgets man is a social
animal, his consciousness is a
product of social relations and
politics is the weapon of the
class struggle and that his philosophy and ideology derive from
the superstructure of our society.

Thirdly, all the old cliches—Berke
Berke's bourgeoisie.

Fourthly, Mr Kahn. Has this dear
gentleman never observed anything and seen the economic,
social and political structure in
its right perspective. He
seems to think that capitalism
is absolute, that there is no
class-struggle and society is
static. Someone should inform
him that society progresses, the
means of productions revolu-
tionise (ie mechanise), labour
is not needed. But capitalism
needs labour to make profit.
Wham. Big contradiction.
Economic crisis. Only one way
to solve it. Social revolution.

Fifthly, the Czech article. When
will the public realise 1) neither
Russia nor Czechoslovakia are
communist/socialist. 2) You
cannot have socialist states. 3)
This crisis is due to Czechoslovakia having a far more
advanced capitalist type economy than Russia, and therefore
wanting to join the also advanced west.

Finally, Chicago- Pacifism
doesn't work. Eugene, if you
want something you grab it,
you don't ask. If you want a
change in society, you have to
smash it first, and only the
proletarians can do that.

In conclusion I would say your
magazine is another product
of the pseudo-radical set. I
wish it wasn't.

Yours sincerely,

Noll Rogall
38 Primley Park Cresc.
Leeds 17.

Dear Sir,

to write on vinyl plastic with
wotever media (um) YOU
CHOOSE! or is consequently
available or PRACTICAL
(for instance strong solvents
are not recommended unless
you wish to produce literature
of the obscure)
EVEN SMUCDXVDESE
but wot about making a
stencil?
wot about it ,,,,,,,???2???????
'the medium of the printed
word is now so outdated that it
is abandoned to dilletantes
whose only qualifications are
their abilities to vary the
parchment'—Khufu, egyptian
pharoh during the 26th century
be inventor of hieroglyph
pictograms which he trans-
ported to china where through
long evolutionary processessses
the complex ideograms of china
developed abasalootaly false
history.

THE JOINT VENTURE
13 ladbroke crescent W11.

Dear OZ,

At the beginning of September
the Turkish government passed
a new passport law. This forbids
hippies or beatniks from either
entering or staying in the
country. Many are being turned
away and 40 hippies staying in
Istanbul were immediately
deported as soon as the law had
been passed. Their definition of
beatnik is bitnik in Turkish. Bit
means louse, so really it's louse-
nik they mean. This means that
anyone who has long unkept
hair and beards, defiled and sor-
did clothes and is penniless, will
not be accepted.

If anyone gets to Istanbul, don't
stay at the Gulhane Hotel or in
the area of Sultanahmet, it's
renowned for its busts. Don't
ever trust a Turk - police rely on
informers.

The best hash (esrar) comes from
either Bursa or Gassantep. Don't
buy form Istanbul, it's too expensive.

There are many of us busted in
Turkey. Turkey is the worst
country in the world to get
busted in. The minimum
sentence given is 2½ hears, the
maximum sentence 30 years,
the inbetweeners as myself
receive 8 years 4 months. We
don't receive amnesties, murder-
ers do.

I was busted in the country with
Pakistan hash (charas). The cha
charas was chatral chatos, each
piece was stamped by an official
stamp that said: 'Chatral charas'
in urdu.

Turkish prisons are like hotels
caged with animals.

Do what you can for us, we need
someone to take notice of our
situation. I've been in nick for
2½ years now and have 3½ more
to do. But think of those with
30 years. I write on behalf of
all of us, it's been the first opportunity. My letters are not controlled, no one in the city of
Erzincan can understand English
well enough. Besides they trust
me. Anyway, if I'm sentenced
for abuse against Turkey and its
laws, my case will be stronger . . .

Robert Pontin
Merkez Ceza Evi
Erzingan
Turkey

PS Once when I was Ankara,
Oz came to me, how about a few
more copies? Sorry I can't send
the subscription money. Your
stickers came in useful. 'CANNA-
BIS' is stuck upon the cell wall.
Ninety five percent of the prisoners are 'heads' here. Many are
serving life imprisonment ie.
caught with 450 kilos or 0. . . 50
kilos of shit and so it goes on . . .
love
RP

2

Dear Richard Neville,

In receipt of yours of Sept. 10, very sorry about never writing that piece on Kingsley Amis (some day it will be done) and yes, I *would* like to "generalise my criticisms of the Underground", elaborating my point about its "political deathwish" (your words, buvo), "phoney culture" (yours again), "etc" (again). The "etc" has me worried, since the other two quoted terms pretty well cover the range of my arguments as first made public in my notorious long letter to the *New Statesman*, a letter which I understand has subsequently come to be regarded down there among you all as the four-cornered, hard-edged perimeter of absolute squareness. Well, even though I would never dream of assigning Underground politics a "deathwish", I still *think* that on present showing they have their own doom built in, whether they wish for it or not. Obviously Underground politics, such as they are, *wish* for most of the things which the liberal-humanist tradition has long cherished as the very opposite of death: love, peace, creativity and the rest of the caboodle. But as Hannah Arendt pointed out at the end of one of her classic studies of totalitarianism, *politics is not the nursery*.

Politically speaking, it seems to me that as long as the Underground preaches revolution it is setting itself up to be knocked off. The revolution it calls for would in fact be the worst thing that could happen to it, since the Underground would be automatically and abruptly taken care of by whatever force emerged to administer the resulting chaos. (This force needn't be the police, by the way: vigilante daddies with a few young mouths to feed would justifiably beat you to death with tea-squares as you tried to grab milk from the crates.) In its heart of hearts, of course, the Underground has no plans for revolution, since this would mean taking over an industrial society which is too complicated for it to understand. Nor does it even have plans for bringing immediate pressure to bear on the people who actually do administer the industrial complex. Perhaps by instinct, certainly not by brains, the Underground seems to have tumbled to the fact that continued and increasingly complicated industrial progress is the necessary precondition of its own survival. The clearest demonstration of this new awareness (a semi-conscious awareness, I fear) is that the Underground, when it fights the police — the very force specifically equipped and paid to deal with street action. As genuine *saboteurs* of the industrial system, the Underground does not rate; although with typically boneheaded ignorance it dismisses the old Committee of 100 stuff as essentially quiescent.

But of course the Underground is right and my generation was wrong on this subject: you can't smash the set-up by peeing down the manhole of an RSG, parking your arse on a V-bomber runway, or even blowing up Battersea powerhouse. The only way to fight City Hall is by providing an alternative mode of existence and keeping it running long enough for the industrial complex to become humanised by penetration and by example. This is the *real* politics of the Underground, a politics it inherited from the CND generation without gratitude or understanding, just as the CND generation inherited the old radical tradition without gratitude or understanding, and so on all the way back to Christ Jesus, whose followers first landed us with the continuous historical problem (not just a difficulty but a *problem* and never to be laughed or sung or "meditated" out of existence) of moving the legions out without moving the priests in. And what I originally objected to about Underground politics I still object to: its pigheadedness about what really *are* its politics, its blindness to the *fact* that it must guarantee the continuity of its own intelligence by clarity and by study, its blindness to the *fact* that a down-grading of technological complexity would mean suffering on a large scale, its blindness to the *fact* that its own present liberty was created in the past by men it has not the knowledge or the discrimination to recognise as heroic, its blindness to the *fact* that any revolution open to a power-grab is a *defeat*.

My idea of unmitigated, catastrophic boredom is to listen to a convocation of dropouts mumbling about Britain's similarity to, say, Greece. The subject of the *differences*, of how these differences came about and how best they can be preserved, never comes up. As a psychological climate, the Underground in Britain is essentially an atmosphere in which some clod getting busted for not being smart enough to hide his pot can imagine himself to be in the same political condition as a middle aged, committed Greek intellectual being tortured for what he knows. And so on around the ring, until every distinction is blurred. We - are - the - Viet - Cong - and - what - is - done - to - the - Viet - Cong is done to us. (And what is done by the Viet-Cong is done by us?) Che lives. (But have you ever had to decide who dies? He had to. Lovely smile, though.) Dixon - of - Dock - Green - equals - Heinrich - Himmler. In this mish-mash of generalised emotion, realities drown. The murderous complications of politics become elementary photographs, the photographs become trendy wallpaper and everyone who is anyone can feel involved, even (especially) those who haven't the imagination to realise that other people's pain *hurts*.

And meanwhile the extension of liberty in these islands is curtailed and its very preservation threatened by the growing disinclination of the infected young to commit themselves to the choices between evils, the long second thoughts and the necessary boredom vital to liberty. Instead of rights, we are offered Love. Love, that magic word whose manic propagation among this generation is Hollywood's final triumph. As if the guaranteeing of personal liberty against abstracted emotion were not the whole of politics in the modern age!

But of course none of this 'Love' garbage could work for a minute without a great deal of equally polarised Hate, which we see venomously directed at trendy symbols like the bourgeoisie (the custodian of civilisation in Europe), liberals (we name no names because we know so few), and regular politicians up to (or down to) and including Johnson. It never occurs to people who *cartoon* politics in this way that they are in fact succumbing to the mental corrosion spread into space and time by the two chief tyrannies of this century. Let me make this point once more, Richard, before I turn to our second topic of the evening: there is only one tradition of thought, that tradition is the liberal-humanist tradition and there can be no simplification of it which is not a distortion.

As to "phoney culture", I need add very little to what I first argued. It seems possible that the Underground is already shaking itself free from its first chaotic democracy (in which *everyone* is "talented") and evolving towards the realities of art, which, as some of your sweet helpless people have doubtless already realised, means some people being more talented than others. But the cultural ambition of Underground people as a whole remains villainous low, and can be raised only when it is realised that no alternative *culture* is possible. An alternative *society* is at least a proposition, but an alternative *culture* is not even a notion. There is only one culture, in which the unique is added to the unique, and to become aware of its eternal laws is a necessary step in realising that life is not a fairy story. A work of art comes out of the alone on its way to the universal and during its passage through the brain of the poor bastard fingered to be its creator he receives a forcible reminder that "self-expression" is strictly for children. Art is individual, but it is not *personalised*, and has very little to do with happiness. The Underground, expressing itself compulsively, has come up with some styles of dress, a few good ways to decorate the walls, some tricks with lights and some copycat graphics: kid-stuff mainly, and fair enough, since most of its members, by the long time-scale of the artistic life, are children still.

The true significance of the Underground is as a political movement and political movements are not in themselves creative all they can create is the possibility for creation.

And after all this, am I basically for or basically against? Basically for: and will remain so until the point when the Underground goes irrational by conviction. That point is not yet, but it could come. Every bad poem, Zen epigram and brutal paragraph brings it nearer.

Clive James,
Pembroke College,
Cambridge.

4

SPIKE

These two reports by Release are, in some ways, a very effective reply to the Flip Top Pot anti-legalisation article in this issue.

Dale is the editor of Interzone A and one of the most active participants in the community around Notting Hill—at one time running a free food and clothing stall in Portobello Road.

ONE

✳ The voice of three Villages—Silenced

Having a party in Notting Hill Gate can be hazardous, but there is nothing more likely to revive the flagging party spirit than a visit from the local constabulary, in force. It seems that the police are attracted by party noises but rather than joining in as guests, they prefer to come uninvited on the pretext of looking for . . . drugs.

Dale's flat was raided in April when there was a gathering of 29 people on the premises. The police managed to find a very small amount of pot, and some skins. Nevertheless they proceeded to arrest all 28 people, the 29th was a Russian Orthodox priest who had been allowed to leave.

At Ladbroke Grove Police Station everyone was charged with being in possession of cannabis, but it was technically impossible for all 28 of the people arrested to have possessed the piece of cannabis and the charges against 24 were dropped at committal proceedings five weeks later. Many of those arrested had spent several weeks in custody because they were unable to find the necessary ties to bail them out. (A magistrate will grant you bail but unless you have a friend who is over 21, a householder with no police record, whom the police consider suitable—there is not much chance of being released before trial).

Dale, and his girlfriend, and two others were the only ones finally charged.

Dale (19) and Kathy (19) were charged with being in possession of cannabis and

of allowing their premises to be used. The other two were charged with being in possession of cannabis; one of them pleaded guilty and was fined £10 at Marylebone Magistrates Court. The other was later placed on probation when the case was heard at sessions.

The police referred the case to the Director of Public Prosecutions who considered it serious enough for his intervention, which automatically meant that Dale and Kathy would have to appear before a Jury at Inner London Sessions.

Four months later, four issues of Interzone A later, and a few days after the arrival of Kathy's baby, the case was heard.

Dale and Kathy pleaded 'not guilty' to both charges, they were found 'guilty' of being in possession of cannabis, and 'guilty' of allowing their premises to be used. The case was remanded so that Mr R.E. Seaton, Chairman of Inner London Sessions, could order probation and medical reports. Kathy was allowed bail, but Dale was remanded in custody. Before the case was finally heard we contacted three people who knew Dale very well, had given him ideas for Interzone A and would act as character witnesses for him. One was a psychologist and two were priests, but Mr Seaton was not persuaded by their evidence to follow any other course than that which the probation officer had recommended. The probation officer's report to Mr Seaton recommended that Dale would benefit from a period of Borstal training.

Kathy was put on probation for two years and Dale was sentenced to Borstal—a discretionary sentence of up to two years.

Borstals are overcrowded, and it is almost impossible to go from the Court to Borstal. So Dale is now in the notorious Borstal Allocation Wing of Wormwood Scrubs Prison, where he could remain

for months, until there is a place for him a at a Borstal.

He is appealing . . .

✳ A True Story

Chris and Alfred were walking home one afternoon when a blue police car pulled up beside them and a couple of policemen got out. They searched Chris and Alfred, but as they found nothing they got back into their car and drove off.

A few hundred yards further on the two boys were stopped again by the same police who had bothered them a few minutes before. This time they were told to get in the police car, and unless you are wearing a pinstriped suit with last terms Eton report in your pocket, it is advisable to do what the police tell you. They were taken to Muswell Hill police station and charged with being in possession of cannabis resin.

—What cannabis resin ! ?

The cannabis resin we found on the pavement when we went back and looked at the spot where we first searched you.

PLANT . . . but Chris and Alfred kept their cool made no statements, and asked for bail. They were allowed bail of £50 of their own surety and came straight round to Release. They had to appear in Court the next morning but we explained that this appearance was just a formality, as the police cannot proceed with a case until they have an analyst's report on the drugs in question. We told them how to apply for legal aid and gave them the name of a solicitor who would fight the case for them.

They were refused Legal Aid, but their solicitor made the necessary inquiries, the results of which were interesting !

Chris and Alfred had been stopped walking up an avenue—at the top of the avenue there is a cinema.

The police said that when they first stopped Chris and Alfred, a policeman who was sitting on the cinema roof had seen Chris drop a piece of pot on the pavement. The two policemen in the car had not seen this surreptitious movement but on talking to their colleague, who by then had climbed off the cinema roof, had decided to go back to the first stopping place and had found the dropped pot.

This seemed a miraculous piece of detective work and their theory was put to the test. Our solicitor with surveyor and photographer made an excursion to Muswell Hill.

They were surprised to find that, from the spot that the police say Chris and Alfred were first stopped, the cinema was completely obscured by trees.

From the .... taking a policeman's eye in place, the area of .... dropping was allegedly ...... places could not be seen.

THE CASE WAS DISMISSED WITH COSTS . . .

TWO

If you're wondering why Brian Jones' sentence (£50 fine) was so light, it's because even the thickest observers realised the stuff was planted.

THREE

For some of us at OZ, the Brighton obscenity trial (Page) was a nostalgic event. In September 1963, the Sydney Stipendiary Magistrate Mr Locke found Australian OZ 6 to be obscene and he gaoled the art director and editors. They appealed, and the conviction was quashed.

Sixteen expert witnesses appeared for OZ, but Mr Locke, the Sydney magistrate, like Mr Ripper the Brighton magistrate, couldn't believe his ears. In his summing up he noted:

'Some remarkable pieces of evidence assist in assessing the weight to these and other opinions expressed by some of the witnesses for the defence. As an example, we find the witness John Olsen deposing, among other things, 'distortion in art is absolutely normal'. In another place he said: 'There is no real world of art that is not distorted'. A second example: the witness AK Stout said 'I do not know what an obscene term is' and in another place he said, 'Four letter words never corrupted anybody'.

Astonished as he was by this kind of testimony, at least Mr Locke did not go so far as to recommend that the witnesses be scolded by the 'University authorities'.

FOUR

David Adams, editor of the forthcoming Notting Hill Herald, explains why

The process of decentralisation has begun. We've seen it in the Digger movement, and we've seen it in Czechoslovakia; we see it in local community centres and in Welsh and Scottish nationalism. Now the process will evolve and, unless something drastic happens, within the next quarter century we shall have returned to village-styled self-sufficient communities linked to the central zone but autonomous in many respects and with a great deal of self-government. Whether these village-styled communities will be so localised as, say, boroughs or counties are now, or whether there will be a compromise and the small communities will be part of a medium-sized community of a state, and the state autonomous within the federation (eg Notting Hill, Camden, etc within London State, London State being part of the UK federation), depends on many things. The point is that the process is one of historic inevitability.

The actual form of the press is fast becoming redundant. There are faster ways of learning about events and more durable ways of keeping a record of important statements. What the newspaper must become is a reflection of and a service to, a community. The reason that national newspapers are becoming valueless is because they are centralised (despite regional editions that only very slightly from the London based edition) and because they are hardly interested in dissemination of information.

A new press must evolve. It will be a product of the community, as in the Status Village Voice, East Village Other, etc are a real part of the community they deal with. The press must become a self-perpetuating force. It initially guides and stimulates the community and thereafter acts as a voice and a synthesis of the various aspects of the community. It must be by the community, for the community and of the community. At the moment I know of no local paper over here that is just this. There are small journals that serve a minority group; there are others that serve a lot of people in different parts of the world. Perhaps the reason is that we are only just beginning to discover our communities. You can't start a local press and form the community afterwards; by our law of historical inevitability the community evolves and produces its own newspaper.

This is why we are publishing the Notting Hill Herald; it has now become an inevitability, as the evolution of Notting Hill into a community that is working for itself is seen to be an inevitability. The Herald has simply come into being; well, not simply, because the community hasn't got far enough yet to be able to dispense with money and we need money to print the paper.

So we are appealing for funds; and not only for the Herald. The Herald will be published by a group called The West London Free Press. Later the WLFP will publish any printed material that fills a gap in Notting Hill. One of the first things will be a free poetry service, subsidised by profits from the commercial productions like the Herald.

At the moment the press, and this applies to local newspapers as well as nationals, is a one-way media—from newspaper to reader. Editors look at events and decide what their readers are interested in. In fact media, by definition, is a two-way rubber ball. Things happen, and they get reflected; ideas are expressed, and they get reflected; moods are present, and they get reflected. Now newspapers make the news; it's a crazy situation but inevitable. If you think of the lack of communication between readers in their environments and the editors in their Fleet Street offices. We will be reflecting an area, acting as a catalyst and, in the truest sense, a medium. We will disseminate information. We will exist only to collect relevant information

tion and pass it on.

If you think you can help, we'll be glad to hear form you. What we really need is money. Once this thing has started, it won't stop. The revenue will pay for the printing with, we hope, some left over for free literature. But the WLFP has to be set up. Donations to: West London Free Press, 1 Glendower Place, SW7. We'll let you know what's happening as soon as.

FIVE

The Assasination of Mavrogenis. Who is next?

On May 29 the body of George Mavrogenis was found in a forest fifteen miles north of Copenhagen. He had been shot through the head. His widow, Brigit Mavrogenis, only stated that she believed his death to be a political murder. Mavrogenis, a member of the Central Unionparty, had once been press attaché at the Greek Embassy in Copenhagen, but after the coup of April 1967, he had quit his post and founded a resistance movement against the dictatorial regime in Greece. In view of the fact that anti-junta resistance groups in Europe are being watched and followed by assassination squads sponsored by the present illegal government in Greece, it is not too much to believe that this is only the first of a coming string of assassination attempts. The junta appears to fear freedom among Greeks outside its well-patrolled borders almost as much as it fears freedom at home.

From: Democrita, June 19

A Quote from the New York Times

'Athens, June 1. The Education Minister, Theophylaktos Papaconstantinou, in a circular made public today, warned that the police had been asked to report, reprimand or even arrest children violating (New Teenage decorum) rules out of school.'

Got any news, information, rumours? Send it to Spike, c/o OZ.

SIX

Second best disc jockey, according to the Melody Maker awards, is Tony Blackburn. Tony was so incensed at John Peel's victory, that he wrote to Melody Maker claiming Peel didn't really qualify as a pop DJ and that the award should go to himself.

SEVEN

After repeated requests for money due, gentle Michael X recently became impatient at the offices of International Times and drew a knife. He left satisfied.

SEVEN

Living up to our reputation for string pulling, nepotism and corruption, the editor of this magazine urges all readers to buy his sister's new novel The Girl who played Gooseberry by Jill Neville. Biased as he is, the editor thinks this book is funny, sad, stylish, unexpected and profound. Buy it and swell the family exchequer. (Weidenfeld & Nicolson 25/-)

Also highly recommended is The Beginning of the End, by Angelo Quattrocchi and Tom Nairn (Panther) with its extraordinary mixture of poetry and logic.

Note to media men: OZ Advertising Manager, John Leaver is nightly washer-upper at Muffins Restaurant in Ifield Road SW10. Come, enjoy scallops mornay, rosemary lamb and tequila; while John's rinsing your dishes you can discuss next month's advertisement.

HUNG·ON·YOU
230 Kings Road
End-of-the World

EIGHT

The Decca bureaucracy is notoriously cowardly and conservative. The only thing they like about the Rolling Stones is the money they earn. Despite fierce battles last fortnight, Decca still refuse to accept the Stones' LP cover and have again delayed issue of the.

Beggars Banquet. Says a Stones publicist: 'Where will it stop?' If we let them change the cover, they'll begin interfering with the lyrics.' Meanwhile their 45, Street Fighting Man, which is not released in England and banned in Chicago, is enjoying discreet brisk sales in One Stop Records (in Oxford Street).

NINE

Both the BBC and Thames television have turned down a Dutch made documentary on the late Biafra, now showing to packed houses in Amsterdam. The film is considered 'too anti British' It depicts, in gruesome detail, the bombing and slaughter, showing how whole generations of Biafrans have been wiped out. The film also details the British arms bargain sale.

TEN

If Middle Earth folds it will be due to the single minded efforts of Superintendent Smith of Bow Street Police Station. His merry men were responsible for the fatal raid on its Covent Garden premises and they've been harassing Middle Earth ever since. When the GLC closed the roundhouse on Saturday 28 September, alternative arrangements were hurredly made at the Lyceum. At 3.30 pm, £350 was paid to its manager for the planned Canned Heat concert that night. A few hours later, Smith's heavies swooped in and warned the Lyceum's manager against accomodating the grooving junkies. Canned Heat was canned once more.

Middle Earth have asked OZ to print the following warning:

In future, anyone found pushing, carrying or fixing will be grabbed and turned over to the police immediately.

UPS

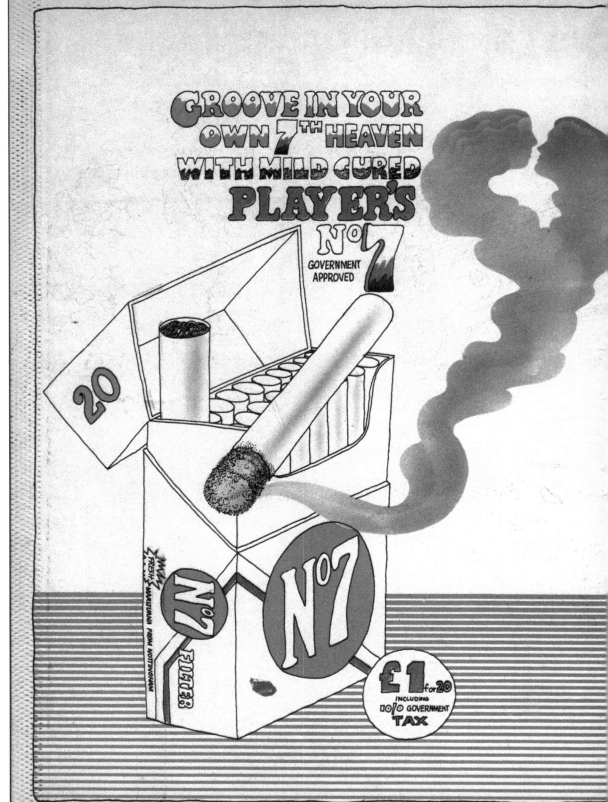

Flip Top Legal Pot

Legalise Pot rallies are so beautiful; hundreds of doe-eyed painted people stirring slowly under the soft sky, bound together by their sense of gentle daring in a common cause, holding smoking incense sticks like they were precious aphrodisiacs or opium pipes at least. Not less beautiful, but probably more so because their beauty is not compromised by utility. If pot is legalised it won't be capitulation to this kind of demand: when our masters decide to have pot on their side it is dubious whether it will be to our ultimate advantage.

It is clear that nobody wants to be penalised for doing something harmless and pleasant, but do we really want our pot legal?

Champions of legality do, because the law against marijuana is too clear an example of the arbitrary nature of the law, but to many of us the notion of law itself is antipathetic. The law exists, we are told, to protect life and property. It protects life by outlawing abortion, euthanasia and suicide, ie: it insists on life even when it is unbearable to the liver. It cannot be proved ever to have prevented a murder or an assault, and can be proved to have legally killed and to have penalised those who refused to fight and kill. Police brutality is legal massacre. In the interest of life, it proscribes marijuana, as a dangerous drug less habit forming than tobacco and coffee and considerably less harmful to the organism than alcohol and aspirin. If the law did protect life or could protect life against war, madness, or disaster perhaps there would be some point in wooing legality, but there seems to be no point at all in respecting it as the safeguard of property. Many of us do not believe in the inalienable right of property, to the extent that we possess little or nothing, and do not complain when it is used or carried off by others, and tend ourselves to use and carry off the goods of others, especially department stores and bookstalls, and yet I do not find posters saying

Legalise Theft.

Everything that I do can be guaranteed to annoy a guardian of the law in a certain frame of mind, and yet I cannot join any movement to

Legalise Offensive Behaviour.

It would be less soft-headed, and consequently more beautiful, if equally futile, to rally in Hyde Park under the banner

Fuck The Law.

The signers of petitions to legalise cannabis go to some lengths to distinguish themselves from the criminal classes. Of the thousands who would sign and maybe did, the publicised names were priests, members of parliament, pop intellectuals, jurists and doctors, stooges of the establishment, some of whom were so rosily innocent of the irrational nature of arbitrary opposition that they cried out in amazement when they were passed over in the race for more eminent positions within the establishment. Others were so firmly entrenched that they didn't have to worry. You can't revoke MBE's.

The legalisation of cannabis has been rejected by a confidential tip to advise the Home Secretary on drugs in Britain. They recommend, however, that the penalties for possessing cannabis should be reduced.

The committee...

The rest of you, stop and consider before you rally again, what legalisation would mean. Our masters will not legalise marijuana until they have worked out how to control it, which means *how to exploit it.* When the cigarette companies have finally lost their battle to conceal the relationship between smoking and lung cancer, they will begin pressurising for legalised marijuana (and ought to be designing the scene right now). Their economic pressure is more powerful and more subtle than the unintelligible ravings of a few unamplified hysterics among the doe-eyed crowds

...judge.

In deciding against legalising cannabis the committee felt that knowledge of its effects was insufficient to justify a change. It was also recognised that legalisation would break international agreements on drugs.

of Hyde Park. Governments get a useful slice of revenue from cigarettes, otherwise tobacco would already have been outlawed. The potential rakeoff from pot is enormous—it's even more than what goes to the pushers.

Then the advertising campaigns will begin: all the young executive prestige shit will gather round the kind of joint one smokes. They'll come in flip-top boxes and be lit with Dunhills, photographed on malachite bedside tables, with automatic pistols and platinum cuff-links. All the slow ritual of rolling a joint, the gentle rhythm of passing it from lip to lip . . . all the communion of the shared conspiracy gone. The smoke won't be as good either, adulterated with commercial products, dry and stale from being too long in the packet, or the shop, or the machine.

Maybe it won't happen that way, only one thing is certain: if pot is legalised, it won't be for our benefit but for the authorities'. To have it legalised, will be also to lose control of it.

The alternative is to join the criminal classes and be done with it. Regard the law as your enemy (it is actually impartial to all but itself) and take steps to lick it. The negro, prevented from joining the whites on his own terms, closes the ghetto to the white man. The pot smoker may reject legality and work instead to promote lawbreaking in that form, as far as possible with impunity. To begin with Stop Getting Caught.

Any London con can tell you that you're more likely to get caught when you aren't doing anything wrong than when you are, so it's nonsense to think that you need not develop any routines to protect yourself because you're not doing anything wrong. The law is not concerned with right and

wrong. Any criminal knows that the police will manufacture any evidence that they cannot find, and better it should be pot than detonators and gelignite, or heroin. He also knows that in all but the rarest cases (like if you're a bishop in mufti) it is worse than useless to claim having been framed. Learn how to deal with the police. The great evidence manufacturing industry is part of that legality pot smokers are so anxious to get on the right side of. Fuck it. (One way you could fuck it, if you are caught, is to insist on the exact amount you were carrying being declared in court, so the cops don't keep half of it to plant on somebody else.)

Most criminals know the law very well: pot smokers don't bother to find out. You should know exactly how little you have to tell the fuzz. If the cops stop you on the street asking what's in your paper bag, especially if it's obviously records, pause before letting them search the rest of you long enough to hurl your gear into the nearest front garden or down the grating or into a crowd, or somewhere. Even if they find it, it's a different matter to prove that it's what you threw. Even if you're not carrying anything you could throw something else just to confuse

things. Another way is to carry some harmless substance like basil leaves, or sugar cubes, or sugar pills, so that they think that they've found the gear and don't bother to fit you up, and only after tests discover their error. The tests are too documented and too public to be rigged (I think). Learn the criminal's rule, to protect your own, especially your connection, and don't as one idiot did toss your gear to someone else when you're getting busted. Remember ignorance of the contents of a parcel is no defence. If you're in a public place which is getting busted drop the gear on the floor because it can't be traced to you and the management is for it anyway, that's if you can't drop it in the can in time. Awful to think of the stuff the fuzz gets hold of for free. Don't leave gear at home: if you must have it around it's safer on you, especially if you're staying with a friend. Don't stockpile it: let the pushers do that: for them it's a calculated risk.

There are more ways out, and we must develop them. If, like Mafia and Prohibition we succeed well enough in breaking the law and not getting caught, it will paradoxically have more effect in getting pot legalised, than all the pious ejaculations and gormless pleas for gentler sentences, because people cannot be allowed to get away with things. We have certain advantages over criminals of a less self-conscious type, so let's use them.

If after all you really must have your pot legal, you can always get a prescription for tincture of cannabis, an innocent corn cure, and have your own bottle of filthy green liquid, and your own little spoon.

Germaine.

Janet Golding

I CAN'T ESCAPE

The emptiness in my arms is an evil force, driving me to inexorable ruin. To satisfy my needs, I am willing to gamble away everything.

by Myra Norris

I had the dream again last night. It was so real that I awoke with my body sweat-drenched. Even after I was fully conscious, I seemed to feel the hands roaming over me, taking their pleasure, meeting no resistance on my part.

I rolled over in our huge double bed. I reached out my hand. My fingers touched Don's undented pillow. I withdrew them as if they had touched a loathsome reptile. With growing awareness, I recalled that Don would be away another ten days. The swing through the mid-west district wouldn't be curtailed for hell or high water. These junkets never are.

And I don't dare complain. I have no right to. The house we live in, the clothing I wear, the insurance policies which protect the children and myself are all very much involved in Don's journeys to his company's district offices.

But as I listened to the ticking of the clock and glanced down the length of my naked body, I knew that I would be taking action again. And the thought sickened me.

"You're no better than a cheap whore," I told myself. The words bit into me with the force of a whip blow. No woman likes to think of herself in these terms.

I rolled over on my stomach and buried my face in my arms. I tried to will myself back to sleep. It was useless. The quivering in my loins, the ache in my belly, the pounding of my heart against my breasts wouldn't allow sleep. Finally I rose and watched the dawn come up in the eastern sky.

At breakfast I managed not to betray my innermost feelings to the kids. I packed their lunch boxes, herded them into the Mustang and got them to school. I hoped that their innocence would not be destroyed by their mother. Yet I knew there was a distinct possibility that it would. Supposing Don found out.

You never can tell about that. You're never safe. There's always the unexpected return, the gossiping neighbor, the telltale clue.

Yet knowing all these things wasn't enough to stop me. I pulled into the parking lot behind the Double E and found a phone booth. I trembled so that I found it difficult to insert the coin into the slot. "Make him be at home!" I breathed.

The receiver buzzed once; twice. Although the day wasn't particularly warm, the clammy sweat broke out along the length of my spine.

Then: "Hello?"

"Jack, darling."

"Hey, it isn't even nine o'clock yet."

"I have to see you. Are you free?"

"For you? You bet your round little bottom. And don't let anybody pinch it until I get there. Give me an hour to shave and clean up."

"The usual place?"

"The usual, naturally."

THE usual place is a suite in a motel near Kennedy International Airport that Jack's firm keeps for visiting firemen. Cars pull in and out all day long and there are never any questions asked.

I could scarcely breathe with the excitement that gripped me. It was an excitement tinged with the worst possible feelings of panic and guilt. *(Continued on page 54)*

(Continued on page 54)

Ho! Ho! Ho!

CONFESSIONS OF A

MY PASSION DRIVES-

I demand the passion and I hate myself for it. My sick hunger has made me worse than a common street-walker, it has destroyed my hope of ever being the faithful woman my husband married.

FAITHLESS SUBURBAN WIFE

Alan Aldridge's book jacket for 'Drop Out' by Robin Farquharson (Blond 25s October). Last winter Dr Farquharson suspended a successful career and 'dropped out': his book is an impression of contemporary society seen from the bottom up.

Revolution '68
The right story's
the left one

So read **The Beginning of the End: France, May 1968** by Angelo Quattrocchi and Tom Nairn, two non-compromising writers of the Left who tell it like it is. Angelo was there. Tom wasn't but what the Hell, he still knows what it's all about better than any press-room full of capitalist mass-media pundits. So will you—when you've read him.

Even more so if you also read **The Student Revolt: the Activists Speak** with contributions, interviews and so on from Cohn-Bendit, the March 22 Committee, etc., etc. **Both 6s** Both published by

(Panther)

MIDDLE EARTH
AT THE ROUNDHOUSE, CHALK FARM

October 12th   Peter Green's Fleetwood Mac
                Joe Cocker
                Doctor K's Bluesband

October 19th   Pink Floyd
                Blue Cheer (the loudest
                group in the world)

For further programme details ring 01-229 1438 or consult Melody Maker.

DREAMING OF A RED CHRISTMAS

David Widgery

It moves. After two decades of devout leaning against locked doors, the left has walked into two or three of the boudoirs of power and begun to convince people about the secret passages they found there. 1968 is decisive historical punctuation quite as important as 1917, 1872 and 1848. What makes it so critical is not just Paris in May or Prague in August or the Gold Crisis which made the bankers hearts go cold everywhere this year, but the impact of all three on people and their politics. The separate proofs add up to a revolutionary theorum. Paris showed the flush of energy and resourcefulness released by workers who according to the script was hopelessly conned, cajoled and cut and dried by the system. Prague (and its echo and cameo in Chicago) which showed again, if further proof were needed after '53 and '56, that the Communist World has nothing to do with socialism and the Free World has even less to do with freedom . . . neither side really objects to slaughter in the streets as long as it stays the right side of the fence. The gold crisis too has collision which ought not to have been able to happen but which has left the banks bleeding and the growth rates amputated. The authorised version of two hostile and incompatible social systems, has been shown, unignorably on 100 million cathode tubes, as two intolerable systems of human human domination. The revolutionaries are those, in the Mekong Delta, the Chicago stockyards, the Oakland courthouses,

the factory action committee and the college lecture hall in France, fighting, sometimes winning, but recognising and naming Capital and its lieutenants and integuments. The left for which for twenty years has been huddled to keep warm round various campfires in the dark and shouting insults at one another, has at last seen the glory of a mass movement without which they looked, and were, a joke.

After France and Enoch in the absence of a popular party, stalinist or social democratic, many workers are feeling the need for politics; many engineers are reluctant about their national strike precisely because they realise that without real politics it will get smashed with both arms tied behind its back. Those who (mis reading Marx) thought that workers had to be driven by misery will see them beckoned by ideas, ideas which take on a power of their own in the world of chimneys and girders. The programme is increasingly simple; the system stinks and it moves over if you push it hard enough.

Just to take one example, that of the struggle of council tenants, now almost entirely working class since the Town Hall has largely replaced the private landlord who can make a bigger profit in building office blocks and middle class commuter estates. In 1915, a group of Glasgow housewives decided to knock the rent increases and they fought on their own with

broomsticks, dustbin lids and pails of water to throw at the Council bailiffs. The court cases were blockaded by thousands of workers from the shipyards, the foundries and the munitions factories. Soldiers informed by letters to the front began to talk of mutiny. In insurrectionary crises, the first Rent Act was passed fixing the rent at the pre-war level . . . many tenants are still living on the gains of this victory. In '39 tenants took over the control of their buildings during rent strikes in Birmingham and the East End, at Langdale Mansions Police had to negotiate with tenants pickets before being allowed through to interview a man who had committed a crime. In St Pancreas in 1960 when 400 police and 28 bailiffs sprung a surprise raid, housewives waving frying pans ran to building workers on the Shell south bank site and and railmen in the Camden Goods Yard who marched back to the estate and routed the forces of law and order. The bailiffs report describes the flat of one of the evicted tenants: 'The original door has been removed and a bulkhead lined with steel plates six inches thick fastened in its place, buttressed with heavy baulks of timber. The windows too, were firmly secured with thick planks. Work was commenced on the door but no impression made. Attention was then turned to the window and a hole made, through which the defendent kept up a steady fire of bottles'. This October 240,000 GLC tenants face the first of four yearly increases in rent with wages frozen and unemployment the highest since the war, there are already signs that if the Council try evictions it could be on the scale of Glasgow, already dockers and car workers have promised support and there have been massive tenant demonstrations in Central London which the press has systematically ignored.

But if the systems growing economic jerkyness will generate new political failure will express itself in the electoral responses of the middle class. Not only does the system creak at its arthritic joints and its trade pulse wander and grow more reedy. But as a civilisation, as a set of abstract values, as a way of life, modern capitalism is not just in a state of terminal melancholia, it has actually ceased to exist. The tone of its ideology is prematurely drained of any optimism, just listen to the language of Humphrey's speeches, stubborn in his tonsils. Its rhetoric meanders from a mystified scolding to an irrational violence. For not only did the end of the Undemocratic Convention in Chicago exemplify the systems inability to recognise the one man, McCarthy, which might be able to save it from within, but McCarthy himself was unable to do anything outside the definitions of the system except go on thinking like Thomas Aquinas and acting like Florence Nightingale.

We are in the process of seeing quite how far most quondam liberals are prepared to go in order to keep their own indignation safely in leash. In the States, the time is long past being against the war, but please Mr President a little less bombing against the draft but Hell we'll go, nothing against pot and LSD we'd love to try some, some day. But now in Britain the tone of public liberalism (fulsome or inwardly degrading on the party in power) is becoming increasingly inconvenient. It should not be lost on us that it is the Observer which is offering bright ideas about anti-riot weapons, William Rees-Mogg who front pages the nicer lies

about forthcoming insurrections and lovable Labour back benchers whining ignorantly about riot suppression.

What the black community and working class militants have known for generations is being painfully discovered by those middle class intellectuals who have previously cherished and disseminated the most endearing illusions about the basic decency of our system. Now even they are coming to realise that modern Britain was built on blood, the ache of mens muscles, skulls and gravestones, and that it was built by gangsters and thieves. The difference is that until recently this bloody part of the business has been done out of sight, in India, Malaya, the far East, Greece and the Labour Camps of South Wales and the Industrial North which are as foreign countries. But now, and from now on, the police courts the cells, the senior common rooms and the graduate employment exchanges is showing the privileged something of the methods the system has used to oppress the rest of the world.

Middle class rebelliousness and bourgeois hooliganism has other intriguing results. It seems to be leading the guilty sons and daughters of the British bourgeoisie to adopt, as a grotesque touchness, the romantic illusion that violence of itself is strengthening and purifying. Certainly the evidence suggests that the revolutionary class is always the subject of attack and that without self defence the active non-violence of socialist society cannot be created. In that sense, soft core pacifism is not only a delusion but a dangerous snare because it leaves the agressor in possession of the initiative. But the sons of gentle folk bragging of how hard they hit a copper is as repulsive as violence for its own sake is anywhere and has nothing, repeat nothing, to do with socialism. The idea of violence as the highest form of class struggle and the superiority of racial nationalism to socialist internationalism are simply crude rationalisations of the absence of mass strength on any mass industrial

support in Britain and the inability of the rationalisers to go about getting any. In all probability, the demands in England to demonstrate 'that power is in the street' will in fact simply demonstrate that power is sitting in front of his TV watching the Golden Shot. Students, layabouts and undergraduates simply lack any point of purchase on the system. Which is not to say there are not a good deal of things that can be done usefully done.

A pleasant start might be for British hippies to stop being sentimental and lazy about the system, and going on as if their highest aim is to teach in oriental beatitude. If one per cent of the celestial beings who say

packed a gross
and commercial
Doors Airplane concert
devoted themselves
to throwing
accurate
yoghurt
bombs at
the
Queen or undressing in Court we would be a lot better off. And the more obsessive of the Guevara fans ought to start realising that out in Sierra Maestre is the council estates and skill of formulating leaflets is more valuable than knowledge of a carbine. And everyone ought to start realising that words like redundancy and unemployment, so effortlessly slotted into polished diagrams means grown men with families and without jobs not sure how to replace last years school uniform which has holes in it, wives forced to do three hours cleaning floors before most of us are up, husbands doing the washing up and sitting around in the kitchen, real holes, real floors, real people. The whole present is about these people, their needs and then fight to defend and win them. The moment is more constructive now than at any time since the War intellectuals of the world,

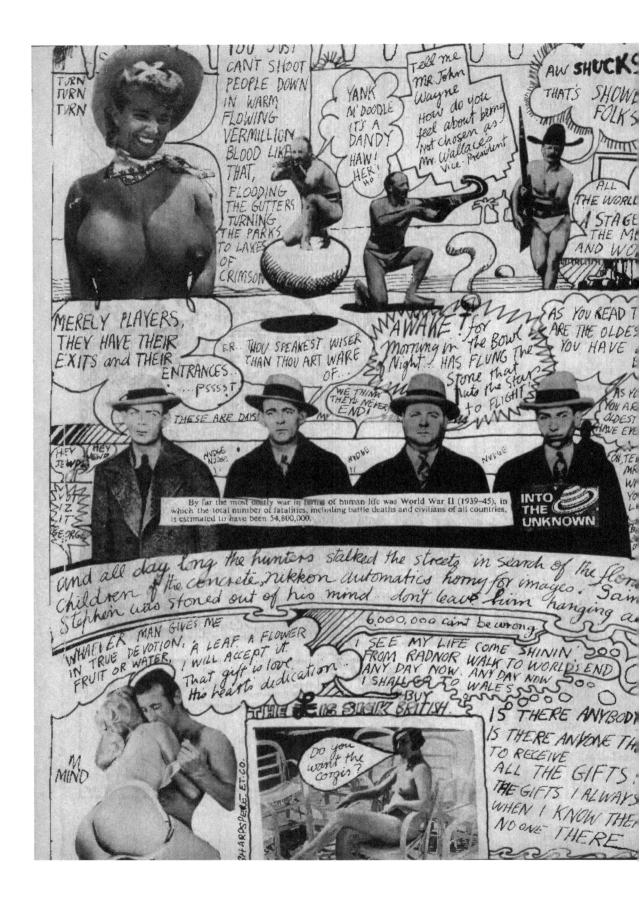

'If you want to make a revolution first take over the television.'

'If only we had our hands on television we could transform society'

'If THEY didn't have firm control of the BBC and the ITV they wouldn't stay in power another week.'

'How true is all that?'

Television is a revolutionary medium but that doesn't mean that it can be used to transform consciousness within any given society. The attitude of people towards the television medium is inherently revolutionary in the sense that it contains a built-in demand to control that medium but television can only illuminate the information about a society that its inhabitants already possess in general terms.

Most public discussion about television programmes isn't fundamentally discussion about quality—it is argument about what ought and ought not to be shown.

If you don't like a book you take it back to the library; if you don't like a play or a film you walk out; if you don't like a newspaper you change to another one. If you hate a television programme you complain to the relevant authorities and ask them to take it off. In every television viewer, and I don't believe there are really any exceptions to this, there is a thwarted programme controller.

In other words with television as with no other medium, there is an automatic demand on the part of the recipients to exercise control.

'At the same time there is an automatic simultaneous demand on the part of the authorities to exercise control. Both government and viewer share the identical underlying supposition, that to communicate pictures to half the population is to be able to mould society. Every individual viewer knows of certain things that he doesn't want his fellow citizens to hear or believe for fear that this will ultimately alter the way society operates; every government fears that its functions will be, in some mysterious way, usurped or its own political structure altered or disrupted, if certain categories of ideas and information circulate on the enormous scale on which the television medium operates. In other words both series of pressures upon television are pressures towards *censorship and self-censorship;* all discussion hitherto conducted about the organisation of the medium of television has been discussion about

ways to tie it up, to prevent it realising its believed potential. But there is in fact no reason to accept that it has any such potential, any power to influence people much beyond the point they've already reached.

Of course television has never operated outside conditions of thorough control of one sort or another in any part of the world; there's no way to test this argument.

But there are certain things we do know. If you use television consistently as a means of lying and distortion you create a situation in which the medium as a whole is disbelieved. The greater the degree of control by government and party over television in, say, the Soviet Union or pre-Dubcek Czechoslovakia, the lower the level of public credence. The same really goes for France.

If Brezhnev himself took control of Czech television and changed all the personnel to suit his own ends (as he might well do) he wouldn't succeed in persuading a significant proportion of the Czechs that the Russian troops moved in to stop a counter-revolution. He might terrorise them simultaneously into signing pieces of paper to that effect but no matter what proofs he might present, if his message failed to match the actual experience of the people watching he would fail to convince them.

Television operates within the area of accepted consciousness. Governments in insist on keeping tabs on it in one way or another 'to keep it out of irresponsible hands' but although television can be used to make the gentle shifts in public opinion necessary to shift Douglas-Home for Wilson or Wilson for Heath no set of hands, however 'irresponsible' could use the medium to shift the system of government out of existence.

But there is still this inherently democratic demand by the viewer to take charge of himself. What about that?

Television seems to bring out the authoritarian in people, whatever their alleged views on politics in general. It has the power to accelerate changes in ideas and tastes but the kind of influence it wields in this field is more apparent than real; a social change engineered by a spate of programmes is apt to evaporate overnight when something else comes along—unless there is a real basis for that change existing quite independently of television.

The point is that the revolutionary element in the nature of television occurs in the instances when it makes the unconscious feelings of masses of people conscious and explicit, when something hits the screen that people already know but didn't realise could be openly stated. Recently you had in Britain a programme that went fairly thoroughly into the question of the behaviour of the police towards black immigrants; previously no-one on a really public medium had drawn attention to a widespread phenomenon of maltreatment. After the programme many papers said the 'police had won' and the usual liberal elements contended that the 'police had lost' and it was left at that; but no-one troubled to find out what had happened to the consciousness of immigrants themselves after the programme. For the first time something that related peculiarly to their experience was dragged into the open and turned into a fixed point of public discussion, known about, argued about. For them the television programmed had of course changed nothing at all as far as their physical well-being was concerned, but it had subtly altered an aspect of their identity as a group within British society.

Television could build upon the desire of the viewer to take charge of it; it has a strange power to take what an individual or a small group realise is happening to them or within them and generalise upon it with an entire society looking on. The problem is how the viewer, on one level participating less in regard to this medium than in the case of any other, thrusts his private or unconscious realisations towards the people who fill the screens. How does the television medium scramble out of the bonds with which the authorities and the viewers continually leash it up and realise a series of potentials that would be profoundly revolutionary?

I don't know. Perhaps you have to have the revolution first.

BARRICADES AROUND THE SMALL SCREEN

You thousands of Underground children who will queue up all night in the cold and pay ludicrous prices to squat on a concrete floor and worship a fashionable, imported pop group, with your vision obscured by a plethora of tv cameras should remember that Her Majesty's Courts provide regularly, free of charge, spectacles of even greater absurdity and entertainment.

One memorable judicial 'happening' was the trial of Michael X at Reading (see OZ No 7) and another was the recent prosecution of Bill Butler in a Brighton 'part-time' Magistrates court.

On August 29, Butler was convicted by a car salesman, a Labour Exchange manager (retired) and an auctioneer's wife for selling obscene prose and poetry, and fined £230 plus 180 guineas costs. When passing judgement, the Chief Magistrate, Mr ('laughing Jack') Ripper commented.

'May I say how appalled my Colleagues and I have been at the filth that has been produced at this Court, and at the fact that responsible people including members of the university faculty have come here to defend it. It is something which is completely indefensible from our point of view. We hope that these remarks will be conveyed to the university authorities. As far as the book Poems by John Giorno, this is the most filthy book I have ever had to read.'

At one stage during the proceedings, Bill Butler was asked by the Prosecution, who hoped to embarrass him, to read aloud from that book of poems by the filthy John Giorno. Butler did so—with a rich, resonant bellow that delighted the gallery, discomforted the Prosecutor and educated the Bench. Another highlight was when the exasperated Prosecutor (Mr Michael Worsley) asked Butler: 'But why do people read such poems?'

'Because', answered Butler wearily, 'poetry is one of the few things left that makes life worth living anymore'.

'Fucknam' by Tuli Kupferberg, a Fug, was one of the items condemned. As the Defence pointed out, it was ironic that this was considered to be dirty, when the butt of its satire, Vietnam, is in reality a far greater and crueller obscenity.

The most comic moments in court were, as usual, provided by the police. One item confiscated was an issue of a New Underground tabloid, 'East Village Other'. The front page pictured a scattering of numbered dots and the headline read something like 'You will be arrested if you join these dots'. The exhibit was tendered with the dots joined. But it was admitted by the Crown that the dots had not been joined by the Defendant. So who had completed the dirty picture? 'Er . . . we did' muttered the embarrassed assembly of plain-clothesmen. (They were not arrested.)

3,000 copies of OZ and some issues of IT were also seized by police at the time of the raid. Although these had been dropped from this prosecution it was clearly hinted at in Court that separate

action may follow against the publishers. We cannot give official opinion on the verdict, because Butler has decided to Appeal and OZ does not possess the immunity of 'The Times' from *sub judice* proceedings. However, know your enemy. We offer a condensation of the Prosecutor's final address to the Bench. It also should be pointed out that almost all of the iniquitous items are available in London bookshops or were at the time of publication. One final sadness; none of the publishers of the works prosecuted (eg. Corgi, and New English Library) offered any assistance to Butler. Evergreen Review didn't even bother to answer Butler's letters.

Extracts from
Mr Michael Worsley's closing speech:

Thirdly I would like to say a word about the defences expert witnesses. I have not called any expert evidence to rebut it and I take full responsibility for this decision. The reason for this is because I rely on your examination (he is referring to the Magistrates) of the works themselves to rebut the defence of public good. It is obvious that these books are obscene and it would not be in the public good for them to be published. The Court is perfectly open not to accept the Defendants experts. I concede that not every page of every work is obscene. One would have different views about whether it is good or bad and this is not a question of whether this is disgusting but whether it is obscene. I rely on this Court knowing a dirty book when they see one despite all the expert evidence and all the high-sounding language which was used.

Fourthly I should now like to say a word briefly about each of the witnesses in turn. First the Defendant Butler he has given his opinion about particular works, for example the pornographic poem. This is unmitigated filth, but Butler said and others said that it had literary merit. Whether Butler is sincere or not I believe he may be, and he may have devoted his life to literature or not, but anyone capable of saying that this poem is of literary merit shows that you cannot rely on their evidence. You have seen this poem, I wonder what this country is coming to, if we can say that this sort of filth has literary merit and should be published in the public interest.

As to Mrs Anne Graham-Bell, she is a lady, if I may say so, of the utmost respectability and honesty. She told us that this material would help publishers, but this of course is irrelevant as we are only concerned with the publication

which was intended under these circumstances. As to the extract from The Story of O in Evergreen 31 she disclaimed any desire to deal with this which shows clear evidence of bias. She thought that once a person became an adult they could not be corrupted, this is of course wrong, as you (the Magistrates) well know. She is not to know the evil to which these sort of things lead.

As to Mr Mottram, he said that the 'pornographic poem' had literary merit. The Defence did not even admit that certain passages were disgusting and obscene they tried to defend everything, even this poem. Mr Mottram is a moral tutor of students, yet he said that if his students could only find sexual fulfilment through sadistic perversion it would be a good thing for them.

Objection by Defence
This was a completely hypothetical point and indeed a silly hypothesis. It was my recollection that Mr Mottram said if they did that and nothing else and if this was the only way they could fulfil themselves there being no other way then it would be a good thing, this changes the context of the remark and, therefore, the shades of meaning given to it.
(There seemed to be some dispute between the notes on evidence taken by the Prosecution and the Defence as to precisely what Mr Mottram did say).

Worsley continuing.

Reference was made to the judgement of Mr Justice Stable in the case of *Secker v Warburg* about the standards of our time. I should like to point out that the material in that case was concerned with a natural love between man and woman not with buggery, sadism, orgies etc. Mr Justice Stable does not countenance or approve the kind of practices concerned here. In many cases he has shown his extreme distaste, dislike and disgust for buggery.

As to *Section 4 (1)* (objects of general concern) which includes political objects for example Vietnam—if one has compassion one does not need to hold the heads of the readers over the muck-heap to express it. This does not drive a decent man to filth.

I rely on you (the Justices) knowing a dirty book when you see one. I would only repeat that you know a dirty book when you see one.

S DIRTY BOOKS

obscenity is official !

Hunke's Journal
Hitler Painted R...
Poems by Bill Deemer
Poems by John Giorno
Ritual
Say My Name by Gibson
I Want to Fuck Ronald Reagan by J G Ballard
Customs No 8 (with 'Fucknam' by Tuli Kupferberg)
Grist
Kulchur No 9 (with 'Toilet' by Le Roy Jones) No 16
          No 19 (with 'Yoga Exercises' by Tom Veith)
Best of Olympia
East Village Other
The Last Times (contains Plymel)
The Seed
Evergreen Review: No 15; No 16 ('Justine' by de Sade;)
No 27 (Robert Ce Soir;)
No 36 (Lovers of Roissy from 'The Story of O' by Pauline Reage;)
No 34 (Last Exit to Brooklyn;)
No 35 (Pinktoes;) No 36 ('Justine' by de Sade)
and Nos 38, 40, 41, 43—50.

G. METSON

A TURNING ON TO THE DIVINE GAME...

The following text is an interview between a group of people, which included children, and Dr Allan Cohen, Counselling Psychologist at the University of California. He was a colleague of Dr Timothy Leary and Dr Richard Alpert during early researches into LSD and similar drugs. His disillusionment with chemicals as a means to conciousness enhancement brought him to Meher Baba who says that true self-knowledge can only be gained through a natural process of evolving and unfolding conciousness. Dr Cohen was recently in London to give a series of lectures.

Q: Meher Baba says that everything is nothing. God is the only reality and that he says to give up drugs. Why should you give up drugs if they aren't real? Its just like a dream you know. You just dream about taking drugs. Like I dream about living. So why give up drugs at all?

AC: *In a dream many things can happen. Some of the events that occur in a dream make me dream more deeply, other events in a dream can help you wake up! If you take as the assumption, as Baba does, that the purpose of life is to fully wake up to who you really are, to infinite God, then there are certain things that help, certain things that hinder. Though all these things are illusory. For example, you could take drugs in a dream! And taking drugs in dreams gets you stoned, and gets you high, and you would perhaps be more complacent, perhaps satisfied in the dream to continue dreaming. In one sense you might do something difficult in your dream that might cause a small nightmare, and that small nightmare might be enough to get you to ask the question, can I wake up? And how can I wake up? Baba is simply saying about drugs, and he says this specifically, that if drugs are a dream into a dream, an extension of illusion, and that taking that dream into a dream as reality is as he says, like taking a mirage to water, and if the purpose of life is to drink of that self knowledge then taking drugs can harm one to waking up.*

Many people who have turned off drugs and moved on to mysticism are the real revolutionaries. They aim at more than change in local policy or revisions in the structure of the national government - they seek a revolution in the nature of man and seek to start with themselves. For many reasons outlined by Meher Baba as well as common sense, 'turning on' keeps you from permanent internal revolution. The perfect men have really changed the world—Buddha and Jesus had neither armies nor thrones. The real revolution is of that conciousness which none can control but yourself and which can even transcend the possibility of frustration. No matter how politically involved you might be, your first objective is to cool your own head, that with advanced love, conciousness and intuition, you might know exactly what to do to get where you know you want to be.

Q: I hear Baba calls himself God. If one man calls himself God, how do you know that he is God?

AC: *What else can he call himself when he is God? He says there is nothing but God. He not only says he is God, he says that ALL are God in varying degrees of consciousness. We are not conscious of our Godhood, and continue to experience the duality of illusion. He has the full consciousness and continuous experience of Godhood, and the authority to say: 'I am God!' He says that he is God in human form, the Avatar, the Ancient One who has come to redeem the modern world.*

Q: What's to stop me going out in the street, going up to someone and saying, 'I AM GOD'? Turning a lot of people on to the fact that I am God.

AC: *Besides bad Karma, you would have to HAVE those qualities which would shake the world.*

Q: If Baba says God is in everyone, why should I bother with Baba? Why can't I look towards myself and find the God within me.

AC: *Because you wouldn't know yourself if you saw it. Because we are not sufficiently conscious, we don't know who our Real Self is. That's precisely the reason why we can't follow it. And that's precisely the reason why we need a master who embodies our Real Selves in a way we can relate to it. In a way that will not fool us or let us down. When one follows his or her ego one is subject to all kinds of illusions and delusions because the ego is NOT the Real Self, and only the Master really knows what experiences one needs to get out of the illusion of self and find one's Real Self. Baba says I AM YOUR REAL SELF. And of course, that he loves you more than you could ever love yourself. Because, you don't know how to love yourself, he does. So it is absolutely essential, that at some stage of the spiritual path for everyone to* get hooked up with a perfect Master. Or to get hooked up with one's REAL SELF.

Q: If Baba is in silence, why does he write so many books and give so many explanations?

AC: Well Baba does say that he's keeping silent this time because for one thing man has had enough words! And its now time to live them. He's also in silence because it has great mystical significance. But about the books, he said that these are books only the words written to satisfy the intellect, the convulsions of mans' mind and intellect. Words are a signpost. At least it points the way to non reading.

Q: If one gets involved with Baba should one drop ones present religion or beliefs, like Christianity or Yoga etc?

AC: Baba says it's not necessary to leave one's religion. He belongs to no religion, in fact he intends to draw them altogether like beads on one string. If you follow Baba then you are a real Christian. Or you are a real Buddhist, because after all you are following Christ or the Buddha in Baba. Furthermore, every religion was based at least on a Perfect Master. Perfect Masters are the same consciousness as is Baba. However Baba does say that concentration on him is the perfect way. Looking into a whole lot of other methods might impede one, so it's best to concentrate one's energy on one source. On one Master.

Q: What are Baba's attitudes on sex and marriage?

AC: Well, Baba says that sex is the major duality of experience. The biggest one. In effect, the experience of being a man or a woman is the most powerful pull towards the illusion of duality. The most obvious crystallisation of that duality is in the physical form. It is trapped in a physical form in our identification as either a man or a woman, which really grabs our consciousness. When all other things can be wiped away we are all still pretty much attached to that kind of distinction. Baba says that because we are attached to the distinction we are unconsciously seeking to unite with the opposite, to become one, which is all motivation is anyway. Thus, the whole business of sex is to get the apparently male, and apparently female regions of consciousness together. Now, the question is, how do they get together? It depends on the part of illusion that one identifies with. If for example one is identifying totally with physical body, then the question of lust crops up. Apparently to get together just physically, well, it doesn't work, just on that level because it intensifies the separateness of the opposite partners. And it makes one acutely aware of missing them if they are not there in their physical body. If greed and jealousy appear we are still I and YOU, and the problem of getting together has not been fulfilled either. Another step up is getting together of the mind, the mental body. Then, possessiveness and lust leave. They cannot be conditions of a mental affiliation. Physical gratification can also not be a limitation to that kind of Love. And that kind is when the person really would like the happiness of the other no matter what. That's a very high form of attraction. That's where the duality starts to break down, because then I am with you wherever you are, and whatever you are doing, and the togetherness is much greater. But that then, is STILL limited because of I love you.   The origin of the sex drive is divine Love, where really the two elements unite into Oneness. This can happen in a pure consciousness, where the drive is not attached to the body, the emotions or the mind. Baba says the value of a really deep and sustained male-female relationship is to bring out all the deepest part of the ego, which has to be transcended.

Q: We were talking about the drive towards One-ness and so on, and the channels to take, but will we, or do you think it possible that evolution will eventually lead us all to God realisation? Like soon, we may be able to communicate telepathically, breaking down some barriers of separateness surely. Does Baba say that we will eventually stop reincarnating, all of us, and God reign only. Or do you always have to involve?

AC: The way Baba talks about it is that evolution is really cyclical that spiritual progress is obviously easier in certain ages. Like it's going to be a heck of a lot easier for all the people around after Baba speaks! That does not violate any of the individual Karma. For example, some cat that might really be zonked by the next Avatar in the Avataric age, seven hundred years from now, might today be a dog.

Mike McKinnery.

For more information on universal love, it's mystical and real meanings; The mechanics of the universe, the perception of illusion, the understanding of true self-knowledge, write to:--
The Universal Spiritual League, 87 Wardour Street, London W1.

poem by C.LOGUE drawn by MICHAEL ENGLISH, from NEW NUMBERS, Spring 69, Rapp & Whiting.

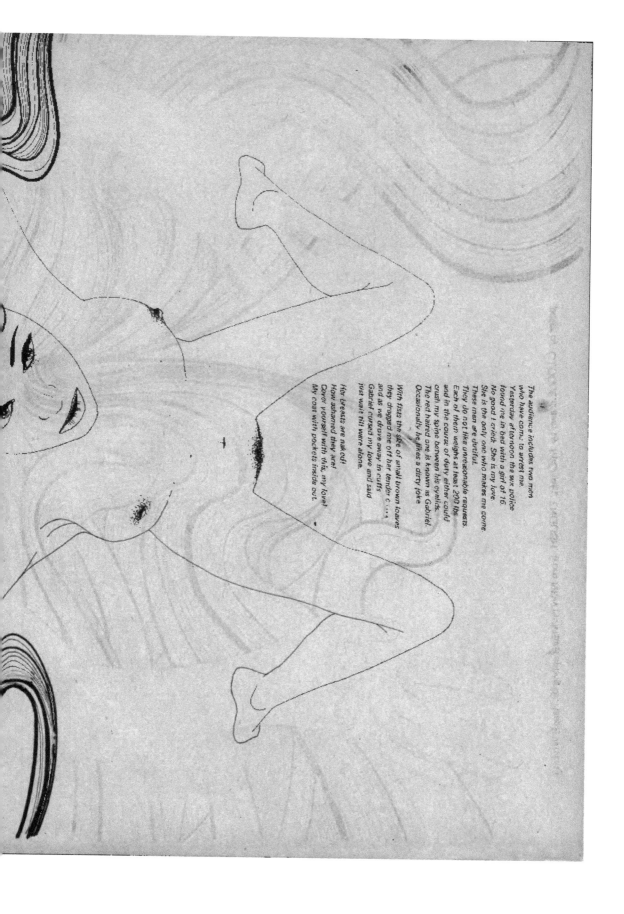

The audience includes two men
who have come to arrest me.
Yesterday afternoon the sex police
found me in bed with a girl of 16.
No good I cried. She is my love.
She is the only one who makes me come.
These men are dutiful.
They do not like unreasonable requests.
Each of them weighs at least 200 lbs
and in the course of duty either could
crush my spine between his eyelids.
The red haired one is known as Gabriel.
Occasionally he likes a dirty joke.

With fists the size of small brown loaves
they dragged me off her tender c....
and as we drove away in cuffs
Gabriel cursed my love and said
Just wait till we're alone.

Her breasts are naked!
How ashamed they are!
Cover yourself with this, my love!
My coat with pockets inside out.

continuity & discontinuity

Edward de Bono.©

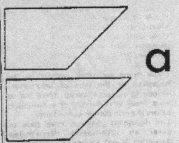

The two shapes shown above would be made out of thin plastic. The idea is to put them together to form a single shape that could be described accurately to someone who could not see what was being done. Almost everyone arranges the two shapes to form the rectangle shown below. This arrangement is either described simply as a rectangle or else as a rectangle that is three times as long as it is broad.

pic B.

A third piece is now added and as before the aim is to arrange all three pieces to give a shape that is easy to describe. Many people have quite a lot of difficulty over this but eventually (with annoyance at their slowness) reach the solution shown below. Other people reach this solution at once. Again this shape is described as a rectangle or as a rectangle that is four times as long as it is broad.

Pic C.

Two further pieces are added and the task is to arrange all five pieces to give a shape simple enough to describe. Most people become completely stuck at this stage. They think for a bit and then set off with a rush only to end up with disappointment at one or other of the shapes shown below. One of these is incomplete since a piece is left out and the other is not simple enough to be described comfortably. Many people give up and declare that it cannot be done.

Pic D.

And yet the answer is extraordinarily simple. A complete correct sequence is

Pic E.

The difficulty is that at the second stage the longer rectangle is indeed the most logical development from the shorter rectangle but use of this longer rectangle makes the third stage inaccessible. If, however, the square had been chosen at the second stage then the third stage follows easily since it just involves making the square bigger.

The plastic pieces provide a simple and visual model of a self-maximising system. At each stage the available pieces are put together to give the best possible arrangement. Unfortunately the system has continuity so the arrangement may not be the best possible pure arrangement of pieces but the best one that follows on from a previous arrangement. The rectangle was the best arrangement at the first stage. At the second stage the longer rectangle was the best arrangement given the preceding shorter rectangle. Yet at the second stage the square was obviously the best pure arrangement.

In order to reach the solution one would have to disrupt the continuity. One would have to refuse to be blocked by the adequate. One would accept the rectangle as perfectly adequate but would go on to discover alternative arrangements such as the square.

The pieces of plastic may be considered as pieces of information and the passive self-maximising system as a model of the information processing system of the brain. Traditionally information processing in the brain has always been regarded as a physical process analogous to the way a man might build a house by choice of units and choice of their distribution and relationships.

A computer is an example of a physical information processing system. In a physical system everything is at rest or in uniform motion in the same straight line unless acted upon by some force. In a biological system nothing is at rest unless so constrained by opposing tendencies.

The principles of biological information processing are fundamentally different from those of physical information

processing. In spite of the traditional view it seems very likely that the brain is not a physical information processing type of system but a biological type.

A physical type of system involves a processor and what is processed. The processor actively works on the material that is to be processed. A biological system is passive and self-organising. The material processes itself. The physical system works by choice within a frame of reference and requires some way of rejecting what does not fit. The biological system works by random generation followed by survival through natural dominance. There are many other points of distinction.

Perhaps the simplest difference to remember is that in a physical system one is not allowed to be wrong at any stage whereas in a biological system it may be necessary to be wrong at some stage.

There is a story about the man who asked a large cigarette manufacturer if he could have the contract for sweeping the floor in their factories. He was given the contract on condition that the waste tobacco was not used in any form which might compete with the firms products. Nevertheless the man made a fortune. No one knew how he had done it. In the end he disclosed that all he had done was to collect the waste tobacco and then dump it out at sea beyond the three mile limit and claim repayment of the duty. So strong is the continuity from the idea of tobacco to its usage that few people guess how the man made his fortune.

Words and categories tend to magnify this inherent defect of the information processing system since they freeze development at one stage. They imply that future arrangements can only be arrangements of these earlier stages rather than a complete disruption with proper reformation of patterns. It is as if in the arrangement of the plastic pieces the rectangle was given a special name and all future arrangements were supposed to be based on this rectangle. This is in fact exactly how many people do tackle the problem.

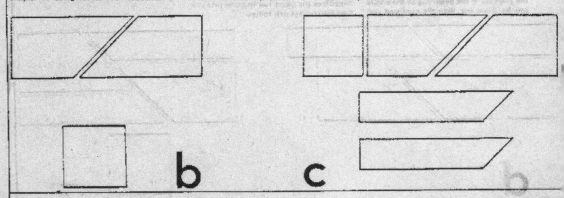

There is a great hunger for hard words, fixed categories and rigid definitions. Most people feel a need for something tangible to build with and to build upon. Useful as this tendency may be in matters of technological development this use of hard words nearly always leads to philosophical word games which are fun to play but as important as nuns' knitting. A caricature of this use of hard words is shown in the supposedly true story of the bank which employed a large computer to work out what characteristics would define the best credit risks among its customers. All sorts of information on each customer was fed in. At the end the computer gave the unexpected answer that the most dependable indication of credit worthiness was being out of a job. The best credit risks were the unemployed! It is easy to see what had happened.

It is not a matter of rejecting the hard use of words as being harmful outside technology. It is not a matter of fleeing from the Western habit of pigeon hole polarisation to the complete Eastern fluidity and rejection of categorisation. It is a matter of using words not as definitions but as triggers. These are soft words. A soft word is a word that triggers off the appropriate response or image. The function of a word is given by its effect not its history. At one moment it may mean something to someone, at another moment something else to someone else. But words can only be used in this fashion if people have had the necessary experience so that the word can trigger off a ready made reaction just as a code number may conjure forth a complete book from the library. Psychology is perhaps the easiest of all fields in which to wallow around in self justifying word games. Instead of borrowing the idiom of such word games one could perhaps develop a direct awareness of the fascinating processes that happen with the type of information processing system we call mind. Such an awareness leads to the emergence of a much more useful idiom. Wordless involvement of the mind as in the problem at the beginning of the article can be more use than the confused and limited gyrations of verbal analysis.

When 'The Five-Day Course in Thinking' was published in America it was interesting that some of the keenest interest was from computer people even though the book stresses the need for discontinuity and the limitations of logical sequence. The interest may have been due to the design of the book not as an attempt to teach anything but as an opportunity for the reader to develop an awareness of the fascinating processes that make up his own individual style of thinking. And in that awareness the computer people are as interested as creative people.

The problems are certainly trivial in the book. But then there is no special switch which changes the system in the brain depending on whether one is dealing with trivial problems or earth shaking ones. It is the triviality of the problem which shows up the nature of the system so clearly. And an understanding of the nature of the system may be far more important than an understanding of the more serious problems since very often these problems are the direct result of the faults of the system. For instance there is a point in the book where philosophical speculation would pronounce a problem to be insoluble and yet the solution is simple in practice. This shows up the limitations of pure detached thinking and the dangers of word-games.

Humour may well be the most significant phenomenon of the mind since it indicates the nature of the system better than does anything else. Humour and the related insight both show how the system is capable of suddenly switching over to a new arrangement of information. A computer is not capable of this sort of behaviour since it operates in a linear fashion which means that at any moment there is only one possible arrangement of information according to the programmed instructions.

There may not be a reason for saying something until after it has been said. Usually a point arises from a context but sometimes the point has to come first and then the context will follow.

It may be necessary to be at the top of the mountain in order to find the best way up. It is usual to move only if there is a direction but sometimes it may be necessary to move in order to generate a direction.

These things are made essential by the behaviour of the type of information processing system involved. There has to be a break in continuity or a disruption before the new pattern can re-form.

The disruption does not itself have to offer an alternative. Nevertheless disruption is not an end in itself but a stage in the development of the new order. For that reason methods of disruption are useless if they impair the faculty for recognising the re-formed pattern even as it snaps together.

It may be wondered what there is to be gained by an awareness of the workings of the information processing system of the mind other than an opportunity to construct new word games. It may be mistakenly assumed that self-awareness is but another name for self consciousness and the rigidity of pseudo-complete analysis.

Apart from the fascination of the process and an acknowledgement of the limitations of the system it is possible to be specific enough to show that there is an important functional word which is missing from every language. In its function the word is as fundamental as the negative which is the basis of the arbitrary and useful yes/no system. The use of this new word could make a difference both to thinking and to behaviour. There is nothing magical about the word which is a practical logarithm. But to gain any acceptance the word would have to emerge into a setting that had some awareness of the thinking behaviour of the mind.

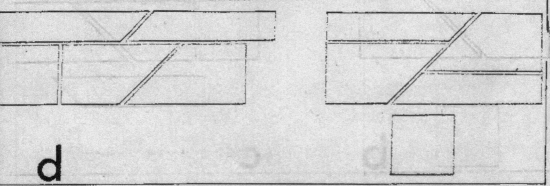

d

For instance if you were asked to divide each of the three shapes shown below into two halves which were equal in size shape and area, how would you do it? More important than just working it out could be an appreciation of why it should be difficult.
What does one know of the mad mud of mind?
Pic. F.

The Use of Lateral Thinking, Jonathan Cape 1967. 18s.
The Five-Day Course in Thinking, Allan Lane the Penguin Press, October 22nd, 1968. 25s.
Edward De Bono, c. 1968.

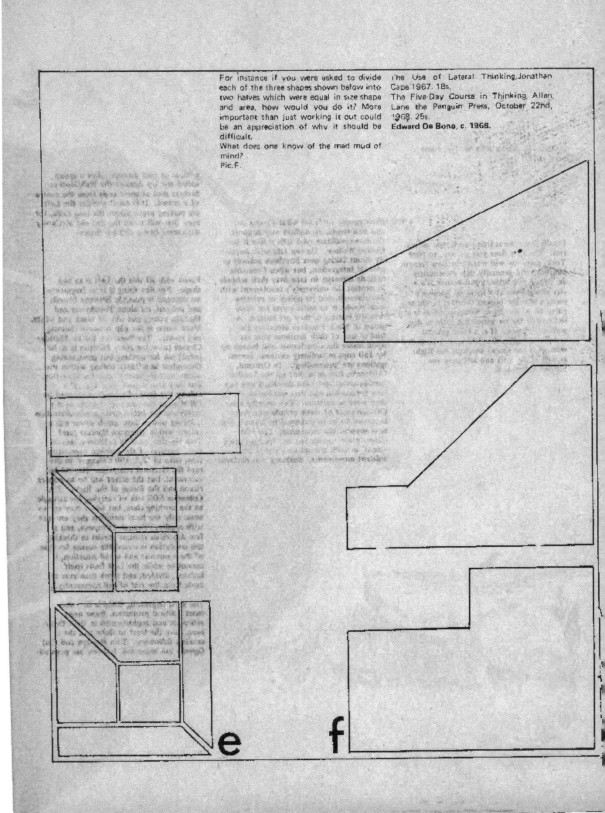

e   f

The State of American protest

by Peter Buckman who has just come back alive.

Finally America is living up to her adjectives. The first time you go, say, to New York, everyone will warn you how frenetic neurotic, and generally sick the country is. When you arrive you discover it's a city that moves at a tenth of London's pace, where the biggest decision is whose party to go to. Now, however, there is a sickness in the air which has little to do with the election. It is a more general malaise, a feeling that life cannot be coped with, that has spread amongst the Right as well as the Left and left only the Yippies untouched.

Most people can't see what's going on, and as a result, 20 million may support the one candidate who tells it like it is: George Wallace. He can talk with impunity about taking over Southern schools to prevent integration, but when Columbia radicals threaten to take over their schools to protest the university's involvement with war research, and its policy of evicting local residents to make room for more research institutes, they get busted. A group of Black Panthers attending the trial of one of their brothers were set upon inside the Courthouse and beaten up by 150 cops in ordinary clothes. Investigations are 'proceeding'. In Oakland, California, two cops shot up the Panther headquarters, and were dismissed and face trial for assault, but that was because they were in uniform. Two months after Chicago most of those people who were supposed to be so outraged by Daley's pigs now support the repression. The FBI alleges grave communist and 'foreign involvement' in both the student and black militant movements. Berkeley was declared a 'state of civil disaster' after a group called the Up Against the Wall/Motherfuckers shot at some cops from the centre of a crowd. It is small wonder the Left are making preparations for long exile, for even that will make the bad old McCarthy days seem like a childish dream.

Faced with all this the Left is in bad shape. For one thing it is so fragmented no dialogue is possible between liberals and radicals, let alone Trotskyites and Maoists, young and old, or black and white. Much worse is the gap between rhetoric and reality. The Panthers, led by Eldridge Cleaver (now the Huey Newton is to be jailed) ask for nothing but guns, seeing themselves as a 'black colony within the white mother-country' ripe for liberation. But they also expect genocide. If a colony like Santo Domingo is invaded by US Marines the moment it looks as if a legally-elected anti-American administration is taking power, how much worse will a colony within American borders fare? Tom Hayden, ex-SDS president, one of the organizers of the Chicago demonstration, talks of '2,3, 100 Chicagos' to disrupt the electoral campaign. He will be successful, but the effect will be to bolster Nixon and the forces of the Right. The Columbia SDS talk of carrying the struggle to the working-class, but when they try to arouse only the local residents they are met with apathy. Though European, and a few American radicals persist in thinking the revolution is round the corner because of the economic and social situation, it cannot be while the Left finds itself isolated, divided, and more than ever remote from the rest of the community.

The most depressing thing is that the most political protesters, those most articulate and sophisticated in their theorising, have the least to show and the smallest following. Tom Hayden and Carl Oglesby are respected, but few are persuad-

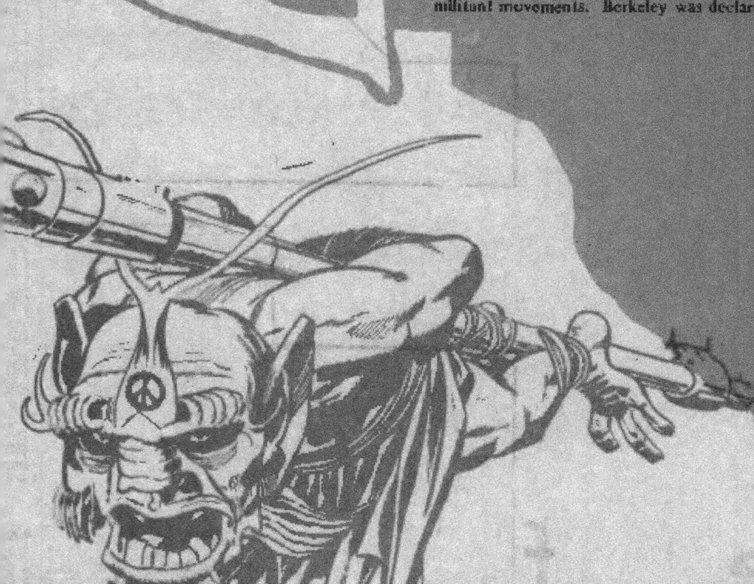

...ed to act on their philosophy, which is to know your enemy—the whole capitalist system—and fight it wherever you can so that groups may be free to 'discover a sense of their own authority and power.' This unfortunately degenerates into isolated incidents of violence whose significance is unclear and whose success so temporary the public is totally alienated. The radicals, moreover, are fatally split between those who believe in the necessity for planning and those who rely on spontaneity. The planners place great emphasis on strategy so that each action is successful in its limited objectives. The spontaneity people believe in 'exemplary action', in an act so daring it galvanises people to do their own thing. That this has had some success—in Berkeley and Columbia, not to mention Paris—has encouraged its supporters to hope for too much from it. No reliance can be placed on the 'masses' to support a revolutionary action if they're getting what they want from the system.

One big claim of the radicals is that their action in Chicago and elsewhere 'polarised' the apathetic and showed the system up for what it was. Fine, but that isn't worth the sacrifice if the effect on the system is negligible, or if all that those fired up by so much brutality are allowed to do is go out and get beaten bloody once again. In an International Revolutionary Students' Conference held recently at Columbia the Germans explained that had spent masses of time discussing theory before acting, so that when the time came everyone would understand what they were doing. No one, it seems, in the American New Left has time for such things.

In this context the only people whose 'exemplary actions' make any sense are the Yippies. They at least bridge the communication gap between theory and action by their life-style, and they are most serious about making people realise how ridiculous the whole thing is. Their throwing of dollar bills from the gallery of the New York Stock Exchange is well-known, as well as their incredibly brave but not remarkably successful actions in Chicago. At least they got good advice: 'Don't call a cop a Nazi pig,' said Abbie Hoffman, 'all he'll do is beat his chest with pride. Call him a sissy nigger-loving Commie fag Jew-bastard. Then he might think you're getting at him.'

The Yippies have ruined the dignity of the Officers Training Corps by miming the drill-routines alongside the cadets, and more recently sent up the sacred House Un-American Activities Committee by appearing before it dressed as witches and casting spells. Most of all they fearlessly live by the do-your-thing-or-fuck-you philosophy that is the only one enjoying a following outside the student body. Young workers see the Yippies having a good time and begin to wonder where it's at. Young radicals are encouraged not to take things so seriously. The trouble is the situation is so serious that when the repression comes—soon—the Yippies will be the first victims. Things will get worse.

R.COBB

STREET FIGHTING MAN

Everywhere I hear the sound
   of marching charging people,
For summer's here and the time is right
   for fighting in the street . . . boy.

But what can a poor boy do
'cept the same old rock roll thing,
But sleepy London town is just
No place for a street fighting man.

Yes I think the time is right
   for violent revolution.
From where I live the game they play
   is compromised solution.

Yes my name is called disturbance
I shout
I scream
I kill a king
I wail at all his servants

But what can a poor boy do
'cept the same old rock roll thing,
But sleepy London town is just
No place for a street fighting man.

Approximately transcribed from:
(Street Fighting Man, Jagger, Richards
Essex Music)

There's a tramp sitting on my
   doorstep,
   Trying to waste his time;
With his mentholated
   sandwich,
   He's a walking clothesline.
Here comes the Bishop's
   daughter,
   On the other side;
She looks a trifle jealous,
   She's been an outcast all
   her life.

The gangster looks so
   frightening,
   With his luger in his hand;
But when he gets home to his
   children,
   He's a family man.
But when it comes to the
   nitty gritty,
   He can shove in his knife.
Yes he really looks quite
   religious,
   He's been an outlaw all his
   life.

Oh the singer he looks angry,
   At being brought to the line,
And the bass player he looks
   nervous,
   About the girls outside,
And the drummer, he's so
   shattered,
   Trying to keep the time,
The guitar players look
   ravished,
   They've been outcasts all
   their lives.

Oh there's 20,000 grandma's
   Waving their hankies in the
   air,
And burning up their tensions,
   Shouting "It's not there."
There's a regiment of soldiers,
   Standing looking on,
And the Queen is bravely
   shouting,
   "What the hell is going on?"
With a blood-curdling
   "Tally-ho,"
   She charged into the ranks,
And blessed all those
   grandma's
   Who with their dying
   breaths,
   Wave "Thanks."

Approximately transcribed from the unreleased
L.P. Beggars Banquet

BFI REPORT
Confidential

According to its memorandum of association the British Film Institute (BFI) was established

to encourage the development of the art of the film, to promote its use as a record of contemporary life and manners, to foster study and appreciation of films for television programmes generally, to encourage the best use of television.

It has a board of Governors. All, according to the Articles of Association, appointed by that eminent artist of the film, that astute recorder of contemporary manners, that the connoisseur of film and television, Chancellor of the Exchequer. As a result there is not one member of the board elected by the 80,000 or so members of the BFI.

Only the Income Tax authorities seem to produce the same sort of helpless rage that the BFI induces in many of those that deal with it. Remember, too, that the BFI gets £300,000 a year, from the Government.

Recently Paul Rotha, Tony Richardson, Ken Loach, John Schlesinger, Susannah York and Clive Donner, amongst others, signed a letter to Jennie Lee, expressing no-confidence in the Board of Governors. Derek Hill (Short Film Service and New Cinema Club) has waged a campaign against the BFI, particularly over the short film issue. At the last AGM some members went along to try and do something about the Board of Governors. They thought that the provision of the Articles of Association about each member having one vote meant something. They soon learnt the dreadful truth about the omnipotent Chancellor. Oz has been given a mass of facts and complaints about the BFI. Some proved innaccurate when we checked them, others are reproduced below.

Stanley Reed, the director of

the BFI, is a good press relations man. Flushed with his success in this field, and the associated one of subsidy-gathering, he has now set his sights at turning the BFI into the Rank Organisation of 16mm. Reed's response to all criticism is a shrug of contempt and the reply that the only thing wrong with the BFI is its lack of money. Look at some of its departments.

1. British Film Institute Production Fund.

In 1951 the film industry gave the Experimental Film Fund £5,000. Over the next nine years it got about £40,000. Out of this came four or five Free Cinema movies (though Every Day Except Christmas and We Are The Lambeth Boys, are Ford-financed). Almost all the fund's films were mediocre or bad, the shows scarcely attended, press comment transparently 'kind', the films wretchedly distributed. Several have never had a booking. Even more startling: of every six projects to which money was given, only one was ever completed.

The Committee administering the fund consisted of an 'inner' committee, empowered to award up to £100 without formality, and a full Committee meeting twice a year. This included such avant garde minds as Sir Arthur Elton, an aged documentarist, Basil Wright, another aged documentarist, Lord Brudbourne, producer of In Which We Serve. The Fund's chairman was Sir Michael Balcon who once told Ken Tynan he could never bring himself to make a film which criticised British institutions such as the army. Neither Elton nor Wright has made a film that wasn't subsidised by government or big business in their lives.

The only passionately concerned committee member was Karl Reisz, who doesn't like anything that's not in the spiritual tradition of Free Cinema i.e. socially conscious left-wing and

tormented by confusion.

Fund footage was a standing joke in London laboratories for years before the fund went broke. About two years ago the Fund was reinvigorated, with £5,000 a new name - excluding the word experimental, be it noted, and Bruce Beresford, a young Australian, in a technical production-liaison post. He is probably the only person in the whole BFI who knows how to put a film together.

Although films have been steadily completed since Beresford's arrival, subsequent distribution of them by the BFI's Philip Strick has been farcical. In one case he sold B S Johnson's film Your Human Like The Rest Of Them (winner of the Grand Prix at the Tours Short Film Festival and Melbourne Film Festival) to the BBC for £75. It should have been sold for about £1,000. The story is a standing joke at the BBC. Most of the films remain unsold.

Why doesn't the BFI sack the dud Committee and set up another with a Peter Brook-Ken Tynan-Bruce Beresford-Don Levy-Stephen Dwoskin nucleus, perhaps? The answer is: the BFI is too enmeshed with its Old, old boys . . .

2. The BFI and Short Films

Short films are demonstrably vital to new talent and to history of the cinema. For years Richard Roud, National Film Theatre (NFT) Programmes Officer, made a policy of making up no programmes of shorts (except the BFI's own, or in response to pressure BFI men Lindgren & Huntley's specialist interest films) and he pointblank refused to help the Short Film Maker's campaign by spotlighting short films.

Just as this campaign was certain to succeed, Reed set up a BFI Short Film Committee. At an NFT Open Discussion on shorts, with Derek Hill, Caroline Heller, John Irvin and others, only one member (Alan Lovell) of that committee turned up. That committee is a face saving sham, to enable the BFI to pretend to a little credit for a campaign which it dare not support because its governors include representatives from

Rank and the ABC; the campaign was in part directed against these two companies. It cannot be too often repeated: the BFI is not, in fact, an independent body.

3. The BFI and The Industry.

The British film industry does a great deal for the BFI. It helps finance it. It gives the NFT free films. It gets very little for its help, since it could run its own archives, stills service, etc, much more cheaply. Sight & Sound, the BFI publication was at one time so contemptuous of British films that pressure was successfully exerted, by one of its industry governors to muffle its criticisms. Another informal regulation forbids the institute to express any definite opinion about censorship. Once again, the BFI is so enmeshed with the old boy net that at every turn this must determine its policies.

4. The BFI as a Competitor.

Derek Hill complains 'No sooner had news of the Short Film Makers' Campaign plans (for a short film festival) been announced than the British Film Institute declared that they were putting together . . . a week of short films at the NFT in August.'

The pattern is quite obvious. Rank and ABC, with their governorships, can dominate the BFI. Reed's empire-building can lead him only along a collision course with every other 16mm interest.

It's up to them to put the BFI in its place.

5. the BFI as a Publisher.

During the mid-fifties, BFI Publications put out a scattering of indexes of film directors. Roud's monograph on Max Ophuls sold all of 200 copies in five years. Its subsequent ventures were few, halfhearted and wretched.

It took a younger critic, Peter Cowie, with his Zwemmer/Tantivy paperbacks, to prove that filmbooks could succeed. Hearing that another younger critic Ian Cameron, was linking up with Nicholas Luard and Studio Vista for another series, the BFI decided, not to collaborate, but to provide (government-subsidised) competition. It linked itself with Secker and Warburg.

The BFI is supposed to further film appreciation. Just how it 'furthers' it may be illustrated by two interesting facts. It repeatedly refused to supply a copy of the NFT's mailing list to Studio Vista, alleging that it was 'out of print'; it was in fact freely circulated in all BFI departments, from which Studio Vista deviously obtained one. It also refused to stock the rival book on Godard, at the NFT festival bookstall, until veiled threats were uttered.

Once again, the pattern is quite obvious. The BFI will go as far as it dare in obstructing the sales of publications other than its own. How this constitutes 'furthering' film appreciation is hard to see. The issues are exactly those aroused by the BBC's subsidising of the Listener, with the difference that the BBC doesn't try to obstruct sales of the New Statesman.

6. The BFI and Critical Opinion.

In a Sight and Sound Article in 1956, Basil Wright said, 'What we need at this stage is an anarchic paper, run by a group of probably rather scruffy young men between about 17 and 22, who will let off squibs and roman candles and rockets in all directions and generally stir up the whole thing.'

The early Sixties saw three such papers—Movie, Motion and Definition. Did Sight and Sound give them any encouragement? It called Definition (from the London School of Film Technique) 'cultural gauleiters', described Movie as out for kicks from violence, and ignored Motion, which had carefully documented Sight and Sound's attitudes. When the London Film-Makers Co-operative was founded, Sight and Sound went out of its way to delve into the political past of one of its members and libellously misdescribed him as a 'professional witness' for the McCarthy Committee.

Sight and Sound also runs the Monthly Film Bulletin and overlaps with the NFT Programmes. It maintains its reputation for 'authoritativeness' by: -
A: Being distributed free to all BFI full members—it automatically increases its circulation by several thousand,
B. All opinions other than its own are either viciously attacked (as above) or ignored. Reference to almost any issue will show reiterated attacks on 'the critics', The NFT programme cite Sight & Sound critics ad nauseam, newspaper critics rarely, and other specialist film critics (from Films & Filming, Movie, Film Culture) almost never.
C: The BFI is an important information centre, and never loses an opportunity to find second 'jobs for the boys'— suggesting one another as festival jury members, press critics, etc. The BFI old boys network includes Richard Roud and Peter John Dyer on The Guardian, Tom Milne on The Observer, Penelope Houston on The Spectator (where politically, her heart, if not her head, is) David Robinson on The Financial Times (though capable of an independent line)

and John Russell Taylor on The Times & The Times Literary Supplement.

7. BFI Response to Criticism

One expects a semi-official body to ignore a great deal of criticism, either for its own good reasons, for hidden reasons (e.g. industry pressure and politics), or through simple lethargy. What one doesn't expect is a vindictive, ad hominem response which, without being the rule at the BFI, is all too common. For example:

When an employee of the Central Office of Information (C.O.I.) made a perfectly fair criticism of the BFI in the correspondence columns of a magazine, a BFI Department Head wrote a personal letter to his Head of Department, on the thin pretext that the letter could be taken as the COI's official opinion; the correspondent almost lost his job as a result.

Again, when Films & Filming criticised the recent increase in the price charged by the BFI for stills, the BFI officer responsible wrote to the editor accusing the assistant editor of abusing the BFI's facilities by paying member's price for stills subsequently used for publication. This accusation was not merely false, but, again, libellous. In point of fact, that assistant editor had, over the past ten years, given the BFI stills library many thousands of stills, on condition of retaining free reproduction rights. Once again, the BFI's response to perfectly reasonable criticism could hardly have been more spiteful and ungrateful.

8. BFI Had Faith.

In the last NFT programme Richard Roud claimed that the NFT had pioneered appreciation of the New York underground over here. Perhaps he can explain why, when he was offered 40 hours of New York underground movies in 1966, he turned them down as of no interest? And why in 1967 he said of two movies by Peter Emmanuel Goldman, 'those have little to do with what is generally known as Underground cinema, which is just as well?' And why, when the current underground programme was arranged with the co-operation of the London Film-makers Co-operative, did NFT programmes and press-sheets bear no credit whatsoever to that organisation?

9. Muddle and Apathy.

A: A student at the London School of Film Technique ran a film society which managed to attract, as its special speakers, men of the calibre of Francois Truffaut, Hitchcock, Fritz Lang, Nicholas Ray, etc.

The BFI is in an unparalleled situation to arrange for such events at the NFT. Over the years it has consistently failed to do so. (In this connection it should be noted that the Berkeley and Rouben Mamoulien programmes were part of a 'package' arranged by a New York archive, to tour all European cinematheques, and the NFT's sole initiative in this respect was making its theatre available).

The recent sessions by Peter Ustinov and Don Siegel represent a new initiative, which should be encouraged—it should also be noted that its inauguration is pathetically tardy.

B: The print copies of BFI releases have been a matter for complaint from within and without the Institute for many years—some sequences, in important films, are virtually indecipherable, others wrongly edited. The BFI has a blanket excuse in alleging poor quality of the original archive print. But according to many BFI staff, this poor quality is a fiction, in many cases; the BFI simply releases the cheapest print, indifferent to its quality.

C: The BFI and CBA services have become so bad, with mislaid and delayed films and acknowledgements, that its usual procedure, to blame the GPO, has worn thin, and the recent Annual Report acknowledges, covertly, the volume of complaints, by pleading that its volume of work has forced it to cut down on its usual 'personalized' service. In fact this 'personalized' service includes putting reels from Film A in the tins of Film B and delays of half-an-hour or more, while

the staff hunt missing films and forms, are the rule at its Film Counter in Lower Marsh.

D: The acquisition of films is equally slapdash. A visiting Professor recently had to make four appointments before the films he was offering were even looked at, a film delivered by hand still hadn't been looked at four months later, despite numerous reminders , and and was simply withdrawn.

10. The National Film Archive:

The National Film Archive, run by Ernest Lindgren has at last count 1899 films—many of them appear to be short films. When you consider that over 2000 overground commercial films are made in the UK and the US each year and when you add the films made in the rest of the world (Japan makes over 300 a year) 1899 is an amazingly small number. Particularly when one learns that 17 of the films are those of Basil Deardon (obscure maker of 40's English films) and that there are no films of Godard, Truffaut or Resnais.

11. BFI Charges:

The NFT obtains its films free of charge from kindly distributors, but its seats cost as much as those at Rank cinemas, even before the recent increase, which brings them up to West End standards. The BFI pleads a loss at the NFT, but in fact its figures on this are entirely theoretical (as its report implies, when speaking of sums deemed to relate to the NFT). A policy of high prices all round bears particularly heavily on undergraduates and other young people whose interest in the cinema is both active and influential, and the BFI should adjust its pricings in an effort to make concessions towards them.

Undoubtedly the BFI performs some useful functions, a few very well. In many respects, however, it is competitive, vindictive, exploitative, selfregarding and irresponsible. As a semi-official body, supported by the taxpayer, and responsible to its members, it has no business to be so. And the groundswell of discontent with its senior members will continue until genuine, not merely token, changes in its composition, its status and near-monopoly position are made.

Rather sheepishly, we should point out that two OZ people, Martin Sharp and Andrew Fisher have both happily made films with grants from the production fund. Sharp (Do you love me Darling) 1968 with Bob Whitaker) Fisher (The Adventures of X, 1967 with Michael Newman)

How to start: 5–12 friends who know and enjoy each other's company can look for a large house of six or more rooms, via an agent, classified adverts etc. for a rent of £10–£12 per week. This works out at about £2 per week each, with two persons sharing a room. Add another 10s each per week to cover overheads: rates, electricity, gas. An initial deposit of £2 10s each should cover the agent's fee. Initially the bare essentials: mattresses, a sofa, some chairs, a cooker, etc. could be purchased either second-hand or on hire purchase, then gradually increased by bargains from jumble sales, auctions, second-hand shops or outright gifts of furniture from sympathetic persons. To provide for this, a common fund should be set up, also to cover cost of minor repairs, decorations, etc. One person (the one with the most stable income) would sign a long lease with the landlord, with option to sublet. In group situations a person's hang-ups from childhood and early adolescence tend to come to the surface. Constant depth communication among all concerned should gradually bring about greater insight and understanding of oneself and others. This is not easy, and is a wisdom gained through tears and crises. But there can also be moments of fun and enjoyment when everyone participates in group singing, dancing, picnics, love-ins, etc. It would be foolish to introduce drugs into the scene, as this would be providing the fuzz with an open invitation to bust

DOWN ON THE FARM

Emmanuel Petrakis,
15 Camden Hill Road,
London SE19.

up the community, and all its constructive aspects as well. If you want a successful community, you had better make sure that the participants share a commitment towards an outside social goal, such as community service. Underground information and liaison service, raising funds for a useful project, etc. Selective screening of applicants and a probationary period for newcomers would tend to protect the group from undesirable or parasitic hangers-on.

There are a number of community houses in London and other parts of the country, each with a different approach (artistic communes, social work, rescue work, with or without sexual freedom, digger-style, Christian philanthropic, vegetarian, pacifist, bourgeois liberal, pot-takers, etc.). one group of about 8 persons, the Phoenix Community, in Crouch Hill, North London, is so well organised, that for £5 per week each member enjoys a private room, evening and weekend meals (they employ a cook), central heating, a large garden, a frig, a washing machine, and a telephone. They have formed a housing association, which has erected a block of flats with communal facilities nearby, and a third house has been purchased for conversion. They hold an open house one evening per month. Besides communal functions, arrangements should safeguard the use of a room for reading, writing, meditation, private interviews, and so on. The Phoenix community provides a quiet library room, as well as a communal lounge.

One way to initiate aspirants into communal living, is for the Underground organisations to rent a large country house near London and other major urban centres for weekend communes. These would give interested radicals a chance to really get to know each other in a functional setting, to explore ideas, and to have a nice time together.

Living together: When two or more persons, who have known each other over a period of time, have discovered common bonds and affinities, and gained affection for each other, they may form a Group Family to give more definite shape to their relationship, and to encourage its expression into deeper and more meaningful channels. In the Group Family, of mutual adult adoption, there is no mine and thine, but "ours": our home is community flat or house, our common fund, our children. Thus we can find happiness through sharing and serving, and live at a deeper level which removes the root causes of much personal and social suffering through isolation. Most of our social evils are the result of our present mistaken concepts and poor human relations, which make strangers of our fellow humans. The Group Family may, in some cases, imply Group Marriage, in the practical if not the legal sense. The family should not be a strait-jacket where too intensive and sometimes explosive relations exist, but a co-operative group sharing a similar outlook on life, always open to include other suitable persons. Older members act in the role of uncles, aunts or grandparents. The younger adults can function as spouses.

Although apparently revolutionary, the idea and practice are not new. They have been successfully applied for many years, with local variations, in the Polynesian Islands, in African communities, in Israeli kibbutzim, among the Eskimos, etc. This way of life is currently practised by some hippies and others in the U.S.A. and the U.K., and by increasing numbers of young p e o p l e   i n   S w e d e n.

Working together: The Alternative Society can only come about through our daily efforts towards economic independence, functional integration, and constant re-education. In the initial stages, community members may have to take on casual work outside the community. The eventual aim, however, should be to provide basic services or make useful goods in order for a group to cover its material needs. What individuals can do in this direction, a group can usually do better. An example of individual initiatives: Ding Dong Cottage in Cornwall, run by Judith and Douglas Cook of the peace movement, who make and sell wooden baby toys. One can also mention diggers who work as part-time gardeners, radicals who earn a living as teachers, James Abel, a libertarian who runs his own printing service, and many others.

If we look at communitarian groups, we can quote Beeville Community in New Zealand, a group of about 30 people who started about 30 years ago from small beginnings as a pacifist group. They are self-supporting on 30 acres, 12 of which are in permanent orchard, and have set up a small precast concrete factory, a modern honey-processing plant and building with 480 bee hives, and a repair workshop.

Another pacifist commune, Koinonia Farm, in Georgia, USA, consists of about 10 adults who make a living by operating a pecan plant to process their pecan nuts, and by selling fruitcakes and pecandy via a small mail order business.

About 11 anarchists live together at Tolstoy Farm, in Davenport, Washington, USA, on 180 acres, 30 of which are tillable. They are proud of their canned and frozen crops, obtain their milk from a cow and some goats, and raise chickens. Their income is supplemented by casual work in neighbouring farms.

There are many other communities, urban or rural, in the US and other countries which have started quite modestly. Some have set up experimental schools, others sustain themselves by making leather goods, children's clothing, tools, watches, etc. In Japan, 30,000 live in 30 communal villages, kibbutz-style. Some of them have built modern factories for making chicken-rearing equipment, furniture, mats, and preserves. There are also workshops and motor vehicles for the needs of the commune and for outside work. There is total economic integration, a high degree of self-sufficiency, and the various needs of commune members are catered for.

In India, the Gandhian village commune movement has spread over the past 15 years and now embraces 60,000 villages with a total population of 40 million people. There, people grow their own food, build their own homes, weave their own clothes, and give their children a basic practical education imbued with co-operative humanitarian values. The work and the proceeds are all shared and no one lords it over anybody else.

In Israel, over 85,000 people live in about 223 kibbutzim (agricultural communes), many of which are reputed in the country for their high cultural and artistic achievements. A number of kibbutzim pool their resources to set up industrial and further education training centres, and to manufacture agricultural and other equipment for their own use and for export.

South America has about 20 worker-run factories, owned co-operatively by themselves, which include the following industries: metal, printing, glass, textiles, transport, flour-mills, etc. The main agricultural co-operatives in Sao Paulo (Brazil) were started over ten years ago by Japanese immigrants who had learned the co-operative idea from Germany (Japanese kibbutzim now send their teenagers to train in Israeli kibbutzim).

French industrial co-operatives, also well-established for many years now, include the various stages of production, from raw material to finished product, in building, electronic testing equipment, deep sea diving apparatus, printing, electrical goods, cookers, refrigerators, etc. The Federation of Communities of Work in Paris produces its own sophisticated periodical 'Communaute', assists new co-operatives, sponsors training schemes, and carries out international research in co-operative ventures from Mexico and Peru, to Algeria (where they built a new village with 1,000 dwellings) and Polynesia (where a co-operative fishing industry is being set up).

We too in the UK can do the same if we but get together with a will to create constructive alternatives to the Status Quo and its robotisation. To do that we need to set up our own Underground Co-operative Bank or Trust Fund to provide interest-free loans to capable but moneyless radicals with skills or good ideas. We also need to establish an information-pool on casual work (without cards and formalities) until our comrades can develop their self-supporting ventures. These could be workshops producing soft cuddly toys, mini-skirts, aprons or other goods, photographic, home repair or duplicating services, or we could run small progressive freedom-schools in working class areas, organise bargain and literature shops, etc. Failure to respond constructively to the challenge of the times might well bring about more personal breakdowns of various kinds, street violence, and fascist repression as is the case in Greece, Czechoslovakia, Spain and South Africa today.

With a view to co-ordinating efforts and providing contacts and information on libertarian ventures, the 'New Life' movement (15, Camden Hill Rd, London SE19) has been publishing 'NEW LIFE', an international newsletter, since 1965. We are now conducting a workshop/course on "The Dynamics of Social Change" to explore together techniques of mutual aid, creative living, practical projects for personal and social regeneration, re-education and psychological re-orientation. We invite all constructive activists to join us in this exciting adventure and to link up with each other. 'It is better to light one small candle than to curse the universe for its darkness' (Chinese proverb).

rock

Richard Meltzer made his controversial debut in *OZ* 11 with *The Anglo American Pumice Factory**, and is this issue we present selections from his unpublished book: *A Sequel: Tomorrow's Not Today*. Extracts were first published in *Crawdaddy*, the amazing American Magazine of Rock, which revealed that Grove Press had "wrestled with Meltzer's book for seven months before finally turning it down because 'they didn't understand it' ". It was written originally in the summer of 1965 for an undergraduate aesthetics course. The editor of *Crawdaddy* writes: "The intent of the book is to simply offer a sideways insight into the workings of rock as an art form; it is certainly the most careful, well handled approach to the subject I've ever seen".

* For those of you who missed the pun: Pumice = light weight rock.

aesthetics

Bob Dylan's greatest dive into the rock 'n' roll domain, Like a Rolling Stone, represents an attempt to free man by rescuing him *from* meaning, rather than free man *through* meaning. John Lennon's two collections of writings, In His Own Write and A Spaniard in the Works, have shown his desire to denigrate all meaning and thus throw intentional ambiguity into all domains of meaning. And very definitely *all* meaning is similar, beginning with the most 'authentic and continuing down the line.

When told by Paul McCartney about a girl he encountered with the idea that God had advised her to marry Paul, 'I was trying to persuade her that she didn't in actual fact have a vision from God, that it was . . .' George Harrison interrupted with, 'It was probably somebody *disguised* as God'. Meaning by any other name, smells about the same. John and Ringo destroy PF Strawson's argument for separation into logical and empirical primacy:

John: 'We're money-makers first, then we're entertainers.'
Ringo: 'No, we're not.'
John: 'What are we then?'
Ringo: 'Dunno. Entertainers first.'
John: 'OK.'
Ringo: ''Cause we were entertainers before we were money-makers.'

Whereas James Joyce attempted to salvage meaning from semantic chaos, John would rather attain a cool semantic oblivion, and thus has written two books intentionally inferior to James Joyce's works.

One of Lennon and McCartney's manoeuvers is to present meaning in such a role that it becomes trite. Thus is the use of 'in spite of' in a positive sense reduced to triviality in 'Yes It Is':

'Please don't wear red tonight,
Remember what I said tonight.
For red is the colour that will
    make me blue
In spite of you
It's true . . .
Yes it is, it's true.'

This very spirit of the song, with its assertively positive title, presents a frightening ambiguity between arrogance and possession of a unique vulnerability. 'When I Get Home' plays upon the mere appearance of a single word, 'trivialities':

'Come on, if you please
I got no time for trivialities
I got a girl who is waiting home
    for me
Tonight.
Wo-wo-wo-I
Wo-wo-wo-I
I got a whole lot of things to tell
    her
When I get home.'

In the midst of apparent 'tragedy' in realising a sudden revulsion at his semi-adulterous involvement with another girl, he can hesitate to give it the meaning of 'triviality'. But the five-syllable word is so strange in such a monosyllabic context that it is rendered incredibly inappropriate, and the need for meaning collapses.

In a world of such things as random values, metaphysical inconsistency, and the constant unavoidable interruption of pure aesthetic perception by random events from within and without, eclecticism is the only valid position; and other stances may be measured by virtue of their distance from the eclectic. Andy Warhol has devised one of the simplest of all schemes, the selection of a popylar motif, from Troy Donahue, to floral prints, to Campbell's Soup, followed by mechanical multiple reproduction of this motif, with the consistency and inconsistency being a function of the mechanism of creation. Rock 'n' roll, however, cannot rely upon the selling power of random circumlocution of the originally acceptable motif, but turns toward the utter compression of popularly acceptable, yet eclectically arranged, images. A Little Bit Better by Herman's Hermits begins with the instrumental introduction from the the Four Seasons' Coca-Cola commercial, procedes with the sinister spirit of the Rolling Stones' Play With Fire (of course rendered innocent by Herman's contradiction), sung with the vocal style of the Zombies, to the tune of Chuck Berry's Memphis, and in possession of a title clearly reminiscent of the recent hit by Wayne Fontana and the Mindbenders, A Little Bit Too Late. Wayne Fontana himself sounded like a clear version of the Kingsmen in his first hit, like the Searchers in his next. The Beatles have taken from visceral jazz saxophonist John Coltrane in Love Me Do, the gay Four Seasons in Tell Me Why, Larry Williams in I'm Down, and Bob Dylan and Scottish marching bands in You've

Got to Hide Your Love Away. They have used elderly African drum in Mr Moonlight, violins in Yesterday, timpani in What You're Doing and Every Little Thing, packing case in Words of Love, and unusual amplification manoeuvers in I Feel Fine and Yes It Is. They have used double tracking on several records, sometimes so obviously that it can be easily noticed (in Hard Day's Night, John Lennon's harmonica line can be heard while he is singing lead vocal in I Should Have Known Better. It does not matter if part of the Beatles' formula is visible; after all, even Lennon's bathing suit is clearly visible in a bathtub scene).

Teilhard de Chardin's philosophy of education as expounded in The Phenomenon of Man is readily visible in the eclecticism of rock. Just as branches of life strive for continuation, sometimes to succeed and sometimes to reach a dead end, with nature always using a multiplicity of interrelated strivings in its drive toward the Omega Point, rock 'n' roll is clearly viewable in terms of crude persistence. As long as a fixture 'works' in the Allan Kaprow usage of the term, it remains in the fore-front and shouts its presence; when it ceases to work it is relegated to relative obscurity until a new context presents itself and allows for favourable reacceptance. No branch can ever really become extinct if it continues to function in the memory, even dormantly, and old but undiscovered branches from both the 'within' and 'without' of things past, as Chardin uses these terms, can always appear in active functions in contemporary rock. The almost forgotten 1957 minor hit by Kathy Linden, Billy, features an expectation of obscenity in its final passage:

'And when I sleep . . .
And when I sleep . . .
I always dream of Bill.'

This anxiety of waiting for the impossible use of 'sleep' in the last line is not too overtly common in rock of any period, but suddenly in the summer of 1965 it arose in Tom Jones' What's New Pussycat? Pussycat lips, pussycat eyes and other pussycat features are mentioned until, with the final verse, the singer is hesitatingly approaching something more openly sexual and finishes, 'You and your pussycat . . . nose'. Here is the appearance of a branch of rock with now at least two evolutionary members, a branch which I can call the 'pussycat school'. Rock has had its 'rain school' (Raindrops, Teardrops, Rhythm of the Rain, Walking in the Rain, etc.), a fine eclectic grouping which is ambiguously between the inner and outer world of artistic evolution. There are even flimsier branches, such as the branch of all songs with 'tell' in their titles. Rock has implicitly operated on this infinitude of random, eclectic evolutionary pathways, something merely suggested by Thomas Pynchon in his V. My categories 'pony tail rock' (the group the Poni-Tails, What Is Love? which describes this emotion as 'five feet of heaven with a pony tail'; Chantilly Lace, with its reference to the hair piece as a criterion of socio-sexual adequacy), 'fear-of-loss-of-being-rock' (Going Out of My Head; Remember, Dion and the Belmonts' absolutely obscure I Can't Go On Rosalie) and 'march rock' (Little Peggy March, the beat of I'll Never Dance Again; the tympani of Every Little Thing, Calendar Girl, which declares, March, I'm gonna march you down the aisle) are as valid as such categories as 'folk-rock', 'Motown rock', or even 'rock-which-legitimately-renders-human-experience' or 'that-which-consistently-conforms-to-the-standards-of-classical-music rock'.

At the same time rock has transcended any difficulties encountered in the sociology of knowledge. Because it is so wantonly eclectic, any moment's linear connections can bear contradictory relationships to those of the next without difficulty. I Can't Stop Loving You has succeeded I've Had It, Tequila had led to Too Much Tequila, and Eve of Destruction and Dawn of Correction have appeared almost concurrently. William James has seen the impossibility of viewing philosophical contructs separate from the temperament which has led to them; rock has never for a second viewed the construct and temperament as anything but the same phenomenon, or noumenon for that matter. Quine has noted, 'The unit of empirical significance

is the whole of rock 'n' roll. The unit of mere influence in the whole of rock 'n' roll, and this is not merely the result of the failure of reduction, if Hegel's unit of historical significance as all of history seems to be. Just as permissable, anyway, is the Kantian position in Summertime, summertime, which resembles Hegel's end of history, 'No more carbon history.'

The periodicity of artistic evolution presupposes questions of evolving legitimacy and disillegitimacy. Once a new approach has been legitimatized through acceptance, it may be repeated, in the case of rock 'n' roll the very process of legitimatization itself can pertain to rock 'n' roll's total picture, and this repetition of course is driven into the ground, just as I have obliterated the concept of cool-blue by overuse so far in this very essay. Rock has dealt with legitimacy and illegitimacy in a manner both frequently and philosophic reputation. Often something aware of being observed is out of bounds in a rock context and utterly often. When Elvis Presley followed his early hard core rock hits with a ballad Love Me Tender, the music of which had been taken from Stephen Foster, certain questions arise. Could Elvis sustain popular musician in the general break out of sense? Was rock 'n' roll, after just three years of its remarkable movement, on the verge of fusion with this popular mainstream? Pat Boone built his entire early career on music ambiguously legitimate for both pop and rock, with titles like Love Letters in the Sand, Anastasia, There's a Gold Mine in the Sky, April Love, When the Swallows Come Back to Capistrano and the classic Friendly Persuasion. Perhaps he was interested mostly in attaining good legitimacy for his own songs, indeed already with a pseudo-rock energy, without concentrating upon how that energy might enhance what he conservatively judged to be legitimate. The Platters, perhaps the biggest group during the early days of rock 'n' roll, seemed to sound so legitimate that they have completely vanished. As rock developed significant change took place, ballads became illegitimate. That is, they were no longer aesthetically good music but were now available for the hip rock 'n' roll, but beauty could now reenter rock 'n' roll with full 'badness' to it, there was no longer a need to equate beauty with the sublime, merely pretty as muzak necessitates, beauty was now free and ontologically energized. 'Soul' encountered a similar problem, rendered completely by Ray Charles. His early sides and manner produced an intense, lyrical hostility that seemed unsuccessfully removed from rock 'n' roll sentimentality

Charles' What'd I Say and Swanee River Rock alienated his work from its earlier more conservative legitimacy and introduced to rock a variety of soul far more 'righteous' than that of rhythm and blues. One of the first great ballads of this new era of rock was Conway Twitty's It's Only Make Believe, perhaps an indicator of the self-cognition necessary for such a transition beyond limitation by dubious distinction. 'People see us everywhere/They think you really care/But we can't can't deceive/We know it's only make believe.' The problem of delegitimatization has sometimes been reduced to a problem of fossilization. The Righteous Brothers' Unchained Melody is a song recorded scores of times in 'legitimate' context, but only they (perhaps only one Brother sings on the record) a dubious triviality now (self) could make it complete. Comprehensible through a rock connection, the idea was to slur the phrases, but only in the final 'that speed my love to me' is that (it is not ideally audible, even inaudible on a faulty transistor radio. Bob Dylan has brought his harsh folk songs of protest into rock 'n' roll by following the latter's pleasure principle: recording for single release (separate form his record albums) those songs which are the most acutely pleasing, as Like a Rolling Stone and Positively Fourth Street.

The usual label, for segments of artistic evolution, 'baroque' and 'rococo', are easily superficial manifestations of this deeper activity. A cursory examination of the terms used to designate some of the second song, a revelatory of an orientation different from that of the traditional forms to which those labels were originally applied. A song can be a 'hit', a 'bomb', a 'smash', or even a 'gasser', kind of destruction is inherent in kinetic success.

Stylistically, Conway Twitty resembles closely Elvis Presley, what is echoed by Terry Stafford, who sounds like Del Shannon. Marianne Faithful can be thought of as an inane Joan Baez. Adam Faith is essentially the same as Jimmy Clanton stylistically and sound-ably. By convenient, match mysteriously, Dee Dee Sharp has exemplified the Orlons, who do approximate the Marvelettes. The 'late great' Buddy Holly was conspicuously heard in the singing of Tommy Roe and Bobby Vee, who has even used Buddy Holly's Crickets. The instrumental sounds of the Tornadoes and of Johnny and the Hurricanes display no distinct difference. Mel Carter is not overly distinguishable from the

'late great' Sam Cooke. Some vocals and harmonica solos by Dylan and Lennon have sounded so related that one rock 'n' roll magazine said that they might be the same person in different disguises. Jay and the Americans sound like the Fortunes, who sound like the We Five, who sound like the Ivy League, who sound like the Beatles, who sound like the Zombies, who sound like the Searchers, who sound like the Everly Brothers, who sound like a multitude of white country blues singers, who sometimes sound like Negro country blues singers, who can sometimes sound like urban Negro blues singers, who sound like the Rolling Stones, who sound like the Nashville Teens, who do not even look like Jay and the Americans.

At the close of Plato's Symposium, Socrates has clinched complete control of the situation and has, by keeping his listeners on the verge of boredom and sleep, forced them into acceptance of anything he chooses. Socrates was arguing with others—not that Aristodemus could remember very much of what he said, for, besides having passed the beginning, he was still more than half asleep. But the gist of it was that Socrates was forcing them to admit that the same man might be capable of writing both comedy and tragedy—that the tragic poet might be a comedian as well. Socrates here has spoken of tragedy and comedy alone as a matter of dramatic reality. John Lennon in a similar position would group together many more things, likely tragedy, comedy, pornography, melodrama, structured philosophy, mathematics and psychology, history, limerick, babble. Drilled beyond speech, one might still indicate the existence of the Over business beyond speech. Mick Jagger actually offers a variation of this position at the conclusion of the Stones Walking the Dog, babbling, 'Dun-dun-dun, duh-duh . . . . . just a working man so profound revelation, he is ambiguously wounded and/or moved of his power to speak coherently or so awestruck that coherent speech is no longer necessary. Anyway, he just babbles.

by Richard Meltzer

All states are police states. But some societies disguised the fact much better than others, above all Britain and North America (the area of 'Anglo-Saxon democracy' in its different forms). Now, the disguise is wearing thin.

SUPPORT YOUR LOCAL POLICE
KEEP THEM INDEPENDENT!

The battles of Chicago and Grosvenor Square have made the biggest holes in it. But the evidence accumulates every day that these were not brutal accidents, that the old garment can not be sewn up around them — that they were, instead, symptoms of profound, irreversible social change. The mystification was founded on a social consensus which is very rapidly deteriorating beyond repair: in effect, society was held together by an ideological and moral cement which made police-type force secondary. And this physical force simply grows in importance as the cement rots away

The most obvious expression of the change is simply growing consciousness of the fuzz as a social fact, and some sort of social problem (which in Britain naturally takes the form of dismay that coppers aren't as wonderful as they used to be). But it has already been registered culturally in a very striking way. No fewer than three movies this year present an image of the police almost unrecognizably different from that dear to American and British cinema in the past: Don Siegel's *Madigan*, Gordon Douglas's *The Detective*, and a British film, Douglas Greene's *The Strange Affair*.

The consensus worked by keeping us convinced that, on the whole, the police was good. It was the upright guardian of an acceptable social structure. The bent cop is a familiar figure in Hollywood convention, but the whole point lay in contrasting him to the honesty of 'the force,' to incorruptible superiors. The common theme of these new films is, by contrast, that the whole force is bent and corrupt in some

way, because it serves a corrupt social order. Instead of showing corrupt individuals in a wholesome system, they show would-be honest individuals in a system so corrupt that they cannot survive it.

Madigan is much the weakest of the three films, although by the best-known director, Don Siegel. A season of his films was running at the NFT when *Madigan* appeared, which included the first-rate *Baby Face Nelson* (1957), *The Line-Up* (1958) and *The Killers* (1964). *Madigan* is much poorer than any of these, but does at least raise a more interesting question than any of them.

Dan Madigan (Richard Widmark) is a semi-corrupt New York detective: he lives on what is called 'police discount' (hand-outs) but has never actually 'sold out a job,'as his complacent superiors put it. But they have nothing to be complacent about, we learn. Police Commissioner Russell (Henry Fonda) is having a furtive affair with a married member of the Womens League against Juvenile Delinquency, and his Chief Inspector Kane (James Whitmore) is bent in half trying to protect his bent son, Patrolman Kane, who just can't live on his salary. Russell has a high reputation as the soul of uprightness. Nevertheless, he bends over double too, to shield Kane and Madigan. He says of Madigan: 'I always feel he's out there doing something I'd rather not know about'. Yet at the climax, when the cops go in after the crazed killer, he can say: 'Be careful, Madigan. Good detectives are hard to come by.'

Thus, everyone is corrupt, from patrolmen to Commissioner. And the system only works by everyone protecting everyone else. But though Siegel discloses this completely bent universe for us, he is absolutely unable to explore its contradictions. More at home with violence (the keynote of his best films) than with the sociological insight which the theme demands, he founders hopelessly back into conventionality. Everyone's rotten, he suggests, but it doesn't matter because everyone is also OK at heart: the corruption is superficial. When the fuzz comes face to face with the real enemy, everything shifts back on to the familiar terrain of cops-and-robbers. Madigan becomes a hero, Russell becomes human, and even the

bitchy Mrs. Madigan (Inger Stevens) finds she can't bring herself to screw the other man.

However, one must accord the film some credit for its extraordinary *ugliness*. Siegel's ageing heroes, brought constantly into lined close-up, and the grainy brutalism of many scenes, accord better with the theme than the sagging story-line.

But *The Detective* takes the theme almost to its logical conclusion.

Joe Leland (Frank Sinatra) is another New York cop occupying a middling position in the police hierarchy, like both the heroes of the other films. The film traces the whole story of his investigation of the murder of a wealthy homosexual, and is most renowned for the boldness of the dialogue, where penises, spunk, and screwing are spoken of fairly casually. But it is another boldness which is really interesting.

Leland's father and grandfather were both cops, and he struggles to keep straight. He represents the old cinema tradition of the honest policeman. His investigation of the murder is really the analysis of the different corrupting pressures to which he is exposed; and the ambiguous 'success' of the search is really his final recognition that the pressures are irresistible, and his decision to leave the force. The 'honest cop' has become a thing of the past.

The film shows police corruption as having three main aspects. First of all, it is a highly bureaucratic institution, torn by a ceaseless, unscrupulous scramble for promotion. Leland guts his promotion to Lieutenant by sending the wrong man to the chair, against his inner convictions. Then when he finds a subordinate using Nazi techniques to extract a confession, he is powerless to protest because it reminds him of what he has already done. Secondly, the policemen are riddled with the petty-bourgeois prejudices of outside society, in a peculiarly crude and rigid form: this is conveyed vividly by their attitudes to the homosexual milieu shown in the film. Leland fights a lone, losing battle for tolerance. Thirdly, the police are helpless before the massive political and financial pressures of an outside society which is itself totally rotten. When some agitators are arrested, Leland remarks angrily that the

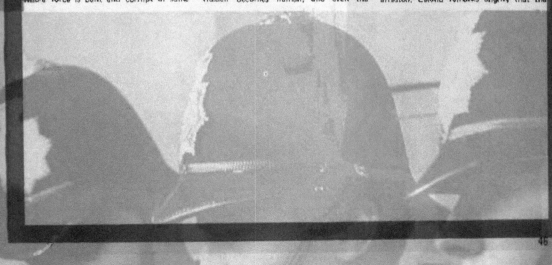

...hine have to 'sit on the lid of the sheltel erbage can', and make the eventual explosion that much worse. Then the shocking truth of the crime emerges. The murderer was a respected pillar of society, who had preferred to commit murder—and then suicide rather than be known as a homosexual, and have his life ruined by the vile prejudices of his bourgeois environment. And he was also the centre of a vast property swindle with vested interests in ghetto housing, in which half the city's upper crust participated.

Thus, Leland succeeds in exposing the 'real villains'. An older type of detective movie would have ended on a brassy triumph-of-justice fanfare at this point. But Leland realises that there is no triumph. The swindle will be back in operation again in six months, whatever happens. It is society. The police force he believed in is there to protect and foster its corruption, not to cure it. He quits, saying that 'there are some battles one can't fight here', but without making clear what they are, or how he will fight them. Played with convincing dignity by Sinatra, Leland is the conventional Hollywood hero figure in a fallen world, a universe whose values have collapsed and left him alone.

Madigan told us that cops are corrupt, but that it didn't matter too much as they are all good guys underneath (it even turns out that a negro preacher's son wasn't roughed up, when under suspicion of sexual assault!). The Detective says that fuzz corruption is only the logical expression of a hopeless social order, hence the one remaining good guy in the world has to pull out.

However, there is still a faint trace of Hollywood's old optimism in the existence of this one good guy. One can't understand how he could have survived so long—what would really happen to an officer who knocked colleagues down every time he saw them being nasty? But anyway, one crusader is left, determined to keep on trying. Americans have conserved that much faith in their dream. In the British anti-fuzz film, there are no redeeming features, no hope, and no hope at all for anyone.

The Strange Affair has two central characters, and of the two P.C. Strange (the titular, less important) (Michael York) is overshadowed by Sergeant Pierce

(Jeremy Kemp), who corresponds to Madigan and Leland in the other films. Pierce is a gritty, angular figure who has made a fetish of police honesty, and consequently detests those who are dishonest. 'There's nothing in this world more despicable than a bent copper!', he warns P.C. Strange. He particularly hates one successful gangster who was formerly a bent copper, and is now in the heroin trade. P.C. Strange is a novice constable who has failed his University exams and naively 'wants to do something useful for society, and that sort of thing'.

The film follows the disillusionment and downfall of both men, but unlike Leland they do not survive catastrophe. Pierce ends up mad, rambling on helplessly about God and the sins of young folk, and Strange is jailed for planting false evidence on a suspect. In other respects, there is a remarkable parallelism between the films: The Strange Affair translates The Detective's critique of the police integrally into British terms. Certain conversations and attitudes echo one another almost word-for-word: for instance, Leland's talk with Curran in the police cafe, and Pierce's talk with Evans in the washroom at New Scotland Yard.

However, the British film is at its best—both more subtle, and much better directed than either The Detective or Madigan. Take the theme of police bureaucracy. Greene manages to convey the essence of this, and also the central dilemma of Sergeant Pierce, in one short, brilliant episode. When Pierce returns to New Scotland Yard, and gets out of his car in the parking ramp, two superiors are looking down at him, framed stiffly in an opening with the building looming darkly behind them. He is angrily rebuked for having failed to 'sign out'. Now he has to go and sign out, and then sign in, so that 'the book' is in order. From their attitude, and his protestations, we gather that his over-earnest eagerness, his anxiety to be a 'single-handed sword of justice' makes him a grain of sand in the organisation, that he is disliked and persecuted for it. As he hurries awkwardly up the ramp, the concrete ceiling shutting out the sky behind him, he already appears vividly as a man alone, increasingly shut up in a private world of rancour and bitterness.

routine talent of Douglas and Siegel very obvious. And he is helped both by a very good musical score by Basil Kirchin (The Detective is burdened by the conventional noises of Jerry Goldsmith), and by a marvellous acting performance from Jeremy Kemp as Pierce. Unfortunately, at his worst he is a lot worse than either of the other two. The weak bits of The Strange Affair are precisely those singled out by most critics as constituting the film's main interest.

All three films counterpoint their view of the police with a story of the central characters' private lives. Here, The Detective comes off best, with a relatively creditable version of that other great American figure, the nymphomaniac. Greene lets himself be betrayed by the swinging-scene mythology into a picturesque vision of a Hampstead nymph and her pornographer guardians: as anyone who glanced at the reviews knows, they make a blue film of P.C. Strange in bed with their ward. This is the same trendy terrain which proved so disastrous in Greene's last film, Sebastian.

Still, the flimsiness of these parts of The Strange Affair is outweighed easily by its virtues: its vision of a London half ruins and half a raw novelty which underlines the archaic routines of the fuzz; its accurate register of the British class hierarchy, both inside the police and in its relationship to the public, where Pierce's desperation is set off against the arrival of a white-robed oriental sage and his crowd of devotees; the quietly convincing picture of the police crusade against youth, drugs, and sex. One can leave the last word to the script: we see Strange and another copper crossing a Notting Hill street, at the same place we saw them previously, on their first patrol, when they knew nothing about it. Now Strange has begun to understand. 'I thought I was going to defend the social order against the incursions of crime and anarchy', he intones, mimicking the kind of voice which later sentences him to two years inside. 'Well,' he goes on, 'that's all absolute rubbish, isn't it . . .'

Tom Nairn

SQUIRREL STOPS A VILLAGE FROM GOING TO THE LOO

Madly lucid

By MIRROR REPORTER

CAREFULLY, a squirrel built up her winter store of nuts . . . and cut off village from its loos.

The larder was in a switch box on top of a pole carrying electricity cables in the Elham Valley, near Folkestone, Kent.

The pile of nuts caused the box to short-circuit.

There was a blinding flash and the squirrel was electrocuted.

All the lights in the valley went out and an electric pump taking water to the hillside village of Rhodes Minnis stopped working.

Serious

For four and a half hours the village had no water . . . and no one could visit the loo.

Santa, Go Home

fright of his face. His new LP cover photo of 21 nude women, ...ed by David Montgomery, who photographs the Queen.

... this bombast - aural and visual ...not hide a fantastic virtuosity of ... playing. The guitar speaks— ...stakably and unashamedly—of a ...up violence and anger, felt by ...rix's entire generation Listen ...o the stabbing, choking, breath-pounding of 'Magic Bus,' ...insky's Symphony in 3 Move-... has got nothing on this— ...less, cursing, rhythmic ... ...tight, fearful.

If you are over 25 you feel uncomfortably aware that Pop is not just music; Something Is Going On Underground. If you are under 25 you are certain that It's All Happening. A curious alliance has been struck between teenagers, the hippies, commercial pop, and the young intellectuals. Somehow all have crystallised into a separate society or 'scene'.

At its centre, the authentic full-time hippies, young, serious, flamboyant in dress, claim to have taken an analytical look at the adult world, experienced a violent revulsion at what they saw, and decided that the only honourable course is to detach themselves, or 'drop out'. International in outlook, they feel they have more in common with their age group in San Francisco or Amsterdam than with older generations, sometimes referred to as the 'grey'. Their ideas are as colourful a grab bag as their clothes. Genuine young curiosity often founders in hippy ideas of 'love' that have only a marshmallow consistency, or in faddy mysticism. But Vietnam and civil rights arouse a common response.

The Underground plans to live peacefully but disparately. It produces and reads its own newspaper, the *International Times*, runs its own boutiques and bookshops, organises its own finances and legal aid for members who get picked up by the police, goes about its own pop arts business. It also likes to go about its own pleasures. This is the point at which it clashes with the 'straight' world since, to break ... s of conventional living, the Underground ... ations produced not only by light shows, ... but also by marijuana and LSD. So its ...d tribal gatherings, its Freak O... police attention.

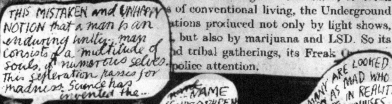

of knowl- edge,

"LOVE SCHOOL"
OF THE STONE AGE MURIAS

Warm, sensual pleasure made easy and without gu...
the expert aim of the notorious, full-breasted ...
whose prehistoric, free-love paradise 300 miles dee...
Indian jungle would shock the hippest, Jet Set swi...

Colonel's daughter
weds a hippy

THE COLONEL'S daughter plumped for a hippy wedding yesterday.

Caroline Barras, 19-year-old daughter of Colonel John Barras, Commanding Officer of Bovington Camp, Dorset, wore green shoes and a borrowed blue-spotted dress.

Bridegroom Barry Thompson, a corporation grass cutter, sported a giant blue paper flower on a tattered jacket worn over a psychedelic shirt.

death.

Anxious to be first in the queue for tickets for a concert by the Rolling Stones my friend and I left the house at 3 a.m. to make our way to the theatre.

We were stopped by a policeman who was to our disgust ignorant of what or who the Stones were.

And so we settled ourselves on the steps of the theatre. Ten minutes later the policeman reappeared on a bicycle and drew from the saddlebag a vacuum flask of hot, steaming tea.

It was lovely. And, by the way, we got our front row seats.—(Miss) ROSALIND BRADICK, Codgordie Avenue, Chingford.

Boob kills marines

Da Nang (Vietnam): A U.S. marine Phantom jet accidentally bombed a unit ... U.S. Fifth Marin... killing six mari... ing eight oth...

MY MOVE? IN HIM WE LIVE AND MOVE AND HAVE OUR BEING OF HEALTHY MIND AND BODY OF A WEAK AND FEEBLE

WOMAN, BUT I HAVE THE HEART DOTH NEED A LANGUAGE ALL NATIONS UNDERSTAND WISDOM SECRETLY THOU SHALT PURGE AND LEAVE HIM LYING WHERE HE FELL BEFORE THE THRONE

OF BAYONETS

LE VOYEUR

the actuality

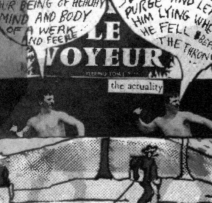

Things go better
wit ke
The Death of
ROBERT KENNEDY
A Family's History
of Tragedy
moment. An attempt
NEWS
OF THE
WORLD
Great Student Plot
shall
..IN UPON ME I AM AN ENGINE THAT MOVES IN PREDESTINATE GROOVES TOMORROW
and TOMORROW, and TOMORROW! CREEPS IN THIS PETTY PACE FROM DAY TO DAY...
TO THE LAST SYLLABLE OF RECORDED TIME AND ALL OUR yesterdays have lighted fools the way...

BETRAYED
Ago
sho
SIEGE
BOMB

you

had peace for a

LIFE'S BUT A WALKING SHADOW, IN A POOR PLAYER, THAT STRUTS AND FRETS

HIS HOUR UPON THE STAGE AS SHAKESPEARE SO WISELY SAID.

THE WORLD'S A STAGE AND THEN IS HEARD NO MORE

?

IT IS A TALE TOLD BY AN IDIOT FULL OF SOUND AND FURY SIGNIFYING NOTHING

LITTLE NEMO IN SLUMBERLAND

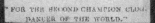

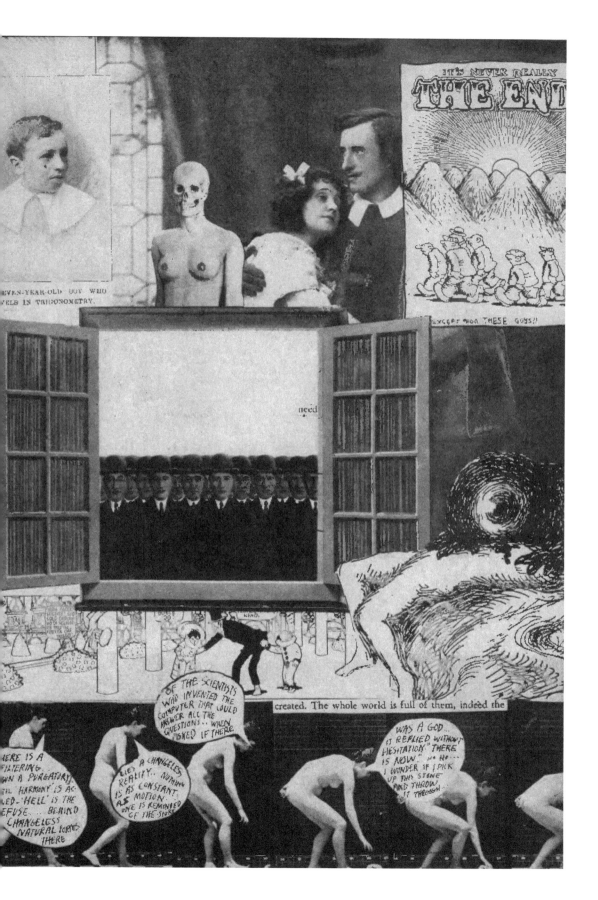

Contents:

Tied to a tree and
BRANDED—
BY MY RAT-PACK CYCLE GANG!

He accused me—
"YOU'D MARRY THE FIRST WHITE MAN WHO ASKS YOU!"

We Were WAY-OUT WEEKEND HIPPIES
We had 48 hours of make-out and freak-out

FREE!

the heart

A LITTLE PICCANINNY AND HIS PONY.

What is the protest for?

It was for this purpose that our rationalizations were

The Miss United Kingdom and subsequent Miss World title brought a total of £3,500 in cash prizes together with a full compliment of lucrative promotional associations with firms as varied in their produce as the International Wool Secretariat on one hand and the mammoth Chrysler Corporation on the other. From "Pure Wool" to 7 litre saloon cars the "critical path" devolves into more permanent and serious pursuits—the next step, according to agent Larthe, is a film test with Hollywood producer Hall Wallis—after that, who knows, the world may be hers to keep. ⟨⊢⟩

THE ICE CAPS are melting

of life?

.. A PROPHETESS ? YEA, I SAY UNTO YOU, AND MORE THAN A PROFITESS — AN UNCOMMON PRETTY YOUNG WOMAN

accomplished cannot be annulled, but only confused.

THIS IS PART OF YOUR TINY TIM SUPER POSTER.

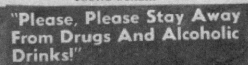

"Please, Please Stay Away From Drugs And Alcoholic Drinks!"

fall of man," may be traced back to that fear); yet the

The owl

IF THE PICTURES we print on these two pages don't make you feel uncomfortable, they ought to. For it is from scenes like this that the rest of the world judges us. And that means judges YOU.

They were taken in the heart of London, still the greatest of capital cities, during the past few weeks. It is a sad fact that they could be taken almost any night . . . and on most days, too.

For months now a steady degeneration has been taking place on London's streets and public places. It has happened so gradually that it has gone almost unnoticed by those people who live and work in the city.

But it has come as a considerable shock to thousands of foreign visitors, who cannot believe that such sights can be tolerated in what was once a proud city.

The truth is that not only are they tolerated, but they are becoming more and more commonplace until they have reached the proportions of a national scandal.

A HALF-HUMAN MOUNTAIN Brings it's wings to bear.

A GARDEN OF ROSES APPEASES ITS LION.

25 WAYS TO RELEASE YOUR HIDDEN SEX POWER
(Continued from page 41)

Who's afraid of Middle Age?

ROBERT LEE MASSIE, *twenty-six, is the product of a broken home and has been a delinquent since the age of eight, finally resulting in the murder of a California housewife whom he was attempting to rob. He has been on Death Row at San Quentin for three years. But, unlike virtually all other condemned men, he adamantly claims his right to execution and has instructed his court-appointed attorneys to cease their appeals.*

"I'm sick of the whole mess. Life never gave anything to me. was always just drugs and alcohol and misery. And I never gave anything to life. I always knew it would end up like this —killing people. That's why I tried to join the Army. At least that way it would have been legal. But they didn't want me. Nobody ever has. So let's get it over with. All I have to say is, see you in the next world."

AMAZING $1 OFFER

4 Exquisite, Wide-Eyed, <u>Full Color</u> Moppet Paintings Reproduced For Your Home

night-bound eyes

to eating of the Tree of Knowledge; perhaps too it was the original meaning of natural death.) Now, faced

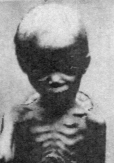

Postmen in Andover have refused to handle their local weekly

newspaper because it has criticised the postal service.

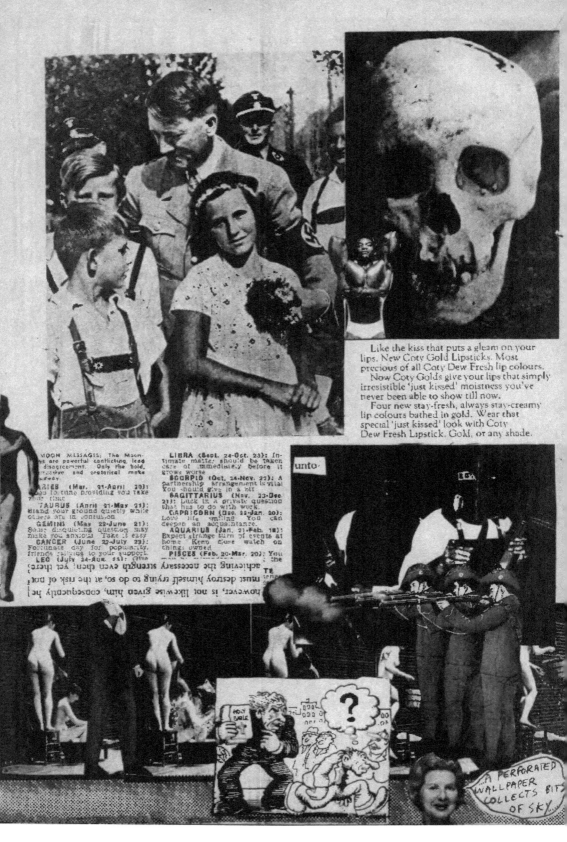

Like the kiss that puts a gleam on your lips, New Coty Gold Lipsticks. Most precious of all Coty Dew Fresh lip colours.

Now Coty Golds give your lips that simply irresistible 'just kissed' moistness you've never been able to show till now.

Four new stay-fresh, always stay-creamy lip colours bathed in gold. Wear that special 'just kissed' look with Coty Dew Fresh Lipstick. Gold, or any shade.

...A PERFORATED WALLPAPER COLLECTS BITS OF SKY...

**I Help Anyone I Can —
st Write To Me."**

the day

RED HORN,
THE THIRD OF THIS
SERIES OF HERO
FIGURES, IS AN
AMBIGUOUS PERSON,
SAID TO BE THE
YOUNGEST OF 10
BROTHERS

, Paul Lawrence Dunbar, having shown us that the educated negro
rite must creditable English verse, offers a book of prose sketches
gro character and manners, called "Folks from Dixie" (Bowden)
tches are of various qualities, but there is at least one masterpiece
nour among them—"Anner 'Lizer." It is a tale of revival times,
is difficult to say whether it is told out of sheer fun or in satire
somewhat business like tone that evidently is not absent from such
ng and emotional epochs. The heroine has the hardest possible
e "git 'ligion," though she is fervent and assiduous, and her credit
meeting is at stake. There comes between her and her goal a
stance that can only shock the nice guid. It was a very amiable,
ry funny circumstance. Her lover, her frivolous, light-hearted,
uiting lover, was her stumbling-block. So, like a woman really in
t, she puts the case straight to him: "I prays an' I prays, an' jes'
begin to heah de chariot wheels a-rollin', yo' face comes right in
on' drives it all away. Tell me now, Sam, ez 's to put me out er
use, does you want to ma'y me, er is you goin' to ma'y Phœbe? I
ints you to tell me, not that I feels pussonally, but so's my min'
at res' spi'ritly." Anner 'Lizer got religion early next morning.
r. Dunbar's simple talk of her struggle and triumph has won him
k of a true humorist.

edge of good and evil in itself, but must endeavor as
well to act in accordance with it. The strength to do so,

THE SKETCH.

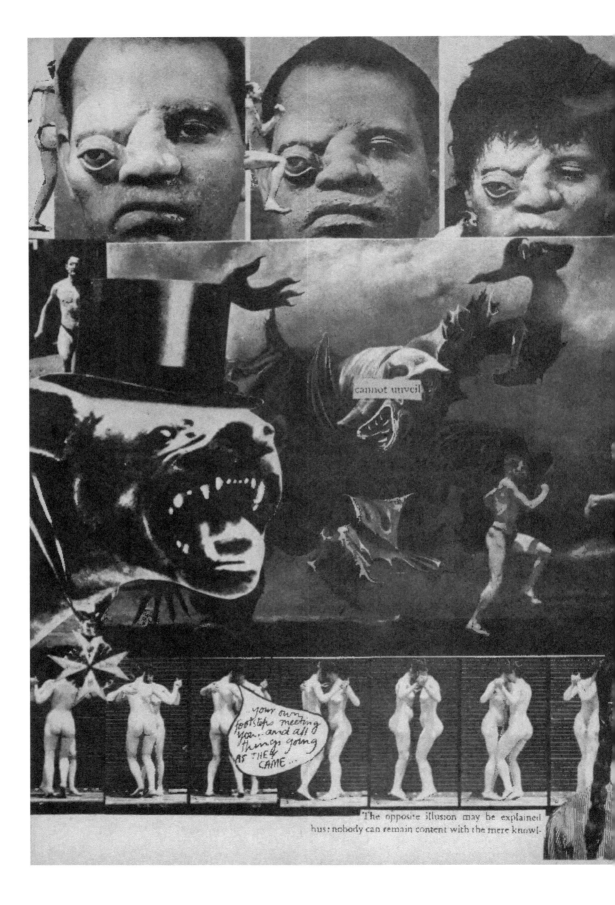

cannot unveil

...your own footsteps meeting you... and all things going as they came...

The opposite illusion may be explained hus: nobody can remain content with the mere knowl-

London OZ is published approximately monthly by OZ Publications Ink Ltd, 38a Palace Gdns Terrace W8. Phone 01-229 4623 . . . 01-603 4205

Distribution: Britain (overgroun Moore-Harness Ltd, 11 Lever Street, London EC1. Phone CLE 4882. (underground) ECAL, 22 Betterton Street, London WC2. Phone TEM 8606. New York DGB Distribution Inc 41 Union Square, New York 10003. Holland Thomas Rap, Regulierdwarsstraat 91, Amsterdam. Tel. 020-227065. Denmark George Streeton, The Underground, Larsbjen straede 13, Copenhagen K.

SMALLS

Oz needs an advertising space salesman. 25% commission — a lot of money to be made. Professionals only.

Results begin. People talk, we rejoice Joirus, OZ Box 16 (1).

DUE TO CIRCUMSTANCES BEYOND OZ'S CONTROL (BUT NOT OF THE NEWS OF THE WORLD) THIS ADS PAGE HAS BEEN CENSORED!

Canned Heat Dig it can you? Get Shout—the soul mag. 27 Kirkstall Rd., London SW2.

Special issue out soon. Subscribe 10/- (4 issues) LINK, 54 Queens Gate Terrace, London SW7.

New scripts of plays and events needed for new West End Theatre Restaurant. Must have sensational content. Vincent Shaw, 1 Old Compton Street, W1. 01-437 1135.

ARTS LABORATORY.
182 DRURY LANE, WC2.
THEATRE and DANCE THEATRE CINEMA, GALLERY, FOOD ETC. Open 6 days a week. ARTS LAB, 242 3407/8 phone for details.

FORUM is a magazine about sex About sexual behaviour, sexual problems, sexual happiness. 'A superbly human document destined to beome the most powerful and controversial socio-sexual arbiter of our time'. Sold by subscription only; Send £3 for 12 issues to: FORUM, dept. 0, 170 Ifield Rd. SW10.

If you

Renovated—Bric-a-brac, Electronic whizardry, Bits Gadgetry, Interior design — Palace Buzz, Coachwork specialists. Whizz kids, Experimental Extravaganza. Right or write to the End, OZ Box No. 16 (7).

LONELY! JOIN THE PATRA CORRESPONDENCE CLUB, friendly, private and confidential. Share your hobbies, find new friends, both sexes, all ages, world-wide.—Send stamp for details, Mrs. P. Gill, 66 Laburnum Rd., Redcar, Teesside, England.

DUREX Gossamer: 7- doz.
DUREX Fetherlite: 10s doz.
AMERICAN SKINS: 38s doz.
Post free from Colne Valley, Mail Order Co. (OZ), 126 The Rock, Linthwaite, Huddersfield.

THE BRITISH POSTER CLUB
10/- offer each month
THIS MONTH
"Swiss Christmas Scene"
from first issue of copyright painting

PLUS
One Carnaby Street "Special"
JOIN NOW!
Send 10/- to
6 Trebeck St.
Mayfair W1.

PATRESC (CLAIRVOYANT)— Tarot Readings by post plus Touchstone/Talisman. Details by post (no callers), s.a.e. please—56 Laburnum Rd., Redcar, Teesside, England.

KONTACT— the new medium for people seeking people. All interests. For current issue send 3/6 to: KONTACT (4), 31 A High Street, Harpenden, Herts.

GET PEACE NEWS, Every Friday, 1s, the Independent Radical Pacifist Weekly. From your newsagent or by subscription from 5 Caledonian Rd., London, N1 (837 4473). Special trial Sub: 6 weeks for 5s post free (students 10 weeks).

OZ is 60c in the USA DENMARK 3 KR GERMANY 1 8DM HOLLAND 2G WHEEEE!

anforum
artaud

SPECIAL ISSUE OUT SOON
SUBSCRIBE 10/- (4 ISSUES)
LINK, 54 QUEENS GATE TERRACE
LONDON, SW7.

Use this form for your small Ads. (see above). Mail to: OZ Smalls, 38a Palace Gdns Terrace, London W8.

Name:		I enclose postal order/cheque for £	s	d
Address				

1/- per word.
Box-numbers 3/-.
Display £3.10.0d per col. inch.
Payment in advance.

Since the Fall we have been essentially equal in our

refuses to account for the deadlock by an error in the original fettering.

would

LADIES AND GENTLEMEN I WOULD LIKE TO SAY THAT THE PEARLS OF A FACE BEDECK HIS RIGHT HAND

THERE IS MORE MONEY TO BE MADE IN WAR THAN IN PEACE!

NOW!

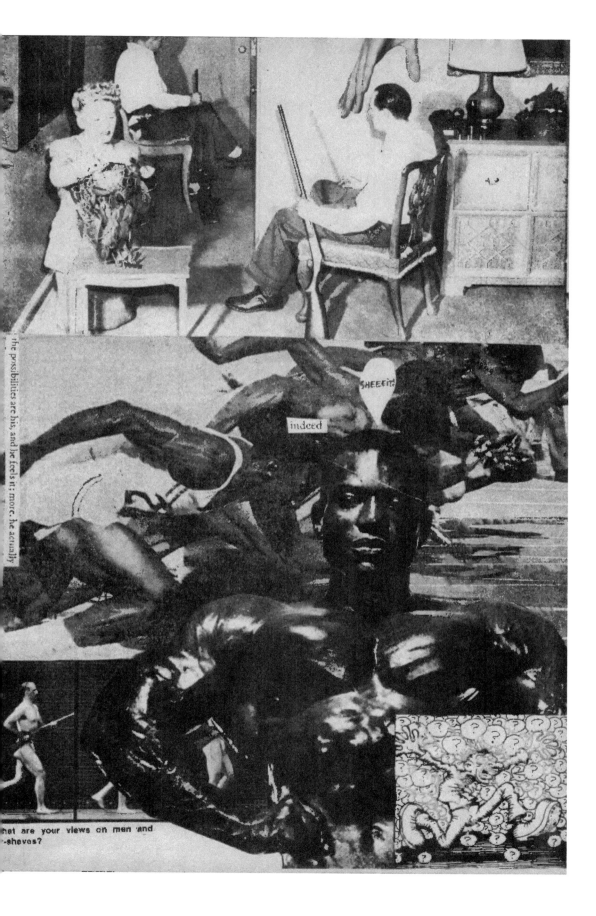

SAVE 4d

I WAN IT!
AND I WAN
IT NOW!

behold

MILLIONS of our readers saw this dramatic
picture in the News of the World last Sunday.
What they didn't know—and what we didn't know
until a letter arrived in our offices—was that behind
it lies a heartbreaking story.
earth, his heavenly collar throttles him, and if he heads
for Heaven, his earthly one does the same. And yet all

O THE
FIERY TEAR
WEPT INTO
THE NIGHT

Why should child
suffer like this?

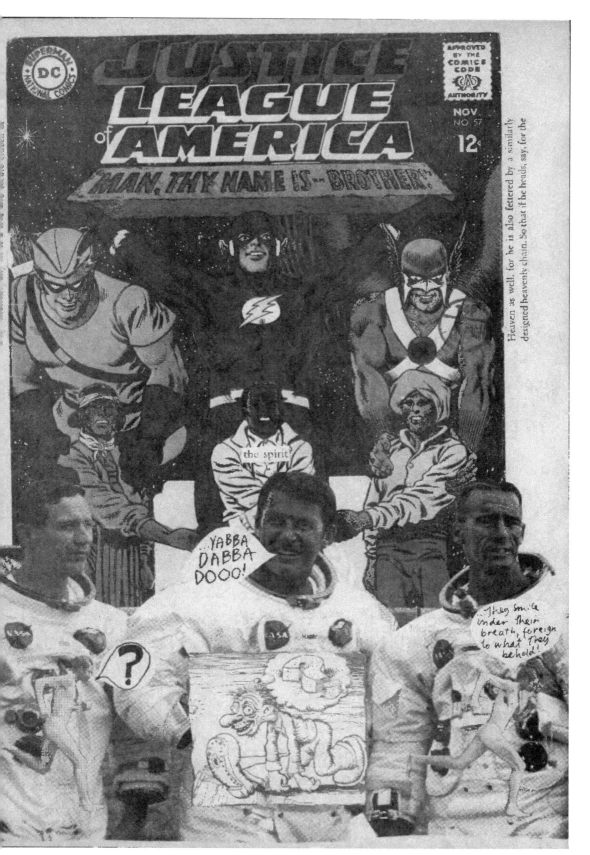

He is a free and secure citizen of the world, for he is fettered to a chain which is long enough to give him the freedom of all earthly space, and yet only so long that

of death,

Perhaps the finest self-portrait

Those TOPLESS California shoeshine parlors ($2 regular, half a buck extra for 2 tone) have already been covered here. But now....to even stand around and WATCH costs a DOLLAR....

I WAS A TIGER IN BED

(continued from page 15)

THE HEATHEN CHINEE.

When the time comes for China to be divided among the nations, a great slice of it, the middle slice, will naturally be placed under the beneficent rule of England; that is, the whole of the Yang-tzi Valley, possibly all the rich province of Szetehnen, and a considerable chunk of the misty mountains of Yunnan, will belong to the Queen. I don't know whether the Chinaman will like it—indeed, I don't know if he very much cares. Last year, when I was attempting to befool myself that I was bicycling right through the heart of China, when really I was walking across it, I went slam-bang across this region that is ultimately to be part of her Majesty's dominions.

One afternoon, I was strolling through the crowded, higgledy-piggledy, noisy, dirty streets of Yunnan-sen, arousing derision from the mob at my tight-fitting cycling-clothes, and striking terror into the hearts of all the little pig-tailed boys with my straggling red beard, when in a curiosity-shop—for I have always had a keen scent for curios—I actually found for sale a half-crown piece. I turned it over with a smile, for the sight was like a picture of home. "This is a curious thing," I said. "Yes, it is," said the long-fanged old heathen who wanted to sell it. "Who is that?" I asked, pointing to the figure of the Queen. "I don't know," answered the dealer, "but I've been told it's the Queen of a far-off country where there are only women."

He was pretty ignorant, was that Chinaman, but he was no more ignorant than other future subjects of her Majesty that I come in contact with. A Chinaman has the conceit of a newly made alderman.

open

FLOAT IN

AND SEE OUR THINGS at

Forbidden Fruit

Clothes, candles, carpets, bags, jewellry, incense, skins, pipes, heads and other imported goodies. 295 Portobello Road. W.10

MASTER PLUNCKFORD AND ALICE.

MARY MACPHERSON, THE SKYE POETESS.

ETTIE CHATTELL AS CAPTAIN BATTLER IN "THE J.P."

the paradisiacal man did; men did not become God, but divine knowledge.

they did not become like God,
but received the indispensable capacity to become so.

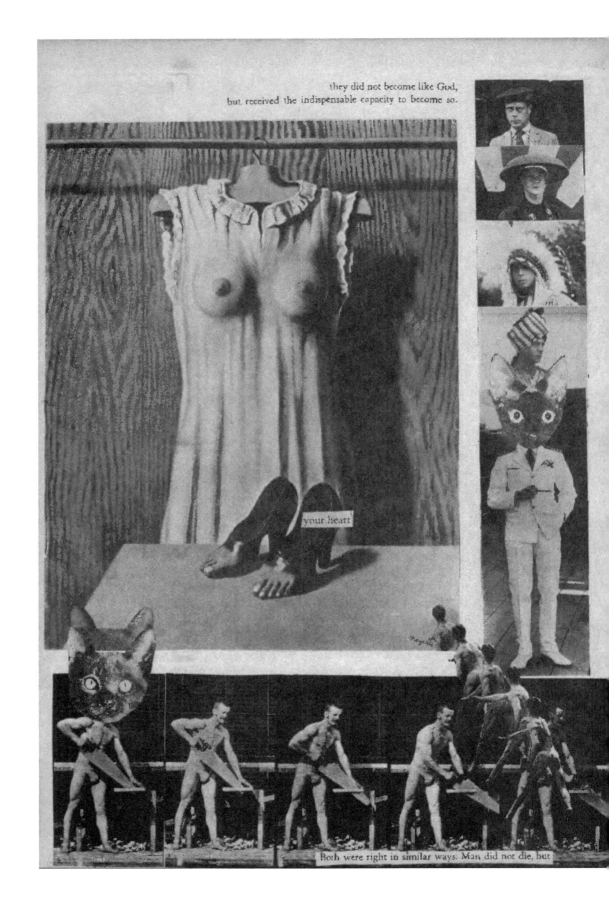

your heart

Both were right in similar ways. Man did not die, but

WINSTON CHURCHILL IN CHICAGO POLICE HORROR
EVENING NEWS
JUST PASSING THROUGH
NIGHT SPECIAL
MAN ON CROSS: COURT CHARGE
HEART MAN CRITICAL BUT STILL O.K!
EVENING STANDARD
VOLCANO HORROR: MANY DI
EVENING STANDARD
wide
BIRTH CONTROL -THE POPE'S RULING
EVENING STANDARD
JACKIE AND ONASSIS -LATEST
EVENING STANDARD
it can be understood so), it would be equality with God. Both were wrong in similar ways. Men did not
YOU CAN AND YOU CAN'T - YOU SHALL AND YOU SHAN'T - YOU WILL AND YOU WON'T - AND YOU
?
WILL BE DAMNED IF YOU DO... AND YOU WILL BE DAMNED
IF YOU DON'T.
die, but became mortal;

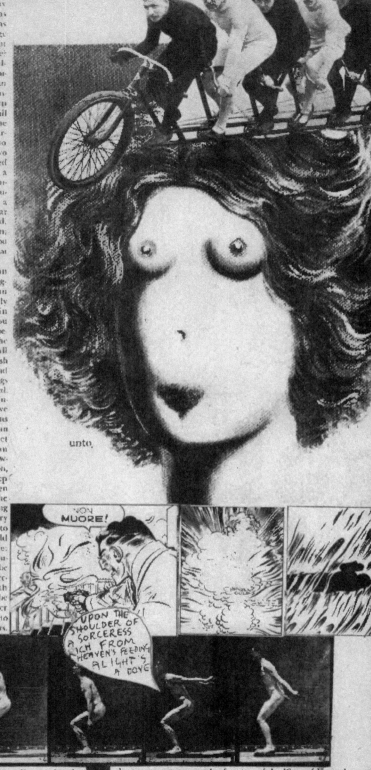

PLAYBOY: Will we be able to find any deep meaning or fulfillment, either as individuals or as a species, as long as we continue to live with the knowledge that all human life could be snuffed out at any moment in a nuclear catastrophe?

KUBRICK: We *must*, for in the final analysis, there may be no sound way to eliminate the threat of self-extinction without changing human nature; even if you managed to get every country disarmed down to the bow and arrow, you would still be unable to lobotomize either the knowledge of how to build nuclear warheads or the perversity that allows us to rationalize their use. Given these two categorical imperatives in a disarmed world, the first country to amass even a few weapons would have a great incentive to use them quickly. So an argument might be made that there is a greater chance for *some* use of nuclear weapons in a totally disarmed world, though less chance of global extinction; while in a world armed to the teeth, you have less chance for *some* use—but a great chance of extinction if they're used.

If you try to remove yourself from an earthly perspective and look at this tragic paradox with the detachment of an extraterrestrial, the whole thing is totally irrational. Man now has the power in one mad, incandescent moment, as you point out, to exterminate the entire species; our own generation could be the last on earth. One miscalculation and all the achievements of history could vanish in a mushroom cloud; one misstep and all of man's aspirations and strivings over the millennia could be terminated. One short circuit in a computer, one lunatic in a command structure and we could negate the heritage of the billions who have died since the dawn of man and abort the promise of the billions yet unborn—the ultimate genocide. What an irony that the discovery of nuclear power, with its potential for annihilation, also constitutes the first tottering step into the universe that must be taken by all intelligent worlds. Unhappily, the infant-mortality rate among emerging civilizations in the cosmos may be very high. Not that it will matter except to us: the destruction of this planet would have no significance on a cosmic scale; to an observer in the Andromeda nebulae, the sign of our extinction would be no more than a match flaring for a second in the heavens; and if that match does blaze in the darkness, there will be none to mourn a race that used a power that could have lit a beacon in the stars to light its funeral pyre. The choice is ours.

unto.

A TUBA LETS LOOSE IT'S BOUQUET OF FLOWERS

NON MUORE!

UPON THE SHOULDER OF A SORCERESS ICH FROM HEAVEN'S FEEDING ALIGHT'S A DOVE

God said that Adam would have to die on the day he ate of the Tree of Knowledge. According to God, the instantaneous result of eating of the Tree of Knowledge would be death; according to the serpent (at least

AMA RIOT

the body

SEIZE HIT BREAK JAIL

'e were expelled from Paradise, but Paradise was
t destroyed. In a sense our expulsion from Paradise

was a stroke of luck, for had we not been expelled,
Paradise would have had to be destroyed.

...IMMOBILIZING
SILENCE. A
LEANING TOWER
DELICATELY
PROPPED UP BY
A FEATHER TAKES
ON A MORE
SOMBRE
TONE

?

AERIAL
EDIFICES
BLUE
THEIR
ECHO.

"I Speak... for the Dignity of Man"

... This dignity cannot be found in a man's possessions. It cannot be found in his power or in his position. It really rests on his right to be treated as a man equal in opportunity to all others. It says that he shall share in freedom, he shall choose his leaders, educate his children, provide for his family according to his ability and his merits as a human being. To apply any other test—to deny a man his hope of life.
because of his color or race or his religion, or the place of his birth— is not .... it is to deny America."

President Lyndon B. Johnson
address to a joint session of Congress, March 15, 1965.

We were fashioned to live in Paradise, and Paradise was destined to serve us. Our destiny has been altered; that this has also happened with the destiny of Paradise is not stated.

DURING THE SUMMER OR OF 1949, MY STUDENT, MISS SCHIFFER, PROVED THAT ANTS ALSO ORIENT THEMSELVES BY THE POLARIZATION OF THE SKY LIGHT!

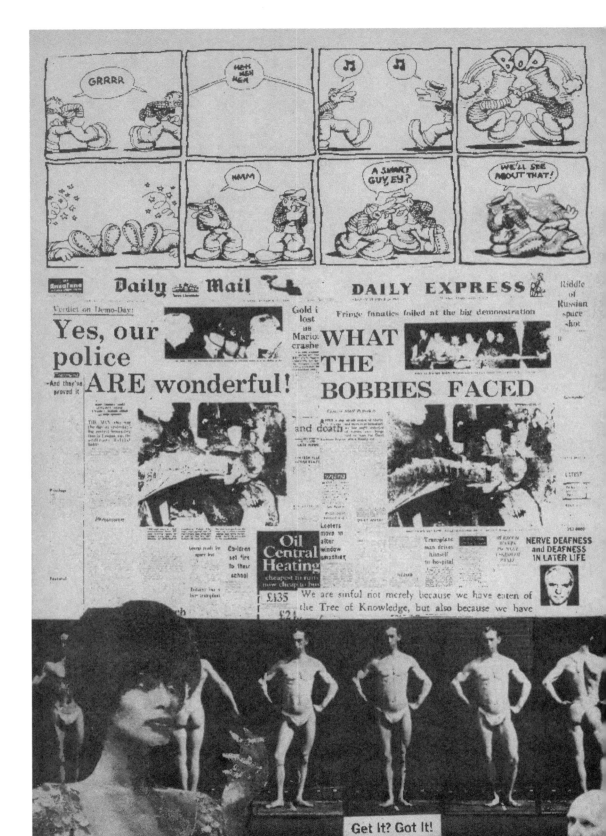

Daily Mirror

In Grosvenor Square, as the great march ends, police and protesters are one, link arms to sing Auld Long Syne

DAILY SKETCH

THE DAY THE POLICE WERE WONDERFUL

Most of the marchers were pretty good, too

And THEY talk about **PROVOCATION!**

The Sketch says: Well done, police

POLICE STAND FIRM AGAINST 4,000

A UNIVERSE WHOSE SIZE BEYOND MAN IMAGINING.

.AND..

The HARI KRISHNA chorus.

SSSHHH.. We scan the TIME SCALE and the MECHANISMS OF LIFE ITSELF FOR PORTENTS AND SIGNS OF THE INVISIBLE.

as the only thinking mammals on the Planet..

WHERE OUR WORLD FLOATS LIKE A DUST MOTE IN THE VOID OF NIGHT, MEN HAVE GROWN INCONCEIVABLY LONELEY... WE SCAN THE TIME SCALE...

?

PERHAPS darling the only thinking animals in the ENTIRE UNIVERSE..→

Why do we lament over the fall of man? We were not driven out of Paradise because of it, but because

SUPER DUPER

Life is probably round.
Vincent

even as the
Maurice and his greatest pride—his new
Rolls-Royce. Pictures by MONTY FRES
PUZZLE FOR CHILDREN
BUT! the SIGNS ARE UNCERTAIN. WE UNCOVER THE BONES OF THE PAST AND SEEK FOR OUR ORIGINS. There is a PATH..
There... But it appears to
HAVE A
MEANING
US.

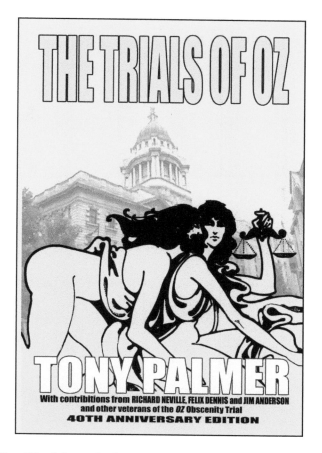

The *OZ* trial was the longest obscenity trial in history. It was also one of the worst reported. With minor exceptions, the Press chose to rewrite what had occurred, presumably to fit in with what seemed to them the acceptable prejudices of the times. Perhaps this was inevitable.

The proceedings dragged on for nearly six weeks in the hot summer of 1971 when there were, no doubt, a great many other events more worthy of attention. Against the background of murder in Ulster, for example, the *OZ* affair probably fades into its proper insignificance. Even so, after the trial, when some newspapers realised that maybe something important had happened, it became more and more apparent that what was essential was for anyone who wished to be able to read what had actually been said. Trial and judgment by a badly informed press became the order of the day. This 40th Anniversary edition includes new material by all three of the original defendants, the prosecuting barrister, one of the *OZ* schoolkids, and even the daughters of the judge. There are also many illustrations including unseen material from Felix Dennis' own collection...

ALSO AVAILABLE FROM GONZO MULTIMEDIA

GONZO
Books

There is still such a
thing as alternative
Publishing

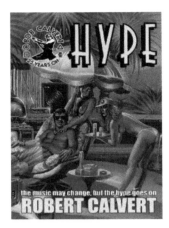

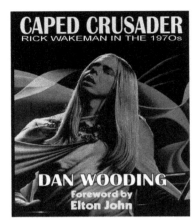

Robert Newton Calvert: Born 9
March 1945, Died 14 August 1988
after suffering a heart attack.
Contributed poetry, lyrics and
vocals to legendary space rock
band Hawkwind intermittently on
five of their most critically
acclaimed albums, including Space
Ritual (1973), Quark, Strangeness
& Charm (1977) and Hawklords
(1978). He also recorded a number
of solo albums in the mid 1970s.
CENTIGRADE 232 was Robert Cal
vert's first collection of poems.

Hype   'And now, for all you speed
ing street smarties out there, the
one you've all been waiting for, the
one that'll pierce your laid back
ears, decoke your sinuses, cut clean
thru the schlock rock,
MOR/crossover, techno flash mind
mush. It's the new Number One with
a bullet … with a bullet … It's Tom,
Supernova, Mahler with a pan galac
tic biggie …' And the Hype goes on.
And on. Hype, an amphetamine hit of
a story by Hawkwind collaborator
Robert Calvert. Who's been there
and made it back again. The
debriefing session starts here.

Rick Wakeman is the world's most
unusual rock star, a genius who has
pushed back the barriers of electronic
rock. He has had some of the world's
top orchestras perform his music, has
owned eight Rolls Royces at one time,
and has broken all the rules of com
posing and horrified his tutors at the
Royal College of Music. Yet he has
delighted his millions of fans. This
frank book, authorised by Wakeman
himself, tells the moving tale of his
larger than life career.

"So many books, so little time."
Frank Zappa

THE NINE HENRYS
By Peter McAdam

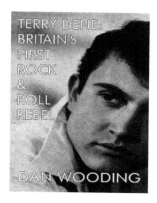

TERRY DENE: BRITAIN'S FIRST ROCK & ROLL REBEL

DAN WOODING

King Squealer

MAURICE O'MAHONEY WITH DAN WOODING

There are nine Henrys, pur
ported to be the world's
first cloned cartoon charac
ter. They live in a strange
lo fi domestic surrealist
world peopled by talking
rock buns and elephants on
wobbly stilts.

They mooch around in their
minimalist universe suffer
ing from an existential
crisis with some genetically
modified humour thrown in.

Marty Wilde on Terry Dene: "Whatever
happened to Terry becomes a great deal
more comprehensible as you read of the
callous way in which he was treated by
people who should have known better
many of whom, frankly, will never know
better   of the sad little shadows of
the past who eased themselves into
Terry's life, took everything they
could get and, when it seemed that all
was lost, quietly left him — Dan Wood
ing's book tells it all."

Rick Wakeman: "There have
always been certain 'careers'
that have fascinated the
public, newspapers, and the
media in general. Such
include musicians, actors,
sportsmen, police, and not
surprisingly, the people who
give the police their employ
ment: The criminal. For the
man in the street, all these
careers have one thing in
common: they are seemingly
beyond both his reach and,
in many cases, understanding
and as such, his only associ
ation can be through the
media of newspapers or tele
vision. The police, however,
will always require the ser
vices of the grass, the
squealer, the snitch, (call
him what you will), in order
to assist in their investiga
tions and arrests; and amaz
ingly, this is the area that
seldom gets written about."

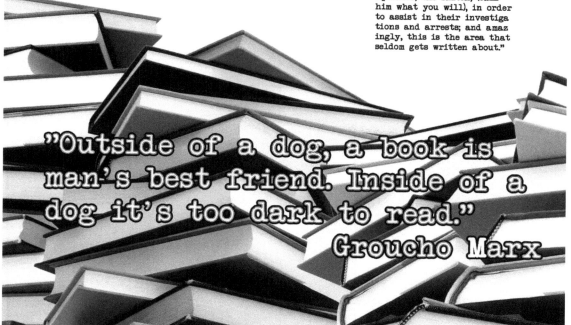

"Outside of a dog, a book is
man's best friend. Inside of a
dog it's too dark to read."
Groucho Marx

Bill Harkleroad joined Captain Beef heart's Magic Band at a time when they were changing from a straight ahead blues band into something completely different. Through the vision of Don Van Vliet (Captain Beefheart) they created a new form of music which many at the time considered atonal and difficult, but which over the years has continued to exert a powerful influence. Beefheart re christened Harkleroad as Zoot Horn Rollo, and they embarked on recording one of the classic rock albums of all time Trout Mask Replica - a work of unequalled daring and inventiveness.

Politics, paganism and .... Vlad the Impaler. Selected stories from CJ Stone from 2003 to the present. Meet Ivor Coles, a British Tommy killed in action in September 1915, lost, and then found again. Visit Mothers Club in Erdington, the best psyche delic music club in the UK in the '60s. Celebrate Robin Hood's Day and find out what a huckle duckle is. Travel to Stonehenge at the Summer Solstice and carouse with the hippies. Find out what a Ranter is, and why CJ Stone thinks that he's one. Take LSD with Dr Lilly, the psychedelic scientist. Meet a headless soldier or the ghost of Elvis Presley in Gabalfa, Cardiff. Journey to Whitstable, to New York, to Malta and to Transylvania, and to many other places, real and imagined, polit ical and spiritual, transcendent and mundane. As The Independent says, Chris is "The best guide to the underground since Charon ferried dead souls across the Styx."

This is is the first in the highly acclaimed vampire novels of the late Mick Farren. Victor Renquist, a surprisingly urbane and likable leader of a colony of vampires which has existed for centuries in New York is faced with both admin istrative and emotional prob lems. And when you are a vampire, administration is not a thing which one takes lightly.

"The person, be it gentleman or lady, who has not pleasure in a good novel, must be intolerably stupid."

Jane Austen

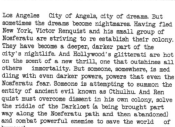

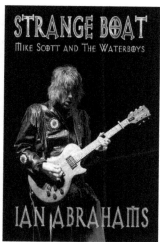

Los Angeles City of Angels, city of dreams. But sometimes the dreams become nightmares. Having fled New York, Victor Renquist and his small group of Nosferatu are striving to re establish their colony. They have become a deeper, darker part of the city's nightlife. And Hollywood's glitterati are hot on the scent of a new thrill, one that outshines all others immortality. But someone, somewhere, is med dling with even darker powers, powers that even the Nosferatu fear. Someone is attempting to summon the entity of ancient evil known as Cthulhu. And Ren quist must overcome dissent in his own colony, solve the riddle of the Darklost (a being brought part way along the Nosferatu path and then abandoned) and combat powerful enemies to save the world of humans!

Canadian born Corky Laing is probably best known as the drummer with Mountain. Corky joined the band shortly after Mountain played at the famous Woodstock Festival, although he did receive a gold disc for sales of the soundtrack album after over dubbing drums on Ten Years After's performance. Whilst with Mountain Corky Laing recorded three studio albums with them before the band split. Follow ing the split Corky, along with Mountain gui tarist Leslie West, formed a rock three piece with former Cream bassist Jack Bruce. West, Bruce and Laing recorded two studio albums and a live album before West and Laing re formed Mountain, along with Felix Pappalardi. Since 1974 Corky and Leslie have led Mountain through various line ups and recordings, and continue to record and perform today at numer ous concerts across the world. In addition to his work with Mountain, Corky Laing has recorded one solo album and formed the band Cork with former Spin Doctors guitarist Eric Shenkman, and recorded a further two studio albums with the band, which has also featured former Jimi Hendrix bassist Noel Redding. The stories are told in an incredibly frank, engaging and amusing manner, and will appeal also to those people who may not necessarily be fans of

To me there's no difference between Mike Scott and The Waterboys; they both mean the same thing. They mean myself and whoever are my current travel ling musical companions." Mike Scott Strange Boat charts the twisting and meandering journey of Mike Scott, describing the literary and spiritual references that inform his songwriting and explor ing the multitude of locations and cultures in which The Waterboys have assembled and reflected in their recordings. From his early forays into the music scene in Scotland at the end of the 1970s, to his creation of a 'Big Music' that peaked with the hit single 'The Whole of the Moon' and onto the Irish adventure which spawned the classic Fisher man's Blues, his constantly restless creativity has led him through a myriad of changes. With his revolving cast of troubadours at his side, he's created some of the most era defining records of the 1980s, reeled and jigged across the Celtic heartlands, reinvented himself as an electric rocker in New York, and sought out personal renewal in the spiritual calm of Findhorn's Scot tish highland retreat. Mike Scott's life has been a tale of continual musical exploration entwined with an ever evolving spirituality. "An intriguing portrait of a modern musician" (Record Collector).

"A room without books is like a body without a soul."
Marcus Tullius Cicero

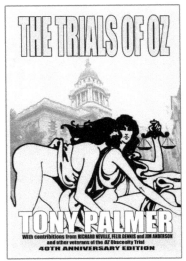

The OZ trial was the longest obscenity trial in history. It was also one of the worst reported. With minor exceptions, the Press chose to rewrite what had occurred, presumably to fit in with what seemed to them the acceptable prejudices of the times. Perhaps this was inevitable. The proceedings dragged on for nearly six weeks in the hot summer of 1971 when there were, no doubt, a great many other events more worthy of attention. Against the background of murder in Ulster, for example, the OZ affair probably fades into its proper insignifi cance. Even so, after the trial, when some newspapers realised that maybe something important had hap pened, it became more and more apparent that what was essential was for anyone who wished to be able to read what had actually been said. Trial and judgment by a badly informed press became the order of the day. This 40th Anniversary edition includes new material by all three of the original defendants, the prosecuting barrister, one of the OZ schoolkids, and even the daughters of the judge. There are also many illustrations including unseen material from Feliz Dennis' own collection…

Merrell Fankhauser has led one of the most diverse and interesting careers in music. He was born in Louisville, Kentucky, and moved to California when he was 13 years old. Merrell went on to become one of the innovators of surf music and psychedelic folk rock. His travels from Hollywood to his 15 year jungle experience on the island of Maui have been documented in numerous music books and magazines in the United States and Europe. Merrell has gained legendary international status throughout the field of rock music; his credits include over 250 songs published and released. He is a multi talented singer/songwriter and unique guitar player whose sound has delighted listeners for over 35 years. This extraordi nary book tells a unique story of one of the founding fathers of surf rock, who went on to play in a succession of progressive and psychedelic bands and to meet some of the greatest names in the business, including Captain Beefheart, Randy California, The Beach Boys, Jan and Dean… and there is even a run in with the notorious Manson family.

On September 19, 1985, Frank Zappa testified before the United States Senate Commerce, Technology, and Transportation committee, attacking the Parents Music Resource Center or PMRC, a music organization co founded by Tipper Gore, wife of then senator Al Gore. The PMRC consisted of many wives of politi cians, including the wives of five members of the committee, and was founded to address the issue of song lyrics with sexual or satanic content. Zappa saw their activities as on a path towards censor ship,and called their proposal for voluntary labelling of records with explicit content "extor tion" of the music industry. This is what happened.

"Good friends, good books, and a sleepy conscience: this is the ideal life."
Mark Twain

The OZ trial was the longest obscenity trial in history. It was also one of the worst reported. With minor exceptions, the Press chose to rewrite what had occurred, presumably to fit in with what seemed to them the acceptable prejudices of the times. Perhaps this was inevitable. The proceedings dragged on for nearly six weeks in the hot summer of 1971 when there were, no doubt, a great many other events more worthy of attention. Against the background of murder in Ulster, for example, the OZ affair probably fades into its proper insignifi cance. Even so, after the trial, when some newspapers realised that maybe something important had hap pened, it became more and more apparent that what was essential was for anyone who wished to be able to read what had actually been said. Trial and judgment by a badly informed press became the order of the day. This 40th Anniversary edition includes new material by all three of the original defendants, the prosecuting barrister, one of the OZ schoolkids, and even the daughters of the judge. There are also many illustrations including unseen material from Felix Dennis' own collection...

Merrell Fankhauser has led one of the most diverse and interesting careers in music. He was born in Louisville, Kentucky, and moved to California when he was 13 years old. Merrell went on to become one of the innovators of surf music and psychedelic folk rock. His travels from Hollywood to his 15 year jungle experience on the island of Maui have been documented in numerous music books and magazines in the United States and Europe. Merrell has gained legendary international status throughout the field of rock music; his credits include over 250 songs published and released. He is a multi talented singer/songwriter and unique guitar player whose sound has delighted listeners for over 35 years. This extraordi nary book tells a unique story of one of the founding fathers of surf rock, who went on to play in a succession of progressive and psychedelic bands and to meet some of the greatest names in the business, including Captain Beefheart, Randy California, The Beach Boys, Jan and Dean... and there is even a run in with the notorious Manson family.

On September 19, 1985, Frank Zappa testified before the United States Senate Commerce, Technology, and Transportation committee, attacking the Parents Music Resource Center or PMRC, a music organization co founded by Tipper Gore, wife of then senator Al Gore. The PMRC consisted of many wives of politi cians, including the wives of five members of the committee, and was founded to address the issue of song lyrics with sexual or satanic content. Zappa saw their activities as on a path towards censor ship,and called their proposal for voluntary labelling of records with explicit content "extor tion" of the music industry. This is what happened.

"Good friends, good books, and a sleepy conscience: this is the ideal life."
Mark Twain

Lightning Source UK Ltd.
Milton Keynes UK
UKHW05f1308260718
326319UK00004B/39/P